Atlantis
and the
Ten Plagues of Egypt

Atlantis
and the
Ten Plagues of Egypt

The Secret History Hidden in the
Valley of the Kings

Graham Phillips

Bear & Company
Rochester, Vermont

Bear & Company
One Park Street
Rochester, Vermont 05767
www.InnerTraditions.com

Bear & Company is a division of Inner Traditions International

Originally published in England in 1998 by Sidgwick & Jackson,
an imprint of Macmillan Publishers, Ltd., under the title *Act of God:
Tutankhamun, Moses & the Myth of Atlantis*

Library of Congress Cataloging-in-Publication Data
Phillips, Graham.
    Atlantis and the ten plagues of Egypt : the secret history hidden in the
Valley of the Kings / Graham Phillips.
        p. cm.
    Originally published : Act of God. London : Sidgwick & Jackson, 1998.
    Includes bibliographical references and index.
    ISBN 1-59143-009-7
    1. Egypt—History—Eighteenth dynasty, ca. 1570-1320 B.C. 2. Bible—
History of Biblical events. 3. Bible—History of contemporary events. 4.
Valley of the Kings (Egypt) 5. Tutankhamen, King of Egypt. 6. Excavations
(Archaeology)—Egypt. 7. Egypt—Antiquities. 8. Atlantis. I. Phillips, Graham.
Act of God. II. Title.

    DT87.P493 2003
    001.94—dc21
                                        2003013006

Printed and bound in the United States at Lake Book Manufacturing, Inc.

10 9 8 7 6 5 4 3 2 1

Typeset by SetSystems Ltd, Saffron Walden, Essex

Contents

List of Maps and Illustrations

Acknowledgements

Graham Phillips would like to thank Chris Stewart, Peter Hull, Simon Trewin, Emma Gibb, Ruth McIntosh, Laura Sujin, Talya Boston, Susy Behr, Wayne Frostick, Simon Cox, Billie Walker-John, Morven Knowles, Lucy Earle, Elizabeth Bond, Gordon Wise and Rodney Hale for all their help. Also, a particular thanks to Andrew Collins, without whose invaluable research this book would not have been possible.

For more information about Graham Phillips, his books, and his research, please visit his Web site at grahamphillips.net

CHAPTER ONE

Imprisoned for Eternity

In the early days of 1907, the wealthy American lawyer and amateur Egyptologist, Theodore Davis, was leading an archaeological expedition in Egypt's Valley of the Kings, just across the Nile from the ancient capital of Thebes. His team included his cousin Emma Andrews, who acted as his personal assistant, the painter Joseph Lindon Smith, who was there to visually document any new discoveries, and the professional archaeologist Edward Ayrton. On 11 January, Ayrton was busy at the northern end of the valley, organizing a team of local workers to clear away a mass of debris that had been strewn around the tomb of Ramesses IX by excavators a few years before. About thirty feet to the south of the tomb's entrance, where the rock face was almost vertical, the workers unexpectedly discovered a deep in-filled trench that had been cut into the hillside centuries ago. Ayrton initially assumed that they had uncovered a ceremonial gully which originally formed part of Ramesses' tomb. However, when they began to unearth pieces of broken pottery predating Ramesses' three-thousand-year-old tomb, it quickly became apparent that the trench must be part of a second and older excavation – an undiscovered tomb.

After further digging revealed a flight of ancient carved steps, the gang continued working all night, uncovering a

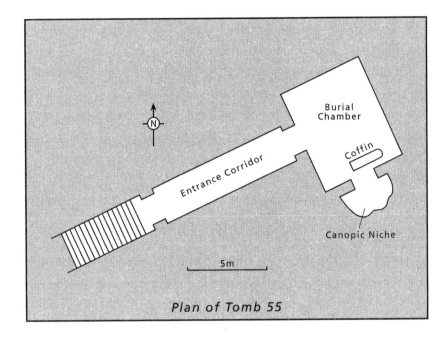

Plan of Tomb 55

stairwell and exposing the stone lintel of the outer entrance to a buried tomb. For a whole week, hour after hour in the dry desert heat, Ayrton kept his men hard at work, removing the rubble from the archaic passageway. Finally, after some twenty-one steps were uncovered, leading deep into the cliff, the workmen came to a solid barrier, an intact limestone wall sealing an entrance two and a half metres high. Delighted, Ayrton realized the implications – the tomb was undisturbed. Yet there was something strange! Usually the entrances to such tombs were embossed with the royal seal of the occupant. Here there was no such seal, just a bare wall concealing an entrance carved deep into solid rock.

An account of the discovery survives in the diary of Emma Andrews, now in the Metropolitan Museum in New York. She tells how almost at once arguments erupted. Ayrton summoned

Davis, who in turn was obliged to inform Arthur Weigall, the representative of the Antiquities Service in Cairo, who immediately arrived to oversee the excavation. Ayrton wanted to waste no time opening the tomb, but Weigall urged caution: the surrounding rubble should be carefully sifted for important archaeological clues before they were forever destroyed by further digging. Davis agreed. As the number of undisturbed tombs found in Egypt could be counted on one hand, the discovery was of immense importance and he wanted an addition to the team: the experienced archaeologist, Howard Carter, who was already in Egypt and staying in nearby Luxor.

Ayrton objected furiously. He and Carter had both been trained by the father of British archaeology in Egypt, Sir W.M. Flinders Petrie, and had since become bitter rivals. Four years earlier, while working for Davis, Carter had beaten Ayrton in a race to discover the tomb of the pharaoh Tuthmosis IV, which contained the most complete war chariot yet found. Carter had thus become the Egyptologist at the centre of world media attention. Other tombs had since been discovered, but they had been empty, long ago stripped of their treasures. Ayrton now had an intact tomb, and he was not prepared to have Carter upstage him yet again. Indeed, Ayrton was sure that they had found the very tomb for which Carter himself was so intrepidly searching: the tomb of the pharaoh Tutankhamun, a shadowy figure from Egyptian history about whom almost nothing was known. The previous year a small cup bearing Tutankhamun's name, together with other materials used in the king's funeral, had been found nearby, leading Carter to believe that Tutankhamun's tomb was somewhere in the vicinity.

Emma Andrews' account is vague as to precisely who ordered the tomb to be opened and the reports of all those involved differ. It is doubtful that Emma herself knew the truth as she was staying on Davis' boat in Luxor and was therefore not present at the time. From what can be gathered, however, it seems that someone, probably Ayrton, ordered the workmen to break down the wall on the night of 18 January. According to Weigall, next morning he and Davis arrived, furious to find Ayrton staring into the dark, gaping hole. Anger soon gave way to astonishment when they saw what lay behind the wall. This was certainly no ordinary tomb. From previous experience, an access corridor should lie directly beyond the bricked-up entrance, yet here there was a second wall, set in mortar and covered with an incredibly hard cement. This time there *was* a seal. The plaster bore an oval impression depicting nine bound captives, over which squatted a jackal: the god Anubis, the eternal protector of the dead, a device common to tombs of the fourteenth century BC.

An unprecedented double barrier! The three forgot their differences and began talking excitedly. There must be some religious significance to the second wall, some aspect of Egyptian funerary belief that no one had previously encountered. It was surely the tomb of someone very special. But who? The jackal seal should have been accompanied by a second seal bearing the name of the pharaoh, yet there was none. Excited by what they had found, Davis was now impatient to enter the tomb, and even Weigall no longer objected. Some of the Egyptian workmen, however, became agitated. Those who had worked on other excavations in the Valley of the Kings knew there was something strange about this tomb. Some voiced concern over unfounded rumours of deadly booby traps – concealed pits or crushing stone blocks – while others were afraid of dangers of a less earthly kind.

In ancient Egypt the afterlife was considered the exclusive domain of the rich and powerful. For the ancient Egyptian, immortality was not determined by moral conduct during life on earth, but was secured by a kind of hereafter insurance. The body was preserved by ritual mummification to ensure the spirit a place in heaven, and it was entombed with its possessions to enrich the life to come. As Egypt grew in power, so did the affluence of its ruling elite, and likewise the treasure hoards of its dead. Tombs became depositories of amassed fortunes to be protected from intrepid thieves, ever prepared to risk capture, torture and brutal execution to plunder the wealth of departed kings. The sepulchres of the nobility became ever more elaborate in an attempt to thwart the tomb robbers: impregnable pyramids, fortified mausoleums, and secret vaults buried deep underground. To whatever plan, concealment or invulnerability, Egyptian tombs were always constructed with one purpose in mind – to keep intruders out. But what Davis and Ayrton had unearthed was an Egyptian tomb unlike any discovered before or since. It was constructed to keep someone or something trapped inside.

What transpired is certainly an episode of some of the strangest behaviour of professional archaeologists in the annals of Egyptology. Instead of a methodical sifting through the rubble between the two walls, followed by the careful dismantling of the inner wall, stone by stone, that should be expected from leading experts in their field, the three ordered the second wall to be demolished with the kind of amateurish pickaxing that only ever happens in the movies. Today, the rushed entrance into this mysterious tomb is considered the sloppiest, most incompetent excavation ever undertaken in the Valley of the Kings.

As the dust settled, for the first time in over three thousand years light penetrated the dark passageway beyond. Just under two metres wide and some two and a half metres high, the narrow corridor sloped downwards into the darkness. As they peered inside a gentle breeze from the valley below blew down the shaft causing something to shimmer and flash in the intrusive sunlight. It was the fine gold leaf that completely covered two huge wooden panels that lay just inside the entrance, resting on top of the limestone rubble that filled the length of the corridor to within a metre of the ceiling. Quickly, the three collected electric lights, tapped from the main supply in the Valley, and, led by Davis, inched their way, one by one, down the ancient passageway. Following up the rear, Weigall paused briefly to examine the panels, making out scenes and hieroglyphic inscriptions which dated them to the mid-to-late fourteenth century BC. The tomb was indeed over two centuries earlier than the nearby tomb of Ramesses IX. Ahead of him, Davis and Ayrton clambered eagerly over the debris, crawling downwards for about ten metres until they emerged halfway up the wall of a single chamber, some seven metres long, five metres wide and four metres high. As his lantern illuminated the vault, Davis was struck by the strangeness of the tomb. The walls, that should have been elaborately decorated with murals and hieroglyphics, were neatly plastered but completely bare.

Below, small glazed earthenware vessels, decorated amulets, more panels and numerous fragments of broken clay were strewn haphazardly across the floor. From the damage and the musty smell that hung in the air, it was clear that water had at some time flooded the chamber. Looking up, Davis could see the cause. A long thin crack running down the length of the ceiling had allowed rainwater, which occasionally scoured down the valley in rare but violent torrents, to seep into the tomb and wreak havoc. Fortunately, not everything was damaged. Davis was relieved to discover that on the opposite side of the chamber there was a deep recess, about one and a half metres square, well above what had once been the water line, upon which stood four undisturbed jars of polished white calcite with beautifully wrought stoppers in the shape of human heads: Canopic jars made to contain the removed internal organs of a mummified body.

As Weigall joined them and their eyes became accustomed to the gloom, they could make out the coffin itself, lying on the floor just below the recess. The wooden lion-headed bier on which it had once stood had long ago collapsed, bringing it crashing to the ground, jerking off the lid and leaving the decaying mummy exposed to the air.

Having clambered down the wall and skirted around the rubble, the three men stood examining the coffin. It quickly became apparent that there was indeed something very peculiar about this tomb. The usual gold portrait mask on the coffin lid, made in the image of the deceased, had most of the face ripped away. All that remained was the right eye, wide and staring. Examining the mask more closely, they could make out, on the forehead, the broken remains of a bronze serpent: the *uraeus*, the Egyptian symbol of royalty. The mummy was not merely an aristocrat, it was a king or queen. But who? An inspection of the inscriptions on the coffin revealed even greater mystery. The name of the occupant in its cartouches – oval designs that surrounded the hieroglyphics of a royal name – had been scratched off. On the mummy itself, the inscribed gold bands that were wrapped around the dressings also had the name of the mummy deliberately cut out. Turning to the Canopic jars, the party discovered that here too the name of the mummy had been removed and inscribed panels on the belly of the jars had been chiselled away.

At first they considered that the damage to the mask had been caused when the bier collapsed, but there was no sign of the missing item anywhere in the chamber; certainly, the obliteration of the name cartouches could not have been accidental. There was only one conclusion: someone had deliberately torn off the face and serpent from the mask, and purposely erased the name of the mummy. As other priceless gold trappings on the coffin had been left behind and the entrance had been intact, this selective destruction could not have been the work of tomb robbers – they would neither have left such gold-work behind nor resealed the tomb when they left. As the tomb seal was contemporary with the tomb's contents, the vandalism must have occurred during or shortly after the mummy's interment. Moreover, as it was an official seal of the period, the stripping of all evidence of the mummy's name, rank and features must have been officially sanctioned.

Looking around, they soon realized that the mummy had also been denied the lavish burial goods that should surround the last resting place of an Egyptian monarch. No weapons or chariots for the occupant to use in the afterlife; no remains of clothes to be worn or food to be eaten; no statues of gods for guidance and protection; no jewels or wealth of any kind – nothing but a few simple amulets, earthenware boxes and jars. Even the wall reliefs to show scenes from the occupant's life and depict his safe passage to the underworld were completely absent; merely cold, white-plastered walls, pitted and stained with age.

The only sizeable artefacts in the tomb, beside the coffin and its bier, were the remains of a number of gilded wooden shrine panels, found dispersed in various locations. The shrine, which was intended to surround the coffin, had not been broken apart and scattered by water; it had obviously never been set in place. Not only had two of its panels been found high up the tunnel, near the entrance to the tomb where they could not have been carried by water, but the shrine itself was incomplete.

What kind of tomb was this? In ancient Egyptian belief, if someone's name was wiped from memory, so also was their influence on this world from the afterlife: a number of Egyptian pharaohs are known to have excised the names of their dead enemies from all inscriptions. Is this what had happened here? If so, the mummy itself should have been destroyed. The ancient Egyptians also believed that so long as the mummy remained, then so did its spirit; some royal tombs of the era had been formally ransacked on the orders of rival successors, and their mummies torn to shreds. Why was this mummy still intact, complete with its gilded coffin, its organs safe in their Canopic jars? Whatever the reason for the curious desecration, it was unlike anything discovered before. The mummy had been robbed of its status and identity – its power to influence the living denied – yet its spirit had been expressly allowed to survive.

Realizing the uniqueness of their discovery, the three men now behaved more professionally, and wisely left the tomb before disturbing it further. The Inspector General of Egyptian Antiquities, Sir Gaston Maspero, was informed and a guard placed on the tomb so that the photographer, a certain R. Paul, could record the contents were they lay, and the expedition artist, Lindon Smith, could draw the panel reliefs of the golden shrine. By the end of the month the contents had been catalogued, drawn and photographed, and everything except the shrine panels and the mummy itself had been removed from the tomb and stored on board Davis' boat moored off Luxor. Yet still they were no nearer to identifying the mummy.

Even by the scientific standards of the time, the first

examination of the mummy, still *in situ* in the tomb, was little more than vandalism. For some unknown reason, Weigall and Ayrton chose to be absent from the stripping of the mummy, and it was left to Maspero, Davis and Lindon Smith to unwrap the three-thousand-year-old corpse. Some idea of the incredibly amateurish way in which they proceeded is provided by Davis' own account: 'When we had taken off the gold on the front of the mummy, we lifted it so as to get to the gold from underneath ... Lindon Smith then pulled out a six-inch long thick sheet of gold. More gold sheets followed ...'

Not only were they more interested in the gold than the historical secrets the mummy could impart, but the unqualified Lindon Smith was allowed to ferret freely around inside the ancient wrappings. Worse still was the way the body was treated once the bandages had been removed. Davis, for instance, prodded at one of its front teeth and by his own admission, 'Alas! It fell into dust.' The unwrapping of the mummy may have been a travesty of scientific method, but the security afforded its burial jewels was a complete joke. The mummy's golden necklace was left lying around on Davis' boat and immediately went missing. A few weeks later, an antiquities dealer in Luxor contacted Davis to tell him he could buy it back if no attempt was made to arrest the culprits responsible for its theft. Davis agreed and paid dearly for its return. The gold bands, however, were lost for ever. An Egyptian laboratory assistant in Cairo – a virtual stranger – had oddly been entrusted with their safe keeping. He promptly ran off with them, never to be seen again.

It is a complete mystery why the men in charge of the operation should have acted so out of character. So unusual was their behaviour throughout the excavation and its aftermath that it has even been suggested that they might have fallen foul of some supernatural influence from the tomb. Maspero was one of the leading Egyptologists of his time – if not the greatest – and as Inspector General was responsible for assuring the highest professional standards from excavators at digs all over Egypt. Likewise Davis, who although not a professional, had been, and would be, responsible for financing and organizing some of the most important archaeological expeditions of the early twentieth century. That they had firstly behaved little better than tomb robbers, and afterwards as complete incompetents, is almost as bizarre as the contents of the tomb itself. As two of Britain's three leading Egyptologists (Carter being the third), Ayrton and Weigall were little better, in the way they ham-fistedly smashed their way into the tomb. But the worst was still to come, as Davis, Weigall and Ayrton, once close professional colleagues, began to bicker among themselves like unruly children.

Shortly after the unwrapping of the mummy, Ayrton did what he should have done before the tomb was opened: he began sorting through the rubble that had been the inner entrance of the tomb in search of the missing royal seal. In tombs of the period, a seal bearing the cartouche of the reigning pharaoh was placed on the entrance of the tomb of any important dignitary. The tomb of a pharaoh himself, however, would not bear the seal of his successor but his own, as the new pharaoh would not officially succeed to the throne until his predecessor was buried. As the cartouches on the coffin and the serpent on the mask headdress specifically identified the mysterious mummy as royal, Ayrton concluded that the missing entrance seal must bear the name of the king who was buried inside. He was certain that it must have been on the inner door, beside the jackal seal, but had broken away as the outer wall fell inwards when the tomb was first broken open. Aided by Emma

Andrews, he painstakingly sifted through the limestone chips for many hours until, piece by piece, the shattered shards of the royal cartouche were recovered. When the seal was pieced together Ayrton was elated: it seemed that he had at last beaten his arch-rival Howard Carter. The seal bore the name of Tutankhamun.

Fifteen years later, and only thirteen metres from the entrance to the mysterious tomb discovered by Ayrton, Tutankhamun's tomb was again discovered, this time by Carter himself. This tomb was filled with the myriad celebrated burial goods and magnificent wall paintings which made it abundantly clear that it was the real tomb of Tutankhamun. Who, then, lay in the tomb that Ayrton had discovered – a tomb that was secured with Tutankhamun's personal seal?

In 1907, even before Tutankhamun's tomb had been discovered, Davis concluded that the mysterious mummy could not be the now-famous king, as it was clearly that of a woman. When they first unwrapped the ancient bandages, the first thing they observed was the position of the arms. The mummy had been embalmed in the pose normally associated with queens of the period, with one arm folded across the chest, and the other by the side, instead of both being folded across the chest like a king. The mummy also wore a queen's crown, as evidenced by the first published report of the mummy made by Walter Tyndale, an observer at the unwrapping. Like everyone else, he took the body to be female: 'Her dried-up face, sunken cheeks, and thin leathery-looking lips, exposing a few teeth, were in ghastly contrast to the golden diadem which encircled her head and the gold necklace that partially hid her shrunken throat.'

Beside the fact that the mummy's arms were in the attitude of a woman, and around its head was a gold band bearing the image of a vulture – the same headdress shown frequently in contemporary portraits of queens and princesses – both the coiffure on the coffin and the figure on the carved stoppers of the Canopic jars were depicted with a hairstyle affected by court ladies of the period. Ayrton, however, emphatically rejected all evidence that the mummy was a queen and not a king. It seemed to everyone that his obsession to outdo Howard Carter and be the first to discover Tutankhamun's tomb was completely clouding his judgement.

What Tutankhamun's entrance seal *had* evidenced, however, was that the body had been entombed sometime during Tutankhamun's reign, approximately between 1347 and 1338 BC. As Tutankhamun's queen was known to have outlived him, Davis decided that the mummy was Amonhotep III's wife, Queen Tiye, who he believed had died during Tutankhamun's reign. As the stopper heads of the Canopic jars were usually made in the image of the person whose organs they contained, Davis drew attention to their similarity to statues of the queen. Moreover, a stone toilet vase found in the tomb was actually inscribed with her name, as were other tiny amulets found in two small boxes. What clinched the argument for Davis, however, were the gilded panels. Forming part of a shrine that was meant to be erected around the coffin, they were decorated in relief with figures of Queen Tiye, and an accompanying inscription declared that it had been specifically made for her.

Ayrton vehemently disagreed: if the carved head on the stoppers really was the likeness of the mummy, why had they not been disfigured like the mask? And if it was Queen Tiye's name that had been so painstakingly eradicated from the mummy, the coffin and the Canopic jars, why so foolishly leave it on the toilet vase, the amulets and the shrine panels? In support of his Tutankhamun theory, Ayrton drew Davis' attention to numerous fragments of clay seals discovered while sorting through the rubble around the collapsed bier which, when pieced together, were found to be impressed with the cartouche of Tutankhamun. He was sure that these had originally sealed boxes of Tutankhamun's burial treasure and had broken off when his tomb had been plundered by the desecrators.

While Davis and Ayrton continued to argue, Weigall came up with a third candidate of his own, suggested by the so-called 'magic bricks'. Common to the period, these four inscribed stones – protective amulets placed in the walls of the tomb at the four cardinal points to safeguard the mummy magically – were always inscribed with the name of the deceased. In this tomb the bricks bore the name of neither Davis' nor Ayrton's candidates, but the king who was thought to be Tutankhamun's uncle: the pharaoh Akhenaten. Weigall was certain that it was his tomb and that his name still remaining on the bricks had been overlooked by the desecrators.

In support of his theory, Weigall drew his colleagues' attention to the inscription on the shrine panel which declared that it had been made for Queen Tiye. It had also been inscribed with the name of the person who had commissioned it to be made; a name that had been erased just like the name on the coffin and the Canopic jars. Surely, he reasoned, this must be the same person who was in the coffin. Why else bother to erase it? From the context of the inscription, the mysterious benefactor could only have been her royal son, her husband's successor Akhenaten. Weigall examined the gold straps encircling the outer wrappings of the mummy, further concluding that these inscriptions could also only refer to Akhenaten.

To settle the argument promptly, Davis invited a European physician living in Luxor to examine the body while it was still in the tomb. The mummy wrappings had decayed through damp and could be lifted off in great pads, exposing the bones from end to end. Examining the skeleton, the doctor quickly concluded that, because of the width of the pelvis, it could only be the remains of a woman. Although the physician was no forensic expert, Davis was satisfied enough with the findings to publish his account of the excavations immediately, under the title *The Tomb of Queen Tiye*.

Although Ayrton dropped his Tutankhamun theory and quickly began searching elsewhere in the Valley of the Kings for his elusive pharaoh, Weigall was not silenced by the results. The mummy's wide pelvis may well be a female feature, he argued, but it also corresponded with Akhenaten's strange physical appearance. In both the statues and the reliefs of Akhenaten found throughout Egypt, he is depicted with a slender feminine waist and unusually wide hips. This prompted many historians of the period to speculate that Akhenaten may even have been an hermaphrodite. Accordingly, the identification of the mummy as female because of its wide pelvis could equally apply to Akhenaten.

Within a few months, both Weigall and Davis were apparently proved wrong. In July 1907, the mummy was sent for complete analysis to Sir Grafton Elliot Smith, Professor of Anatomy at the Cairo School of Medicine. He found to his intense surprise that, instead of the body of an old woman that Davis had led him to expect, he had been sent the remains of a young man who had apparently died in his early twenties. Other eminent experts were called in and all agreed that it was unquestionably the body of a young male, and definitely not that of an older woman. Not only was the mummy not Queen Tiye, but neither could it be Akhenaten, as he was known to have reigned for at least seventeen years and had been well over thirty when he died.

A further discovery made during Elliot Smith's examination

of the mummy was that the gold vulture band around its brow was not a female crown, as first thought, but a 'vulture collar' of male pharaonic burials. The mis-identification was due to the fact that it had fallen up over the head when the bier collapsed, giving it the appearance of a headdress. The mummy was therefore not only unquestionably male, but also a king.

So who was the mysterious mummy in Tomb 55? And why, when he was undeniably a king, did his tomb not bear his own seal? The answer to both questions appeared to be that he was one of Tutankhamun's discredited predecessors, placed in the tomb during Tutankhamun's reign. As the mummy was too young to have been Akhenaten, and the tomb of Akhenaten's immediate forebear, Amonhotep III, had already been discovered in the western Valley of the Kings in 1799, both were ruled out as possible candidates.

Eventually, the development of modern forensic techniques enabled a likely relationship to be established between Tutankhamun and the mummy. In 1963, an examination of the remains by a team of scientists, led by Professor R. G. Harrison of Liverpool University, not only showed beyond doubt that the subject was male and had died around his twentieth year, but it revealed that he shared the same blood group and type with Tutankhamun's mummy: the two were so closely related they were almost certainly brothers.

Although there are no surviving records specifically referring to a brother of Tutankhamun, a shadowy figure emerges from Egyptian history just prior to Tutankhamun's reign who may have been just that. During the last years of Akhenaten's reign, a few carved portraits of the royal entourage include someone identified as Ankhkheperure, and bearing the appellation Nefernefruaten, 'Fair is the beauty of the [god] Aten'. As this was a title used by Akhenaten's queen, Nefertiti, the appellation would suggest that Ankhkheperure was related to her. As she had no sons, then he was probably a nephew, and possibly Tutankhamun's brother. Ankhkheperure appears to have dropped Nefertiti's title at the end of Akhenaten's reign in favour of his birth name Smenkhkare, 'He whom the spirit of [the god] Re has ennobled', and, as Ankhkheperure Smenkhkare, his name appears on a number of stones, finger rings and furniture trappings found on the site of Akhenaten's royal palace at Amarna in Middle Egypt.

Smenkhkare (pronounced *Smen-car-ray*), as he is generally called for convenience, appears to have become Akhenaten's chosen successor, as a carved limestone portrait of the two of them, side by side, and both wearing a royal serpent, was found on the site of the Great Temple at Amarna in 1933. It also seems certain that he succeeded Akhenaten, as a scene in the tomb of Meryre, the overseer of Akhenaten's harem at Amarna, shows him in the accoutrements of a reigning pharaoh with his name enclosed in a royal cartouche. No records of his reign have yet been discovered, although it does not seem to have been a long one. An inscription on a honey jar docket discovered at Amarna shows that Tutankhamun's reign began in the same year that Akhenaten's ended, and a wine jar docket also found at the site, dated to the first year of Tutankhamun's reign, is inscribed with the words, 'wine from the estate of Smenkhkare, deceased'.

If Smenkhkare was the mysterious mummy in Tomb 55, then the sealing of the tomb with his successor Tutankhamun's cartouche means that it must have been reopened within a few years of the original interment. Indeed, this is exactly what the evidence from Tutankhamun's own tomb reveals.

From more than a century's excavations in the Valley of the Kings, a fairly detailed picture of contemporary royal burials has emerged. Within a series of chambers housing opulent grave goods and an ornate Canopic shrine, the king's mummy would be enclosed by a series of progressively smaller wooden shrines, together with a decorative frame over which was draped an embroidered linen cover. Within the shrines stood a stone sarcophagus containing a nest of three coffins, one fitting neatly inside the other like a set of Russian dolls. All that remained in Tomb 55, however, was the innermost coffin, the Canopic jars, a few minor artefacts, and the dismantled shrine panels. It is quite clear from tell-tale clues in the tomb that it originally contained far more. The broken clay seals that littered the floor reveal that treasure boxes had been broken open and removed, and the shrine panels being stacked as they were against the wall, with more in the entrance corridor, indicates that they were in the process of being removed when the operation was for some reason abandoned.

In 1907, Davis discovered something in Tomb 55 which seemed unimportant at the time, but later led directly to the whereabouts of the plundered treasures. Two gilded copper discs, worked in the shape of flowers, were found among the debris near the stacked shrine panels, and correctly identified as pall medallions from a shrine drape. Two decades later they were found to be identical to the medallions sewn on to a black linen pall covering the inner shrines in Tutankhamun's tomb. But the shrine pall is not the only item that was looted from Tomb 55 to furnish so lavishly the tomb of Tutankhamun. On both the gilded shrines and the stone sarcophagus in Tutankhamun's tomb, original text had been erased and reinscribed with Tutankhamun's name. The second of Tutankhamun's three coffins was also appropriated: its gilded portrait mask bears no resemblance to Tutankhamun's appearance on the other two coffins or on his statues. The same likeness can be seen on the lids of four gold coffinettes, used instead of Canopic jars to contain the king's internal organs. Made to exactly the same design, they and the coffin clearly all belong to one set that was made for someone else. When he was clearing the tomb, Howard Carter was amazed to discover that inscriptions on the interior of the coffinettes had the owner's cartouches altered, and closer inspection revealed evidence of the original name: Ankhkheperure, the throne-name of Smenkhkare.

As Carter continued to clear the tomb of its hundreds of precious artefacts, item after item was found to have belonged to Smenkhkare. Treasure boxes bore his name, as did various figurines; even much of the jewellery that so intimately decorated the mummy had been appropriated from the tomb of Smenkhkare. Just how many of Tutankhamun's fabulous grave goods had been appropriated is now impossible to determine, as most bear no name at all. However, when he had finally finished clearing the tomb in 1929, Carter estimated that a considerable part of Tutankhamun's celebrated treasure may have once belonged to Smenkhkare.

A remarkable postscript to this discovery is that the king's golden image from the lid of the second coffin is today almost invariably used to illustrate text books, holiday guides and posters. This famous image that the world has come to recognise as Tutankhamun – the imposing pharaoh, hands crossed majestically over his chest to hold the pharaonic crook and flail – is not, it appears, Tutankhamun at all, but his enigmatic brother Smenkhkare.

So little attention has been drawn to this fact that in 1963, when D. J. Kidd, the medical artist to the faculty of Medicine at Liverpool University, made a facial reconstruction from the skull of the Tomb 55 mummy, he was surprised to find that the resulting features bore a striking resemblance to the face of Tutankhamun from the famous middle coffin. Unaware of

Carter's original discoveries, a number of scholars took Kidd's work to suggest that Smenkhare and Tutankhamun were identical twins. Not only do Tutankhamun's other coffins show that this was not the case, there was also about a decade's age difference between them. It seems much more likely that facial reconstruction of the Tomb 55 mummy matches Tutankhamun's image on the middle coffin because the coffin originally belonged to Smenkhkare.

Tutankhamun, or someone working on his behalf, is almost certainly responsible for the strange condition of Tomb 55. Looting the tomb to furnish his own may explain the lack of burial goods, but the macabre desecration of the mummy still remains as mysterious as ever. If Tutankhamun detested Smenkhkare to the extent that he robbed his tomb and expunged his name, why not destroy the mummy altogether? Why deliberately leave it safe in its golden coffin, with its organs undamaged in their Canopic jars? The desecrators had seemingly taken the trouble painstakingly to remove all evidence of his name and identity from both, evidently in the belief that this would negate his influence from the afterlife, yet they had deliberately left his mummy and organs fully intact so that his spirit would survive. This seems to make no sense, unless of course it was intended as some kind of curse. The desecrators' apparent intentions are clarified by two aspects of the strange entombment: the lack of decorations in the burial chamber and the condition in which the tomb was left.

The wall decorations of a royal burial chamber served a very important purpose, as they depicted the journey of the pharaoh's soul to the next incarnation – the realm of the gods. Without such decorations the king's spirit could not leave its resting place. Furthermore, the way in which the tomb was abandoned and sealed is evidence that they not only feared the pharaoh's earthbound spirit, but made doubly certain that it could not leave the tomb.

The final condition of the tomb shows that the desecrators had ultimately been scared out of the place before they had finished stripping it of all its treasures. The shrine, for instance, had been dismantled and stacked against the north wall and was in the process of being removed, when suddenly, and for no apparent reason, it was completely abandoned and the tomb was sealed up. As two of the valuable shrine panels were left within a few feet of the entrance, the desecrators must literally have dropped them and fled. The fact that they had time to brick up the entrance with these valuable gold-covered artefacts lying within arm's reach, could only mean that the outer portal to the tomb was regarded as a magical barrier against whatever evil they imagined to be inside. To re-enter, even by a few inches, was presumably considered too perilous. Whether they had to complete the procedure in a specific period of time, or whether they had been spooked by something in the tomb itself, we shall never know. What is apparent from the discovery of chisels, a mallet and other workmen's effects found lying on the floor of the burial chamber is that the desecrators departed so quickly that they even left their tools behind. The unusual entrance, therefore, appears to have been prepared as a magical barrier, not to protect the tomb from influences from the outside as was usually the practice, but to prevent whatever was inside from escaping.

It would seem that Tomb 55 was not so much a final resting place as a prison. In the eyes of his contemporaries, Smenkhkare must have committed a crime so heinous that oblivion was not considered sufficient punishment. Rather, they had sentenced him to spend eternity sentient and alone in the silence and darkness of this empty underground vault.

What Smenkhkare had done to warrant so unique and terrible a fate is mystery enough, but his interment in the funerary effects of a woman is even more puzzling. The coffin and Canopic jars had been carefully modified to make them suitable for a pharaoh, with, for instance, a beard being attached to the chin of the face mask, and inscriptions had been altered from feminine to masculine genders. The question is, were these items from the original burial, or were they substitutes from the time of the desecration? Although it has been suggested that the items were the originals – female equipment appropriated and altered to accommodate Smenkhkare because he had died suddenly, before his own burial equipment was ready – this does not sit with the evidence. We know from Tutankhamun's tomb that Smenkhkare did have his own elegantly designed organ coffinettes fully prepared, so there was certainly no reason to use the female Canopic jars. The balance of evidence clearly indicates that the mummy's final condition was the work of the desecrators. This reasoning is further supported by one of the gold mummy bands from Tutankhamun's tomb, which was found to have originally been inscribed with the name of Smenkhkare. This intimate funerary item comes from the very mummy of Smenkhkare, and clearly demonstrates that his remains were completely re-dressed by those who had plundered his tomb.

It now seems clear that the desecrators believed that, for their ritual violation of Smenkhkare's remains to have its desired effect, it was necessary to replace the mummy in a new coffin and the organs in new Canopic vessels once the originals had been looted. However, was the fact that they were female burial accoutrements of special importance? Were the woman's coffin and Canopic jars simply discarded items that were at hand and used for expediency, or was there some specific purpose in using female equipment? The answer appears to be that it was deliberately chosen, as the mummy itself was laid out in the attitude of a woman, with only one arm across the chest rather than both.

What can be gathered from this assorted evidence is that shortly after Akhenaten's death, Smenkhkare was entombed conventionally with his own elaborate grave goods. Sometime during the next nine years of Tutankhamun's reign, the king's followers had plundered Smenkhkare's tomb to furnish Tutankhamun's own. Then, in the belief that they could doom Smenkhkare's spirit to survive imprisoned in the tomb, they completely refurnished the mummy and its organs in a macabre transsexual fashion. In the hope of shedding more light on the thinking behind this morbid procedure, attention must turn to the identity of the woman for whom the burial effects were initially intended. Presumably, the excised cartouches had originally bone her name, and perhaps the torn-away face mask had even been in her likeness.

In the 1980s, when the German scholar Rolf Krauss attempted to put a name to this anonymous woman, he discovered something that, far from throwing new light on the mystery, simply made the matter all the more perplexing. From thorough examination and microscopic analysis of the inscribed panels on the Canopic jars, he recovered hieroglyphics that had been all but obliterated. They revealed that a female title had indeed been removed from columns of text and replaced by that of a man. Incredibly, however, it was not the name Smenkhkare, as Krauss expected, or any other title pertaining to that king, but Neferkheperure – the throne name adopted by Akhenaten. Following this discovery, other eminent authorities, such as Cyril Aldred, curator of the department of Egyptian Art at the

New York Metropolitan Museum, re-examined the inscriptions on the coffin itself and concluded that they too had been reinscribed in a context that was only applicable to Akhenaten.

These new findings, taken together with Weigall's earlier identification of contextual references to the same pharaoh on the now-lost mummy bands, illustrate almost conclusively that the intimate burial apparatus in Tomb 55 was expressly adapted for Akhenaten, and not for Smenkhkare at all. Yet how *could* the mummy be Akhenaten? Although his mummy has never been found, unless virtually every eminent Egyptologist for more than a century has been completely mistaken, Akhenaten was far too old to have been the mummy in Tomb 55. If it was a king from the period immediately preceding Tutankhamun, as dated and determined from every item in the tomb, and it was the age indicated by the most modern forensic techniques available, then it could only be Smenkhkare.

The enigma of Tomb 55 as it now remains is not only a complete mystery, it is utterly bizarre. A body which is almost certainly Smenkhkare is heartlessly robbed of its riches, subjected to an odious ritual curse, laid out in the parody of a woman, and re-interred in a queen's funerary equipment which had already been adapted for another man. Add to this the fact that the 'magic bricks' had been made for Akhenaten's tomb, the shrine had been made for Queen Tiye's, and the treasure boxes removed from the tomb had been sealed with Tutankhamun's cartouche, and we have a mystery so complex that it has remained unsolved for almost a century.

With the mystery of Tomb 55 there begins an exciting historical detective story. Unfolding step by fascinating step, a trail of ancient arcane clues ultimately takes us way beyond the borders of pharaonic Egypt. It is an investigation which leads to startling new evidence of an epoch-making cataclysm, and rediscovers the most extraordinary series of events ever to have shaped the course of human history.

SUMMARY

- Ancient Egyptian tombs were always constructed with one purpose in mind: to keep intruders out. In 1907 archaeologists discovered a new tomb in Egypt's Valley of the Kings. Known as Tomb 55, it was unlike any Egyptian tomb ever discovered. Rather than to keep intruders out, it was designed to keep someone or something trapped inside.

- The mummy was still in its gilded coffin, but all evidence of its identity had been removed.

- In ancient Egyptian belief, if someone was buried without their name they could not enter the next world. It would seem that Tomb 55 was not so much a final resting place as a prison. In the eyes of his contemporaries, the occupant must have committed a crime so heinous that oblivion was not considered sufficient punishment.

- Forensic tests carried out in 1963 finally identified the mummy as the Egyptian pharaoh Smenkhkare, the brother and predecessor of the famous Tutankhamun.

- Sometime in the middle of the fourteenth century BC, Tutankhamun had apparently robbed his brother of his funerary goods, subjected him to an odious ritual curse, laid him out in the parody of a woman, and reinterred him in a woman's funerary equipment which had already been adapted for another man. The enigma of Tomb 55 is so perplexing that it has remained a mystery for almost a century.

CHAPTER TWO

Prelude to Heresy

When Tomb 55 was so mysteriously sealed sometime in the late fourteenth century BC, the Egyptian kingdom had already been in existence for almost 2,000 years. The great pyramids of Giza had been standing silently for over a millennium, but there was still another thirteen centuries before Egypt's last pharaoh, Ptolemy XV, the son of Cleopatra, was murdered on the orders of Caesar Augustus and Egypt became the personal estate of the Roman Emperors. Ancient Egypt was by far the longest-lived civilization the world has known; yet for nearly all its three-thousand-year history, its religious beliefs remained fundamentally unchanged. The one occasion the nation did experience a religious revolution, however, just so happens to have occurred during the lifetime of Tutankhamun and Smenkhkare. Before we can ascertain if there is any correlation between this and the enigma of Tomb 55, we must first appreciate the extraordinary nature of Egyptian culture.

During the European Renaissance, when interest in the ancient world was rekindled, Egypt's wondrous ruins refused to surrender their secrets. Unlike the language of the Greeks and Romans, ancient Egyptian had not been a living language since Egypt came under the sway of the Arab world in the second half of the first millennium AD and Arabic became the national

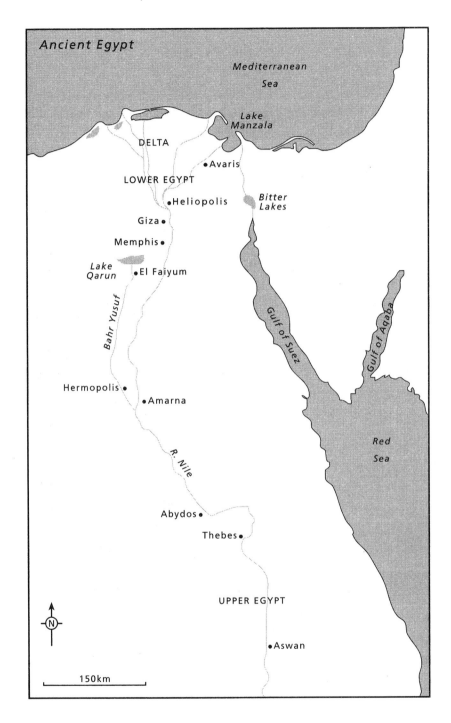

Ancient Egypt

Mediterranean Sea

Lake Manzala

DELTA

•Avaris

LOWER EGYPT

•Heliopolis

Bitter Lakes

Giza •

Memphis •

Lake Qarun

•El Faiyum

Bahr Yusuf

Hermopolis •

•Amarna

R. Nile

Gulf of Suez

Gulf of Aqaba

Red Sea

Abydos •

Thebes•

UPPER EGYPT

N

•Aswan

150km

tongue. The land of the Nile was filled with the imposing monuments of a once-mighty people: temples, pyramids, tombs and palaces, covered with tantalizing inscriptions that no one could understand.

Egyptian writing, in the form of simple pictograms, first appeared around 3000 BC and was soon developed into a system of decorative hieroglyphics, used to inscribe monuments, together with hieratic script, a simplification of hieroglyphics used for speed of writing on papyrus. For years the translation of these exotic symbols defied all attempts, and it was not until the end of the eighteenth century that it was at last made possible by the discovery of the Rosetta Stone. This slab of black basalt, found near the town of Rosetta at the mouth of the Nile in 1799, bore a lengthy inscription dating from 197 BC. As the stone carried the same text in Egyptian hieroglyphics and in a known language, Greek, it enabled the French scholar Jean François Champollion to work towards a complete decipherment of hieroglyphics by 1822.

Even though the myriad inscriptions that still survived could now be read, it soon became clear that day-to-day records of ancient Egyptian life were few and far between. Only from 332 BC, when Alexander the Great annexed the country and made it a satellite nation of the Greeks, is there a clearly documented history of ancient Egypt. The Greeks brought a new concept to the culture, recording contemporary events for historical posterity; something which the Egyptians themselves appeared to have considered pointless. Egyptian writings had almost exclusively concentrated on commercial, commemorative or religious matters. Even those historical events which the translation of hieroglyphics did reveal were found difficult to date or to fit into a chronological framework.

Ultimately, five inscribed monuments were discovered to

reveal the names and order of succession of many of Egypt's pharaohs. The Palermo Stone, a black diorite slab dating from around 2470 BC, recorded a series of early kings; a Royal List from the temple of Karnak included the names of those who preceded Tuthmosis III around 1500 BC; and a Royal List from the city of Abydos, made by Seti I around 1290 BC, named the seventy-six kings who proceeded him, as did two duplicates made by his son Ramesses II. Unfortunately, as an historical chronology these lists are almost useless on their own, as they fail to provide the length of each reign. Luckily, however, one ancient text still survives which does: a list of some 300 kings written in hieratic script on a long sheet of papyrus dating from around 1200 BC. Now in the Turin Museum, the so-called Royal Canon not only gives the order of succession, but also provides the exact period of each reign, right down to the months and days. The problem, however, was that at the time it was rediscovered there was no way to determine how the list related to the modern calendar. Which year did it start and which year did it end? Consequently, the dating of Egyptian history proved a nightmare, with scholars disagreeing with one another sometimes by centuries. Historians needed points of reference: other datable events with which to link the pharaohs' reigns. It was no use looking to ancient Egypt's contemporary neighbours. Until the time of the Greeks their historical records were little better. It fell to astronomy eventually to resolve the matter. Some of the pharaohs' reigns could be precisely dated due to ancient astronomical observations and a lucky mistake in the Egyptian calendar.

The ancient Egyptians knew that the year consisted of 365 days, but they made no adjustment for the additional quarter day, as we do now by adding a day every fourth year. Civic activities, administrative meetings, tax collections, censuses and so forth were arranged according to a 365-day calendar, but religious activities were tied to celestial events, such as the midsummer sunrise, or the spring equinox, that occur at the same time each 365-and-a-quarter-day solar year. Accordingly, the Egyptian civil and solar calendars gradually moved out of synchronization by a day every four years until, after 730 years, midsummer's day fell in the middle of winter. Because they had no idea that the year was determined by the length of time it took the earth to orbit the sun, this discrepancy perplexed the ancient Egyptians, who every few centuries would find the seasons apparently reversed. On one papyrus dating from the thirteenth century BC, a mystified scribe records: 'Winter has come in summer, the months are reversed, the hours in confusion.' It would take a further 730 years for the solar calendar to catch up with the civil calendar, so only every 1,460 years would the two calendars properly align.

As the brightest star in the sky, Sirius was considered to be of great magical importance, and each year on the day of its heliacal rising – its annual reappearance in early July – an important religious festival took place. Accordingly, when this festival coincided with the first day of the civil calendar, every 1460 years, it was considered a particularly special time: the beginning of a new eon called the Sothic Cycle (after Sothis, the ancient name for Sirius). Such an occasion is known to have been celebrated by the Roman occupiers of Egypt in the second century AD. A coin was issued to commemorate the event during the reign of the emperor Antoninus Pius in AD 139. As this only occurred every 1,460 years, by counting backwards we can work out that the same thing had also happened in 1321 BC and 2781 BC.

Against these important dates, specific years in the reigns of kings from the Royal Canon of Turin could be determined. One of the kings included in the list was Senusret III, and a contemporary inscription records that in the seventh year of his reign the heliacal rising of Sirius occurred on the 226th day of the civil calendar. As it took four years for the calendars to move out of alignment by one day, then for the calendars to be out of alignment by 226 days meant that 904 years (226 × 4) must have transpired since the beginning of the last Sothic Cycle in 2781 BC. Accordingly, the seventh year of Senusret III's reign must have been in 1877 BC. Another such sighting is recorded in the ninth year of the reign of the pharaoh Amonhotep I. It happened on the 309th day of the civil calendar, meaning that 1,236 years had transpired since the beginning of the Sothic Cycle in 2781 BC, making the ninth year of Amonhtep's reign 1545 BC. With these and other such recorded sightings it was possible to date the reigns of a number of kings recorded in the Royal Canon. As this list gave both the successive order of the kings, together the length of their reigns, by counting backwards and forwards from the known dates, it was possible to work out when each king's reign began and ended. For example, if the seventh year of Senusret III's reign was 1877 BC, his reign must have begun in 1884 BC; the recorded nineteen-year reign of his predecessor, Senusret II, must therefore have begun in 1903 BC; the recorded thirty-four-year reign of this king's predecessor, Amenemhet III, must have begun in 1937 BC, and so on.

There was a problem with this procedure: as it took four years for the calendars to move apart by a day, the heliacal rising of Sirius would occur on the same day for four consecutive years. Consequently, unless a specific hour was recorded from which to calculate on which of these four years the sighting was made, any date determined from this point of reference could be out by four years. However, this was a minor difficulty compared to problems arising from the Royal Canon itself, in that it was badly damaged, leaving many gaps in the chronology. Even the surviving sections were questioned. Could a list of kings prepared around 1200 BC really be an accurate record of events occurring over a period spanning some two thousand years into the past? Although the eventual scientific dating of archaeological discoveries tended to tally with the dates derived from the Royal Canon, these techniques, such as radiocarbon dating, allowed for a considerable margin of error. From a combination of all these procedures, however, a rough chronological framework of Egyptian history has now emerged. All the same, academic arguments continue. Even recognized authorities can disagree with each other by thirty years or so concerning events in later Egyptian history, and sometimes by as much as a century regarding earlier times.

The only actual history of ancient Egypt to be written in pre-Roman times was compiled by King Ptolemy I's chief adviser, a priest named Manetho, when the Greeks annexed the country in the late fourth century BC. Although, among other things, it provides the names of kings who reigned after the period covered by the Royal Canon of Turin, much of the detail of Manetho's work has been lost. Only selected extracts now survive in the work of later writers, such as the Jewish historian Josephus, who quoted widely from it in the in the late first century AD. From these selected extracts, however, we can gather that the ancient Egyptians divided their history into separate epochs, each beginning once a new royal family, or dynasty, attained the throne. Most modern historians, wishing to avoid being drawn into arguments over specific dates, utilize these historical divisions and refer to events having occurred during a particular dynasty, of which there appear to have been thirty-one before the Greek annexation of 332 BC. With each dynasty being referred to in numerical order, events are ascribed to the First Dynasty, the Second Dynasty, the Third Dynasty, and so on. Today historians further group these dynasties into seven separate periods, each being an era with specific historical characteristics:

Dynasty	Period	Approximate Date
1–2	The Archaic Period	3150–2686 BC
3–7	The Old Kingdom	2686–2181 BC
8–10	The First Intermediate	2181–2040 BC
11–13	The Middle Kingdom	2040–1782 BC
14–17	The Second Intermediate	1782–1570 BC
18–20	The New Kingdom	1570–1070 BC
21–31	The Late Period	1070–332 BC

With a comprehensive list of Egyptian pharaohs, a knowledge of their place in the sequence of events, and an approximate chronology of their reigns, scholars were able to piece together the archaeological and textual evidence and reconstruct the long-lost history of ancient Egypt.

Egypt was a land of stark natural contrasts, the so-called Black Land, a rich, narrow agricultural strip running along the Nile, and the aptly named Red Land, the inhospitable desert to either side. Originally, there was also a political division; an imaginary line drawn roughly through what is now Cairo divided the country into two separate kingdoms: Lower Egypt, around the Nile Delta to the north, and Upper Egypt which stretched to the south as far as modern Aswan. (The Lower and Upper refer to the course of the Nile.) The oldest surviving historical record from Egypt dates from around 3100 BC. Known as the Narmer Palette, it is an inscribed piece of dark green slate showing a victorious king in two separate scenes. Identified as King Narmer, he is shown in one scene wearing the crown of Upper Egypt (known as the White Crown), and in another wearing the crown of Lower Egypt (known as the Red Crown). It is now believed that the palette commemorated the unification of the two kingdoms and the birth of the Egyptian nation. It fell to Narmer's successor, Hor-Aha (a name meaning 'Fighting Hawk') to establish the First Dynasty and found the capital city of Memphis, just south of the Delta apex. It was not until around 2686 BC, however, that Egyptian civilization really came of age with the beginning of the Old Kingdom. During the four dynasties which it comprised, the power of Egypt expanded considerably, due to the increasing centralization of government and the creation of an efficient system of administration.

From the very beginning, Egypt was a culture obsessed with royalty and death. Although Egypt had a pantheon of gods, the principal deity was the sun god Re (also called Ra), for whose worship a massive religious centre had grown up at Heliopolis, some fifty kilometres to the north of Memphis. It was believed that Re had once ruled over Egypt personally but, wearied by the affairs of mankind, had retired to the heavens, leaving the pharaohs to rule in his stead. Called 'the son of Re', the pharaoh was considered a half-human, half-divine being, through whose body Re himself could manifest. However, as the falcon god Horus was the protector of Egypt, the king was also seen as his personification. By the Third Dynasty, therefore, Re and Horus had been assimilated as one god: Re-Herakhte. Depicted as a human male with a falcon's head, this composite deity was considered both the god of the sun and the god of Egypt, and his incarnation on earth was the pharaoh himself. Only the king could expect an individual eternity with the gods, everyone else could only hope to participate in this vicariously, through their contribution to his well-being. This applied as much after the king's death as it did during his life. It was believed that the dead pharaoh's spirit would only survive if it periodically returned to earth for sustenance, in the form of food, drink and other material offerings – something that necessitated having a body to return to. The process of mummification was therefore developed by preserving the body with natron, a dehydrating agent applied to the skin beneath bandages. The king was then entombed with his possessions to be utilized in the afterlife, and surrounded by religious illustrations to assure him power and protection in the next world. These elaborate interments were originally housed in so-called mastaba tombs, a series of chambers cut down into solid rock, above which stood a brick-built superstructure resembling a miniature royal palace. The entire area was then enclosed by a defensive wall and guarded around the clock. The mastaba tombs were therefore not so much final resting places, but *dwelling places* of the dead.

Although it seems that devotion to the king could ensure his subjects a place in the next world, the quality of the afterlife depended on what they took with them. This meant that the nobility also had themselves mummified and entombed as elaborately as possible. They constructed their smaller mastaba tombs around that of their beloved pharaoh, in the belief that they would continue in his service in the life to come. Conse-quently, a great necropolis – a city of the dead – grew up near Memphis at Saqqara, and to cater for the opulent funerary activities a massive industry developed. In addition to the ever-growing priesthood, who attended to the dead by receiving offerings and carrying out unceasing rituals, a wealthy middle class emerged: the craftsmen who built the mausoleums, and the artisans who produced the exquisite jewellery, amulets and burial equipment which furnished them. By far the finest, most lavish and numerous artefacts manufactured in Egypt at this time were intended only for the tomb.

As the funerary industry grew, so did organized crime. Despite the vast numbers of guards and others in attendance at Saqqara, gangs of ingenious robbers still managed to plunder the tombs. To counter this menace, safer and altogether more imposing tombs were conceived – the pyramids. The first of these was designed and built by the royal vizier (chief minister) Imhotep for the pharaoh Zoser around 2650 BC. This huge construction, which still dominates the ruins of Saqqara, was originally designed as a mastaba tomb, but later alterations and additions created a stepped pyramid in which a series of six mastaba superstructures of decreasing size were placed one on top of the other. Although the largest feature of the burial site, Zoser's pyramid formed only part of a complex of monuments designed to imitate the main elements of the king's royal court as it had been in life. Within a white limestone wall that encircled the compound, there stood an array of religious buildings, courts and a mortuary temple where extravagant offerings could be continually made.

It was not long before the more familiar smooth-sided pyramids began to appear. Various explanations have been offered to account for this development. It may have been an architectural device to conceal the entrance from thieves – who nevertheless plundered them all – or it may have represented a sun's ray, symbolizing the power of the principle god Re. Modern commentators have attributed the pyramid with astrological, mystical or even alien significance; the only thing of which we can be certain, however, is that they were seen as a link between heaven and earth. The name 'pyramid' is a Greek word, and was the term the Greeks used when they first encountered these monuments. The Egyptian word for these structures was *mer*. Meaning 'Place of Ascension', this name clearly implies that the Egyptians of the Old Kingdom saw the pyramids as the means by which the pharaoh could ascend to the realm of the gods. In these new constructions the king was no longer buried underground, as had been the procedure with the mastaba tombs, but in a chamber within the pyramid itself. Nevertheless, like the earlier tombs it was still adjoined by a mortuary temple where offerings could be received.

Around the middle of the third millennium BC, the Old Kingdom reached the zenith of its achievements with the construction of the great pyramids at a second necropolis near Memphis at Giza. It was once believed that the great pyramids were constructed by huge armies of slaves, but it now seems far more likely that they were the work of a willing populace. The construction of the royal pyramid complex became the focus of society, of paramount importance, not only to the king, but all his subjects, whose existence in life and after death depended on his soul's survival. The largest and most spectacular of these was the pyramid of Cheops, built for the pharaoh Khufu around 2580 BC. Described by the ancient Greeks as the First Wonder of the World, it was originally 147 metres high – the tallest building on earth until the nineteenth century. Incredibly, its base covered thirteen acres – an area so vast that it could accommodate the cathedrals of Florence, Milan, London's St Pauls, Westminster Abbey and St Peter's in Rome, and still have room to spare. Exactly how it was constructed, even now, remains a mystery. From excavating contemporary habitations at Giza, archaeologists have estimated the maximum possible size of the work force which cut and hauled these thousands of tons of rock into place. Equipped only with simple tools, it should have taken them generations to build the pyramid of Cheops, yet the whole gargantuan undertaking was apparently completed during Khufu's reign of just twenty-three years.

The national obsession with the royal dead finally brought about the death of the Old Kingdom. The incredible drain on the economy required to build, furnish, staff and maintain these enormous burial complexes finally bankrupted the country. Even the monarchy was ruined: in addition to preparing his own burial complex, the king was expected to repair and provision those of his predecessors, as well as provide tombs for his own family and court. Before the Old Kingdom ended in political fragmentation around 2181 BC, considerable military and technological advances had been made, however. Egypt's armies were structured into efficient fighting units, sea-going vessels traded the Mediterranean, and learned scribes were writing with ink on papyrus sheets manufactured from reeds. Sadly, this finely balanced, well-ordered society collapsed into the chaotic conditions of an era now called the First Intermediate.

During this time the centralized government at Memphis was overthrown, and an age of continual fighting resulted between local warlords and provincial rulers. Around 2040 BC, after about a century and a half of civil strife, a fresh era emerged from a strong line of rulers from Thebes in Upper Egypt. Once they had reunited Egypt to form the so-called Middle Kingdom, the Theban pharaohs instituted a scheme that they hoped would stabilize central government and preserve their hold on the throne: the system of co-regency. By placing his own son and heir on the throne nominally to rule alongside him, the pharaoh ensured that after his death there could be no arguments over succession as the new king was already officially in power. There was also a nominal alteration in the religious status of the monarchy at the birth of the Middle Kingdom. During the preceding period of instability, a powerful cult dedicated to the god Osiris had grown up at the city of Abydos. In Egyptian mythology Osiris was the ruler of the netherworld and Horus was his son. However, the newly powerful pharaohs were still seen as the divine sons of Re-Herakhte, a deity which had previously assimilated Horus. A compromise concept ultimately resulted in a kind of archaic trinity: Re remained the principal deity but, as ruler of both heaven and earth, he had two separate aspects. As the ruler of heaven he was Osiris, and as ruler of earth he was Horus. The king was therefore still the incarnation of Re, but while he was alive he was Horus and when he died he became Osiris.

Apart from these few adaptations, the Middle Kingdom was in essence a watered-down version of the Old Kingdom: the pharaohs were still buried in pyramids, although less opulent, and they were still expected to funnel wealth to the priesthood. It was not only the temple of Re-Herakhte at Heliopolis, the temple of the creator-god Ptah at Memphis, and the temple of Osiris at Abydos that required the king's financial support, but the newly powerful sect of the wind-god Amun at the pharaoh's native Thebes. A new temple was established near the city at Karnak which grew ever greater in wealth, size and prestige throughout the era.

Before the Middle Kingdom began to succumb to foreign invasion around 1782 BC, the country enjoyed the benefits of significant technological innovations. The invention of the furnace bellows and the smelting of bronze made for better tools; there were tremendous advances in methods of irrigation; and with the invention of the horizontal loom came an impressive range of fabrics. The Egyptians of the period were even supplied with copious quantities of alcohol, thanks to the introduction of new agricultural methods and the mass cultivation of grapes. And all this before the inhabitants of Britain had even got around to building Stonehenge.

The so-called Second Intermediate began when a series of Semitic kings, from around what is now Israel to the east of Egypt, began seizing control in areas of the Nile Delta. Known as the Hyksos – meaning 'Desert Princes' – their military innovations gave them an incredible advantage over the Egyptians. Not only did they introduce the horse and chariot to warfare, giving them immense tactical supremacy, but they were also far superior archers, employing the more effective compound bow. The whole of northern Egypt fell to the Hyksos around 1720 BC when they stormed Memphis and sacked the city. For 150 years the Hyksos kings governed northern Egypt, making their own capital at Avaris at the eastern edge of the Nile Delta. Only southern Egypt – Upper Egypt – remained in native hands. Here, the Egyptians finally managed to emulate the superior military innovations of the Hyksos, and around 1570 BC the Theban prince Amosis reconquered northern Egypt and inaugurated the so-called New Kingdom. So began the Eighteenth Dynasty, into which Smenkhkare and Tutankhamun were eventually born.

The Hyksos period was especially significant in the country's long history, in that it profoundly changed the Egyptians' attitude to the outside world. Previously isolated from foreign aggression, the Egyptians had happily traded with their neighbours without considering it necessary to conquer them. Now, however, they were forced to recognize that, unless they kept their neighbours under control, it would not be long before Egypt's wealth would again attract invaders. From the outset, the pharaohs of the New Kingdom established a larger, more professional army, adopted expansionist policies and began the foundations of the world's first empire.

Egypt of the New Kingdom made its capital at Thebes, where a new necropolis was chosen in the bleak western hills. In this barren gorge, known today as The Valley of the Kings, the Egyptians abandoned their earlier custom of building pyramids, perhaps because of their vulnerability to tomb robbers, and opted instead for deep rock-cut tombs. It has been suggested that the area was chosen as the royal burial site because the valley is overlooked by a natural cliff formation that resembles a pyramid. However, it was probably chosen for practical considerations, the narrow valley being relatively easy to guard. Here the tombs, consisting of a series of stairwells, corridors and chambers cut into the mountainside, were ingeniously designed to defeat the tomb robbers.

Unlike the earlier burial sites, the Valley of the Kings was used almost exclusively by pharaohs. (Only from New Kingdom are Egypt's rulers actually referred to as pharaohs. Coming from the term *pr-o*, meaning 'great house', it seems to have pertained to the ruling house, or dynasty of Thebes.) Many tombs in the valley still retain a royal sarcophagus and have walls decorated with carved and painted scenes designed to assist the king in passing from this world to the next. These tombs have provided modern scholars with a wealth of information concerning the contemporary religious beliefs, customs and living conditions. Among other things, the tomb scenes illustrate the entire funerary practice, from the initial preparations to the ceremonial processions and the final interment.

The New Kingdom was the strongest and most expansive period in Egypt's history, and the colossal works of its kings, their temples, palaces and monuments are the most numerous of any era. We can even gaze upon the very faces of many of the New Kingdom pharaohs in a special room at the Cairo Museum. When the New Kingdom finally collapsed, these despoiled mummies had been removed from their tombs by loyal priests and hidden nearby in two great caches. Here the fifty-six remarkably preserved bodies remained undisturbed for almost three thousand years until they were rediscovered in the nineteenth century.

Around 1500 BC, the New Kingdom saw the greatest expansion of the Egyptian empire under the pharaoh Tuthmosis III. Often described as the Napoleon of ancient Egypt, Tuthmosis was a militarist who ensured that his campaigns were recorded for posterity. From the inscriptions and illustrations on the granite walls of the sanctuary at Karnak, we learn that he wreaked revenge on the hated Hyksos. He marched against their strongholds at Gaza, Yehem and Megiddo, taking them all within seven months. Even while Megiddo was still holding out, Tuthmosis led a second army to invade Syria, fought decisive battles, captured three cities and returned to his capital to celebrate his victories. By the end of his reign Tuthmosis had captured 350 cities throughout the eastern Mediterranean, conquered Nubia to the south, Libya to the west, and Syria and Canaan to the east.

On the religious front, the cult of Amun had already gained in importance during the Middle Kingdom under the patronage of the Theban pharaohs. Now the more powerful New Kingdom kings associated this deity with their own fortunes. With the wind-god Amun having assumed a premier place in the pantheon of Egyptian gods, he too had to become one with the supreme deity, Re. Accordingly, they were merged as the god Amun-Re, now represented in completely human form. As with Re and Re-Herakhte before him, Amun-Re was the father of the king. As the Old Kingdom had become obsessed with the dead, the New Kingdom became obsessed with the worship of Amun-Re. From about 1567 BC, Amun-Re became the chief deity of all Egypt and his temple cities of Karnak and nearby Luxor were expanded to an unprecedented size. Although the New Kingdom did nothing to rival the constructional achievements of the great pyramid, these huge temples were gigantic complexes of shrines, courts, halls and processional ways covering hundreds of acres. It is estimated that at the height of the empire's power an astonishing 60,000 people staffed the temple of Karnak alone: a multitude of priests, scribes, servants and religious officials, whose essential purpose it was to conduct the intricate daily rituals deemed necessary to assure the blessing of Amun-Re and the continued prosperity of Egypt.

With the foundations of the empire having been firmly laid by Tuthmosis III, and then consolidated by three successors, the subsequent reign of Amonhotep III in the early-fourteenth century BC was the most prosperous and stable period in Egypt's history. International trade flourished, tributes flooded in from foreign lands, and the god Amun-re was venerated like no other god before. When Amonhotep's son, Akhenaten, succeeded to the throne around 1364 BC, everything mysteriously changed. Trade tricked to a standstill, the empire disintegrated, and Amun-Re was abandoned. Even today, no one really knows why. Called the Amarna period, after the site of a new capital built at the time, it is by far the most obscure era of Egyptian history. Nearly all official records of the period were destroyed by later pharaohs who considered it to have been a dark age of heresy. Yet it is during the Amarna period that we find ourselves in the age of Tutankhamun and Smenkhkare, and the time of the mysterious desecration of Tomb 55.

Even before the discovery of their tombs, Tutankhamun and

Smenkhkare were both known to Egyptologists though various inscriptions recovered from excavations. From the historical context of the inscriptions, it was apparent that they had lived during the early New Kingdom and had been Eighteenth Dynasty kings, yet, oddly, neither of them appeared on any royal list. Eventually, the reason became clear: like the other two kings of the Amarna period, Akhenaten and the pharaoh Ay, their successors had erased their names from history. In the eyes of later generations, they had committed acts of unsurpassed evil.

At the beginning of his reign, suddenly, and for no apparent reason, Akhenaten decreed that a new god, a minor solar deity called the Aten, should replace Amun-Re as the chief god of Egypt. Within a short time, he went even further and did something completely alien to everything in Egypt's ancient culture: he proclaimed that the Aten was the *only* god. After abolishing the priesthood, altering all religious practices and initiating a complete change in the style of ceremonial art, he recalled the imperial army to Egypt to work on the construction of a massive new city he deemed should be built at Amarna in Middle Egypt. That he should have completely upturned every aspect of a two-thousand-year-old civilization and reduced the mighty army to humble bricklayers is strange enough, but the fact that everyone appears to have gone along with it all is utterly mystifying.

For centuries, through thick and thin, the religious institutions of Egypt had remained virtually unchanged. The gods Horus, Osiris and Amun may have been assimilated into the principle deity, but it was essentially the same god, Re, worshipped in precisely the same way. Other gods had always been necessary, religious festivals remained essentially unchanged, and commemorative art had been rigidly tied to a specific orthodox style. Even the minor changes, such as the introduction of the co-regency and the assimilation of the gods, had followed periods of national upheaval. Yet with Egypt apparently in the most powerful and stable period of its history, Akhenaten changes everything.

It is not just a question of why he should have done all this, but how he got away with it. The kings of the New Kingdom did not exercise such unchallenged authority as those of earlier generations. In theory, the king still had absolute power, but in reality this power was dependent on the continuing support of many other departments, in particular the priesthood. When the royal succession was disputed or there was a weak candidate, the priesthood could exercise unchallenged power by expressing or withholding divine approval. Moreover, if a king was considered unfit, the priesthood could also rule that he should be replaced. Although the pharaoh was seen as the son of Amun-Re, he was not actually considered an incarnation of the god; rather, a temporary vessel for the god to inhabit. Only when someone was actually appointed pharaoh did the god enter his body. If the circumstances arose which offended the god, the deity could quite easily inhabit the body of someone else. Accordingly, the Egyptian priesthood could simply have found another, more appropriate candidate for Amun-Re to inhabit and install him as pharaoh. In Akhenaten's case, the fact that there appears to have been no attempt to remove him is doubly puzzling. By abolishing the god whom he was supposed to personify he was actually nullifying his own authority.

It has been suggested that Akhenaten may have had the universal support of both the army and the civil authorities. Yet they too had every reason to oppose the king. With the growth of military power there existed a regular and powerful army and a hierarchy of senior officers. The expansion of empire had also

brought about an essential civil service of advisers and adminis-
trators. At Thebes this powerful bureaucracy was staffed with
officials who dealt with the efficient organization of revenue and
expenditure, the armouries, the granaries and the department
of public works. Everything Akhenaten did went against the
army's interests by neglecting the empire and leaving it virtually
undefended, and against the civil authorities' interests by abandoning Thebes and almost bankrupting the country by building
an extravagant new city.

Akhenaten's revolutionary changes were seemingly in no
one's interests. However, they must have had the support of
nearly every aspect of the Egyptian hierarchy. Otherwise, the
usurped priesthood could have impeached him on religious
grounds, the bankrupted nobility could have overthrown him
in a palace coup, and the humiliated army could have mutinied
and seized control.

Had they all gone along with it because they too had
suddenly, and wholeheartedly, adopted Akhenaten's new god?
It hardly seems credible. From what we can tell, the Aten, the
god he established as the sole god of Egypt, was virtually
unknown before Akhenaten's time. There are only a few brief
references to the Aten, and then only as a minor sun god. The
Aten seems to have been of no real importance and was revered
by almost no one. From all outward appearances, what Akhenaten did would be like the Pope declaring that Jesus Christ was
no longer the saviour and that everyone must worship an
obscure saint like St Neots.

That an institution that had survived so long should be so
completely overturned, seemingly unopposed, and replaced by
a completely new god, religious concept and mode of worship,
is completely mind-boggling. The only rational explanation is
that there had been some unprecedented national upheaval –

something so remarkable that it completely challenged the entire social and religious fabric of Egypt. History, however, tells us nothing. Any records that may have existed were destroyed at the end of the Amarna period, when the old institutions were re-established and a wholesale attempt was made to eradicate all record of Akhenaten and his religious heresy.

There is almost certainly a link between this, one of history's greatest unsolved mysteries, and the enigma of Tomb 55. Akhenaten's name was found to have been erased from one of the shrine panels in the tomb, implying that Akhenaten had been a part of whatever sins Smenkhkare was imagined to have committed. More significantly, as the female coffin and Canopic jars in Tomb 55 had been specifically adapted for Akhenaten before being used for Smenkhkare, the bizarre desecration would seem originally to have been intended for Akhenaten. Smenkhkare certainly co-ruled with Akhenaten, and immediately succeeded him and, from all we can tell, shared his revolutionary ideas. Had Smenkhkare's tomb therefore been violated because of his role in establishing the new religion? Although this would tie in with the anti-Atenist reprisals a few years later, it does not fit with the reign of Tutankhamun, in whose name the desecration was evidently carried out.

When Tutankhamun became king, Akhenaten's cultural revolution had been in effect for well over a decade. As he was only about eight at the time, Tutankhamun's chief minister, Ay, appears to have been chiefly responsible for governing the country for the first few years. With Egypt close to bankruptcy and the empire in tatters, Ay and Tutankhamun soon abandoned the city of Amarna, returned to Thebes and restored Amun-Re as principal deity. However, both Tutankhamun and Ay continued to tolerate the Aten religion. This is demonstrated, for example, by the many items in Tutankhamun's tomb which were decorated with depictions of the Aten, which even included the royal sceptre and throne. Indeed, as neither Tutankhamun nor Ay, when he succeeded Tutankhamun as pharaoh himself, made any attempt to reinstate the priesthood, the restoration of Amun-Re was seemingly a token gesture to appease opposition, rather than a heartfelt religious conversion. The later attempts to eradicate all evidence of the Aten religion, and those who sanctioned it, even shows that Tutankhamun and Ay continued to venerate the Aten. Along with Akhenaten and Smenkhkare, inscriptions concerning Tutankhamun and Ay were erased from monuments, their statues were defaced and destroyed, and their names were omitted from the list of kings.

Tutankhamun and Ay may not have been so fanatical as Akhenaten in their devotion to the Aten, but they made absolutely no attempt to suppress the new religion. Consequently, it is difficult to see either of them desecrating Smenkhkare's tomb simply because he had been an Atenist. Nevertheless, there does appear to have been something linking Smenkhkare with Akhenaten lying at the heart of the Tomb 55 enigma. We must therefore attempt to reconstruct the Amarna period by piecing together the few scraps of historical evidence that still survive, and search for any clues that may help us unravel the ever-more-bewildering mystery.

SUMMARY

- Even before the discovery of their tombs, Tutankhamun and Smenkhkare were both known to Egyptologists though various inscriptions recovered from excavations, yet, oddly, neither of them appeared on any royal list. Like two other kings of the period, Akhenaten and the pharaoh Ay, their successors had erased their names from history. In the eyes of later generations, they had committed acts of unsurpassed evil by proscribing the traditional gods and establishing a new monotheistic religion.

- At the beginning of his reign, Akhenaten decreed that a new god, a minor solar deity called the Aten, should replace Amun-Re as the chief god of Egypt. Within a short time he went even further and did something completely alien to everything in Egypt's ancient culture: he proclaimed that the Aten was the *only* god. That he should have completely upturned every aspect of a two-thousand-year-old civilization has mystified historians for decades.

- There is almost certainly a link between this, one of history's greatest unsolved mysteries, and the enigma of Tomb 55. Akhenaten's name was found to have been erased from one of the shrine panels in the tomb, implying that Akhenaten had been a part of whatever sins Smenkhkare was imagined to have committed. More significantly, as the female coffin and Canopic jars in Tomb 55 had been specifically adapted for Akhenaten before being used for Smenkhkare, the bizarre desecration would seem originally to have been intended for Akhenaten.

- Smenkhkare certainly co-ruled with Akhenaten, and immediately succeeded him and, from all we can tell, shared his revolutionary ideas. Smenkhkare's tomb may therefore have been violated because of his role in establishing the new religion. However, although this would tie in with the anti-Atenist reprisals a few years later, it does not fit with the reign of Tutankhamun, in whose name the desecration was evidently carried out. It is a mystery, therefore, why Smenkhkare's tomb was desecrated.

CHAPTER THREE

City of the Sun

About halfway along the Nile, between the Mediterranean Sea and what is now the Aswan Dam, lies the sandy plain of Amarna. Here, Akhenaten's capital lay ruined and forgotten for almost three thousand years before it was rediscovered in the early nineteenth century. In this scrub-covered desert tract around the village of Et Til (also called Tell el Amarna) on the east bank, low mounds of pebble-strewn rubble were all that remained of the once splendid city. The first proper account of the site was made by the British explorer John Gardner Wilkinson in the 1820s, when he surveyed a number of rock-cut tombs discovered in the hills to the east of the village. Although at the time the hieroglyphics could not be read, Wilkinson nevertheless realized that their decorations were unlike any previously found in Egypt. Concerned almost exclusively with the activities of a royal family, these illustrations differed markedly from the traditional religious or militaristic mode. The king, queen and several daughters were not depicted as triumphant conquerors, smiting their enemies, but in everyday domestic scenes, feasting, relaxing and embracing one another. Neither were they shown engaged in the formal cultic practices of the time, but in an altogether more dynamic attitude of worship. Likewise, their subjects, who would usually have been portrayed as sombre

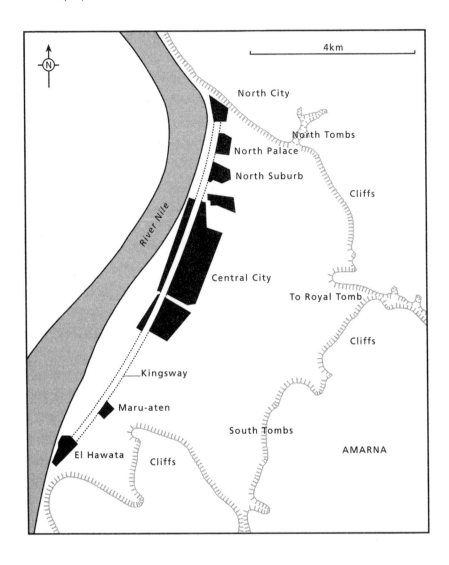

onlookers, were shown as a joyful congregation, dancing, singing and waving palms. Even the artistic style was distinct. The principal figures were not afforded the formal bearing of might and grandeur, but a demeanour of grace and sensuality, while a normally rigid and static affectation was replaced by a sinuous, more relaxed mien. Everything about the tombs was in stark contrast to the Egyptian norm. Gone entirely was the funerary ambience which pervaded the tombs at Thebes and Saqqara, and even the usual gods were absent from the scenes. It was quite clear that the people of Amarna had customs and religious beliefs very different from those practised elsewhere in ancient Egypt.

Early Egyptologists began referring to these people as 'disc worshippers', as the upper part of nearly every scene was dominated by a glyph depicting the sun's disc, from which shone forth a dozen or so rays, each ending in a hand holding an *ankh* (the symbol of life). So different was everything about the Amarnans that some scholars even concluded that they had not been Egyptians at all, but foreign settlers who had merely adopted the Egyptian language. Even when the hieroglyphics were eventually deciphered, it was some time before their identity could be determined. Throughout the site, the figures of the royal family had been defaced and their cartouches erased from inscriptions. This excising – clearly an act of desecration contemporary with the ruins – had been so thorough that it was hard to find an intact royal name, or any clue to the meaning of the revered disc. Nevertheless, there had been oversights in places difficult to access, and the arcane ruins began to relinquish their secrets. The king found to have been the previously unknown Akhenaten, the son and successor of Amonhotep III; his queen had been Nefertiti, the mother of six princesses but apparently no sons; and the strange sun glyph was found to represent a single deity called the Aten. The entire city was dedicated to this god and was even named after it. Called Akhetaten – 'the horizon (or seat) of the Aten' – the city was occupied for less than two decades, before being abandoned to the mercy of the desert.

Sadly, many of the inscriptions and illustrations no longer exist. Following various German, French and British expeditions to Amarna during the nineteenth century, the local population began to resent foreign intrusions. To deter the Europeans from returning, they began to smash statues and destroy carvings and reliefs. Thankfully, however, many of them were copied by these early visitors. The last scholar to work at Amarna before the destruction was Norman de Garis Davies, the surveyor for the British-based Egypt Exploration Fund in the 1890s. Over a period of six years he painstakingly copied all the decorations that still survived in the cliff tombs and published them in his six-volume *The Rock Tombs of El Amarna*. Together with some earlier drawings in the Berlin Museum, made by a German team led by Egyptologist Richard Lepsius in the 1840s, they were almost the only means by which later scholars could piece together the lifestyle of the citizens of Akhetaten.

The first archaeological excavation of Amarna was carried out by Ayrton and Carter's mentor, Flinders Petrie, in the 1890s, and for the first time the colossal scale and splendour of the city became apparent. Akhetaten was a straggling metropolis built along a ten-kilometre stretch of the Nile: a northern town with its royal palace and suburbs, a central city with its sacred temple, and a southern town with its mansions for the upper classes. The whole city was constructed around a great forty-metre-wide processional way, now referred to as the Royal Avenue or Kingsway, which swept down from the northern palace and on through the central city, where it was flanked by a series of official buildings, a ceremonial palace, and the new style, open-air temple to the Aten. There were many smaller temples too, such as the sun kiosks along the routes to the cliff tombs to the east of the city, where devotees could bask in the life-giving rays of the sun. This central city seems to have been an administrative and religious centre, deserted at night except for guard patrols. Its day-time population of priests, clerks and artisans probably commuted from the suburbs, while the high officials had a separate district of mansions which stood in extensive grounds, surrounded by the lesser habitations of their attendants.

A specific feature of these great residences revealed just how different Amarna was. In one of the principal rooms there was a shrine consisting of a niche in which stood an inscribed and decorated stela. Similar shrines housing such a stela – an upright stone slab or pillar – were common to larger dwellings through-out Egypt and were dedicated to a particular deity or ancestor venerated by the residents. In the Amarna mansions, however, the decorations depicted no such gods or ancestors – only Akhenaten and his queen, accompanied by one or more of their daughters as they worshipped the Aten. The larger mansions even had their own chapels adorned with statues and votive images of the royal family. It was clear that Akhenaten not only dominated all official ceremony, but private prayer and medi-tation as well.

It was the same in the nobles' tombs, which would normally be decorated with scenes from ancient texts, such as the *Book of the Dead*, in which various gods would be depicted in order to invoke their influence as guides and guardians in the afterlife. These elaborate burial chambers were built to the same basic plan as those at Thebes, but were decorated very differently. Unlike the Theban tombs, the wall reliefs all focused on the king and through him the Aten. Akhenaten, usually accompanied by Nefertiti and a number of daughters, was shown engaged in various ceremonial activities, such as proceeding in a chariot along the processional way to worship at the temple of the Aten.

Akhenaten's image completely dominated the city, and in life the man himself ensured that his subjects were continually aware of his physical presence. We can see from the tomb illustrations that the royal palace had an architectural feature unique to ancient Egypt: a special window where the king and his family could appear before their followers. Like the Pope from his balcony overlooking St Peter's Square, from here Akhenaten would regularly address his subjects *en masse* in a way that no other Egyptian pharaoh seems to have done.

Amarna was ringed by a natural amphitheatre of cliffs on both sides of the Nile, where a series of fourteen immovable tablets, ranging from two to eight metres in height, were hewn into the rocks to delineate the city's sacred perimeters. These boundary stelae, carved with reliefs showing Akhenaten and his family adoring their god, had been inscribed with lengthy decrees made by the king. Not only were they damaged, like the rock tombs, by the hammers of the local populace in the late nineteenth century, but they further suffered the far more devastating attentions of treasure hunters. A legend had grown up that Ali Baba's secret treasure-cave was somewhere in the area, and in 1906 one of the stelae was actually blown to bits with dynamite in the mistaken belief that the entrance lay beyond it. Thanks to early explorers like the Scottish laird Robert Hay in the 1820s, however, original drawings of the stelae still survive in the British Museum.

Erected while the city was being built, the boundary stelae enable us to reconstruct something of the city's brief history and the thinking behind its creation. Now identified by a different letter, three of them bear a series of initial proclamations that are dated to Year 5, Month 8, Day 13 of Akhenaten's reign, while the others bear proclamations made exactly a year later, and all but three of these bear a postscript of Year 8, Month 5, Day 8. From the assorted inscriptions we learn that eight months into the fifth year of his reign, Akhenaten came to Amarna officially to found the city, set up an altar and establish the city's perimeters, and by the end of his eighth year construction was largely completed.

In the initial proclamations we are told that something terrible had happened which had evidently persuaded Akhenaten to build the city. The king declares that something had been heard which was more evil than what he had heard in the fourth year of his reign, more evil than what he had heard in his first year, and more evil even than what his predecessors Amonhotep III and Tuthmosis IV had heard. What was this evil? Could it offer a clue to the mystery of Smenkhkare's eternal imprisonment in Tomb 55?

Infuriatingly, this inscription had been badly damaged even when the early explorers made their drawings and we can no longer tell what the great evil was meant to be. This damage was clearly the work of Akhenaten's anti-Atenist successors, and seems to have been an attempt to eradicate what would otherwise have been a vital clue as to what lay behind the establishment of the new religion. All that can be discerned from the surviving text is that certain observances could somehow make amends, such as festivals of the Aten, the imposition of dues, and an enigmatic reference to the land of Kush to the south of Egypt.

We can tell, though, from the surviving inscriptions that the changes wrought by Akhenaten were truly revolutionary. In

the undamaged section of the text that follows we learn how
Akhenaten founded the city in the location he believed the Aten
originated:

> His majesty mounted a great chariot of electrum, like the
> Aten when he rises on the horizon and fills the land with
> his love, and took a goodly road to Akhetaten, the place of
> origin which the Aten had created for himself that he might
> be happy therein. It was his son, the only one of Re, who
> founded it for him as his monument when his father
> commanded him to make it. Heaven was joyful, the earth
> was glad, every heart was filled with delight when they
> beheld him.

Akhenaten himself then vows that he will build the city in that
particular location and nowhere else, and no one – not even the
queen – will persuade him otherwise. He continues by listing
the buildings to be erected on the site, including an estate of the
Aten, a temple of the Aten, and a 'house of rejoicing'. There
were also to be built the apartments of the pharaoh and his
queen, and tombs were to be prepared for them and their
daughter Meritaten in the eastern hills. He goes on to declare
that if any of them died elsewhere they must be bought back
here for burial.

From the later proclamations, dated exactly a year after the
first, we learn that the king is now residing in a tent in the city,
from where he set out to re-establish his decrees and make a
new vow. Accompanied by Nefertiti, Meritaten, and a second
daughter, Meketaten, he mounted his state chariot, drove to the
southernmost edge of the town and swore that he would never
again leave the holy city. He then travelled to the northernmost
boundary and repeated the oath. Finally, in the eighth year of

his reign he travelled around the boundaries reaffirming the city's perimeters, presumably now that construction was completed, and inscriptions were added to some of the stelae to commemorate the event.

Apart from revealing something of the city's sacred associations, the stelae further acquaint us with the growing royal family. Depicted either as reliefs or statues, the king and queen are first shown being followed by their eldest daughter Meritaten, later joined by the second daughter Meketaten, and finally by a third, Ankhesenpaaten. Although this would seem to suggest that Meketaten was born after the proclamations of the fifth year, and Ankhesenpaaten after the proclamations of the sixth year, we know from the reliefs in the rock tombs that they both had children of their own within twelve years. It would seem, therefore, that the daughters were only included in the royal entourage once they reached a certain age which, going by their depictions, would seem to be somewhere around five.

The extent to which the royal family had broken with tradition is demonstrated by their attire. Although the habit worn by the king conforms to contemporary royal fashion – a kilt tied around the waist by a broad sash from which hangs an apron in front and an imitation bull's tail behind – his upper body is often bare, lacking the usual collar and armlets. Also the queen, although wearing a traditional robe with a shawl covering one shoulder, wears no jewellery. Likewise, the daughters' traditional gowns lack the customary adornments; even their hair, which is plaited into the conventional side-lock of infancy, is not confined by the usual slide.

Perhaps the most important aspect of the boundary stelae is the insight they provide into Akhenaten's unique religious status and his personal attitude to the god. In the initial proclamations Akhenaten addresses his courtiers and nobles, informing them of his plans for the new city. He tells them that the Aten himself directed him to this site, and they respond in praise, accepting that the god communed solely with the king and with no one else.

From the rock-tombs we can gather that Akhenaten had not only usurped the priesthood as sole spokesman for divine will, but had personally replaced the old funerary deities. Although the traditional funerary practices such as mummification and the depositing of grave goods with the deceased were retained, the wall reliefs show that Akhenaten had taken over the role previously played by gods like Osiris in caring for his subjects in the afterlife. It is to him they pray for favours in both life and death. An inscription in the tomb of the courtier Parennefer, for instance, calls Akhenaten 'Lord of Burial', while one in the tomb of the chief minister Ay asks Akhenaten for 'a life prolonged by thy favours'. Another inscription in Ay's tomb further echoes the acceptance of Akhenaten's infallibility: 'Thou arisest fair in the horizon of heaven, O living Aten, beginner of life ... there are none who know thee save thy son Akhenaten. Thou hast made him wise in thy plans and thy power.'

Akhenaten is unquestionably the one and only prophet of the Aten, and the boundary stelae provide a rare insight into how Akhenaten personally regarded his god. The initial proclamations include a text praising the Aten, seemingly in Akhenaten's own words:

> The great and living Aten [damaged section] ... ordaining life, vigorously alive, my father [damaged section] ... My wall of millions of cubits, my reminder of eternity, my witness of what is eternal. He who fashions himself with his own two hands, he whom no craftsman has devised, he who is established in rising and setting each day ceaselessly,

whether he is in heaven or earth, every eye beholds him without hindrance while he fills the land with his rays and makes everyone to live. In seeing him my eyes are satisfied daily when he rises in the temple of the Aten at Akhetaten and fills it with his own self by means of his rays, beauteous with love, and embraces me with them in life and power for ever and ever.

Although Akhenaten, like other pharaohs, sees himself as the son of a god, his god is very different from other gods. In the phrase, 'he whom no craftsman has devised', Akhenaten affirms that, unlike other gods, the Aten cannot be represented by a physical likeness. Indeed, throughout the site the Aten is only ever represented by the sun disc symbol, and never by a statue or image – human or animal. Since the earliest dynastic times the gods of Egypt had been thought to inhabit their images, and the making of such idols was rigidly defined in the sacred texts. Once the image was made and consecrated it was regarded as a living being: it lived in its own 'great mansion', where it was tended by servants (the priests) who not only clothed and fed it (in the form of offerings), but actually woke it in the morning and put it to rest at night. All this ritual was condemned by Akhenaten, who prohibited the making of any such image of the Aten.

The manner in which Akhenaten acted as both ruler and supreme prelate can be gained from the inscriptions in various tombs. Although the king still bears the title the pharaohs had used since the Old Kingdom – 'Son of the Sun-God' – he now he has an additional title: 'The Beautiful Child of the Aten'. It would seem that Akhenaten wished to distinguish himself from all his predecessors, in that he was not merely the vessel of his god, a nominal son, but of the same substance as his god, literally his offspring. Moreover, it would seem that Akhenaten and the Aten were seen to rule Egypt side by side. A particular event referenced in the tomb of Meryre, the overseer of the royal harem, is dated to year 12 of Akhenaten's reign, and the same event referenced in the tomb of the high steward Huya is dated to the twelfth year of the reign of the Aten. Evidently, like a king and his son, the pharaoh and his god were regarded as co-regents.

Although Akhenaten is the sole spokesman for his god, his family apparently shares something of his divinity. Indeed, it is only they who are privileged to include the Aten in their names. Beside Akhenaten, whose name means 'Living spirit of the Aten', only his offspring such as Meritaten, Meketaten and Ankhesenpaaten, and his queen Nefertiti, whose title was Neferneferuaten, 'Fair is the beauty of the Aten', are granted such a distinction. In both the tombs and on the boundary stelae, the subjects which occur most frequently are the royal family making offerings before altars, bestowing decorations on favoured courtiers, and eating and drinking together at home. In all these scenes, no matter who else is present, the rays of the Aten only ever touch the royal family's bodies or hold an *ankh* – the symbol of life – to their nostrils, an honour denied all others, no matter how high their rank. It seems that the royal family was regarded as a holy family, and their daily prayers replaced the rituals once performed by the priesthood to keep the world in motion.

Although, in theory, the pharaoh had always been absolute ruler, his religious role was more that of an icon or figurehead. The priesthood had the real authority in sacred matters. This is why the pharaohs had so indulged them, sometimes to the extent of their own ruin. It is wrong to think of the Egyptian priests simply as ministers of a modern church, attending to the spiritual well-being of their congregations. Various gods were considered responsible for the forces of nature, cultural accomplishments and fortunes of war, and each of them had to be appeased. The multitude of priests who saw to their veneration would have been regarded more like workers in the modern utilities industries than clergymen – essential to keep the wheels of the nation turning. In many ways Egypt was structured like a technological civilization without technology. As modern civilization would collapse without its power workers, Egypt imagined it would collapse without its priesthood.

The general populace played no part in the temple activities. They did not go there once a week to worship or pray, or visit the priests for seek solace or to ask for guidance. In fact, if they did attempt to enter a temple they would probably have been executed for sacrilege. Personal religion was a personal matter: the state and priesthood couldn't care less which gods you prayed to, or venerated with altars in the privacy of your own home. In Amarna, however, all this changed. Although there was still a priesthood of sorts, the royal family carried out the principal veneration of the god, and it was to Akhenaten you prayed to secure favours and blessings from the Aten.

Akhenaten had, it seems, abandoned superstition, rejected graven images, and instigated a monotheistic faith. Just one of these innovations would have been unique for the period, not only in ancient Egypt but anywhere in the contemporary world. However, he apparently went even further – for the first time in history he made state religion accessible to the masses. At face value Akhenaten would seem to have been a religious visionary, years ahead of his time.

Since the discovery of ancient Amarna, scholars have regarded Akhenaten as everything from a mystic to a maniac. The first, Flinders Petrie, saw him as a gentle sage and a moral philosopher: 'No king of Egypt, nor of any other part of the world, has ever carried out his honesty of expression so openly ... Thus in every line Akhenaten stands out as perhaps the most original thinker that ever lived in Egypt, and one of the greatest idealists of the world.'

Over the following century Akhenaten was seen in many different lights. In 1911 Arthur Weigall saw him as a great reformer, in the 1920s the British Egyptologist James Baikie saw him as a utopian romantic, and in the 1930s the philologist Alan Gardiner saw him as a godless heretic. Opinions range from such extremes as Akhenaten the pacifist to Akhenaten the religious fanatic. Even today the debate continues, the problem being that the evidence appears so contradictory.

At first glance Akhenaten would seem to have been a kindly idealist. Other pharaohs are depicted, without fail, as austere personifications of absolute power; they are seen leading armies into battle, smiting enemies or sitting in judgement. Akhenaten's portrayals completely depart from this stereotype, depicting him as a caring, loving human being. Again and again, Amarna reliefs show him in intimate detail as a family man with his children on his knee, caressing them or dangling trinkets for them to snatch. He is even seen kissing his wife. A particular scene in the royal tomb actually shows him groping for Nefertiti's supportive arm as he sorrowfully mourns his daughter's death. No other pharaoh would dream of having himself revealed in such a familiar fashion. He also seems to have been an animal lover – unlike other kings of the dynasty he is never depicted hunting for sport. Akhenaten clearly sees himself as the benevolent and caring sovereign, something which one of his titles was chosen to emphasize: 'The good ruler who loves mankind'. Moreover, the king seems to have rated honesty as the prime virtue. Everywhere we find inscriptions using a phrase which appears to have been something of a royal motto: 'living in truth'.

A popular theory in recent times has been to regard Akhenaten as a mild-mannered dreamer who lived in a world of his own and had no real authority over his country. Regardless of the merits or flaws of his regime, Akhenaten clearly had the personal influence to instate his religion, control the army and contain opposition. Any notion of some dainty young romantic skipping his way through the great temple at Karnak, clapping his hands and shouting 'everybody out', is clearly absurd. The deposition of the mighty priesthood would have required amazing resolve, remarkable aplomb, and the strategy of a *coup d'état*. Even if he played no direct part himself, he must either have had widespread support or an iron grip on power. Either way, Akhenaten was no idealist with his head in the clouds, but a strong and determined leader.

Akhenaten certainly had no interest in maintaining the empire, however, which rapidly disintegrated during his reign. We have first-hand evidence of his personal responsibility for this predicament, thanks to a remarkable discovery made in the late nineteenth century. In 1887, a peasant woman digging for fertilizer among the ancient ruins of Akhetaten unearthed a cache of over 300 inscribed clay tablets now called the Amarna Letters. Written in Akkadian, a Babylonian dialect which became the international diplomatic language of the ancient Near East, they were dispatches received from Asiatic envoys during Akhenaten's reign. They included repeated appeals for help in overcoming local insurrections and external aggression, and numerous communications from antagonists bandying accusations at one another, all of which went unheeded. Akhenaten was obviously far too busy playing prophet to concern himself with foreign affairs.

On the other hand, Akhenaten was definitely no pacifist. The Amarna reliefs repeatedly emphasize his military authority. In many he is shown wearing either the Blue Crown or Nubian wig, both part of the king's military paraphernalia, rather than the ceremonial crowns of Upper and Lower Egypt. Scenes of military activity abound in Amarnan art: parades and military processions are commonplace, while soldiers are seen everywhere, guarding temples and palaces or manning the fortified watchtowers that bordered the city. According to American Egyptologist Alan Schulman, who made an extensive study of the military background to the Amarna period in the 1960s: 'If we may take the reliefs from the tombs of the nobles at face value, then the city was virtually an armed camp.' There can be little doubt that Akhenaten not only enjoyed the full support of the army, he revelled in military might.

This seemingly paradoxical nature of Akhenaten's reign has led to opposing academic camps – 'Akhenaten the righteous' versus 'Akhenaten the despot' – with each of them emphasizing either the militaristic or the domestic scenes in support of their case. This dispute is nothing, however, compared to the most hotly debated issue of all – the mystery of Akhenaten's extraordinary physical appearance.

In all the Amarna depictions the king's physique is distinctly feminine, with heavy breasts, swelling hips and ample thighs. Since he occasionally wears a long clinging robe similar to a woman's gown, some representations of the king were at first confused with those of his queen. In many of the reliefs, without accompanying inscriptions, there is no way of telling if Akhenaten is a man or a woman. In the late nineteenth century, the French scholar Eugène Lefébure even surmised that Akhenaten had really been a woman masquerading as a man. He drew attention to Hatshepsut, a female pharaoh earlier in the eighteenth dynasty, who had herself represented in male clothing and a pharaonic beard attached to her chin. However, Akhenaten's profile is not only effeminate, it is also deformed. The legs, for instance, are fatty around the thighs but spindly below the knee, making them look like emaciated chicken legs. There are also malformations to the skull, face and neck: the cranium is excessively large, as are the mouth and jaw, which hang down over an elongated neck.

These abnormalities have led various pathologists to suggest that Akhenaten may have suffered from a disfiguring disorder known as Frohlich's Syndrome. A complaint in which male patients exhibit physical peculiarities similar to Akhenaten's, it is caused by damage to the pituitary body, a pea-size gland at the base of the brain which secretes hormones controlling the function of other glands. The subsequent effect on the thyroid gland, which controls growth and metabolism, can result in features such as a lantern jaw and extended neck; damage to the hypothalamus, responsible for water distribution, can result in the accumulation of fluid in the cranial cavity which can enlarge the skull; and interference with the adrenal cortex, influencing the secretion of natural steroids, results in a feminine-like distribution of fat around the breasts, abdomen, thighs and buttocks. Invariably, Frohlich's Syndrome afflicts the gonads, rendering the patient sterile.

This last condition presents a serious objection to attributing such a disorder to Akhenaten. Far from being sterile, he seems to have sired at least six daughters, three of whom specifically bear the title: 'The daughter of the king, of his loins, born of the Chief Wife Nefertiti'. Although it has been suggested that the onset of Frohlich's Syndrome may not have occurred until after Akhenaten children were conceived, this seems highly unlikely, if not impossible. Firstly, there is the nature of the disease itself:

cranial enlargement from the condition would need to have occurred early in life, before the bones of the skull could harden and close, and hydrocephalus (fluid on the brain) would invariably result in mental retardation leaving Akhenaten incapable of functioning as the dynamic ruler he appears to have been. Secondly, he was fathering children years after he is depicted as if suffering from the disorder: towards the end of his reign he had three more daughters from Nefertiti, and possibly another by a second wife Kiya. It is quite impossible for someone with such apparent vigour, libido and sexual virility to have suffered from Frohlich's Syndrome to the extent that his representations imply.

There is, in fact, persuasive evidence to suggest that Akhenaten did not have the curious physiognomy the reliefs and statues would have us believe. Although in the official representations of the king he is shown with the peculiar anatomical features, in a number of private representations he is depicted looking quite different. Two statuettes in the Louvre in Paris, dating from well into Akhenaten's reign, are excellent examples. The painted limestone pair statuette of Akhenaten and Nefertiti, and the yellow steatite statue of a seated Akhenaten, both show him looking as normal and healthy as anyone else. There is no enlarged cranium, no extended jaw and no womanly curves. These and similar figurines were made for the household shrines of the nobles, who would have been all too familiar with Akhenaten's true appearance. Such representations would obviously have had sentimental value, showing the Akhenaten they personally knew, rather than the divine son and prophet of the Aten.

It seems almost certain that Akhenaten's semblance was deliberately distorted in a manner which was seen to symbolize significant religious attributes. Not only is Akhenaten depicted in such a way, but to a lesser extent so are his family and high officials. With Nefertiti it is most pronounced. In some of the later Amarna reliefs it is difficult to tell her and her husband apart. She is shown with an absurdly long neck, massive cranium, a huge mouth and protruding jaw. In her case, we know for certain that her true appearance was very different, thanks to a number of far more flattering representations, particularly the famous bust found by the German archaeologist Ludwig Borchardt in 1911. While excavating what had been the studio of the royal sculptor Djhutmose at the Great Palace at Amarna, Borchardt found a number of plaster casts, sculptor's studies, half finished statues, and heads and busts, which threw entirely new light on the methods of portrait sculpture in ancient Egypt. The most astounding piece in this collection was a life-size painted limestone bust of Nefertiti which is thought to have been a master study for lesser sculptors to copy. Now in the Berlin Egyptian Museum, this renowned bust shows a beautiful woman with none of the exaggerated facial features shown in the reliefs. Also, a similar, but unfinished plaster mask of Akhenaten was found. Although he does have a long face and a full mouth there are none of the distorted features we usually find.

Others also emulated the 'royal deformities', but the lower the rank, the less pronounced. The young princesses are often endowed with enlarged skulls, serpentine necks and excessive bodily curves, but not the exaggerated facial features of their parents; while the lesser courtiers only have one or two such peculiarities, like the excessive cranium of the courtier Paren-nefer and the pendulous breasts of the chief sculptor Bek and the chicken-legs of his wife.

It would seem that the depiction of these curious physical characteristics was connected in some way to Akhenaten's personification as the son of the Aten. Before he assumed the role, a year or two into his reign, he is shown looking quite normal, even in official representations such as those at the temple of Luxor. Reliefs in the tomb of the royal vizier Ramose at Thebes actually chronicles the apparent metamorphosis of the king. He changes from normal appearance in scenes concerning his advent to the grossly distorted appearance by the time the Aten has assumed prominence within a couple of years. This transformation surely indicates that artists had been directed to depict him in this way once he had undergone his religious conversion. Indeed, inscriptions made by the chief sculpture Bek actually suggest that they were Akhenaten's personal instructions. On a quartzite stela in the Berlin Museum, found at Heliopolis in the 1880s, and reliefs carved on rocks at Aswan, Bek describes himself as 'the apprentice whom His Majesty taught'. It would seem that, as master of works, Bek was responsible for implementing and regulating these new artistic conventions.

The bodies of two members of the Amarna royal family still available for medical examination are Smenkhkare and Tutankhamun, and both have an unusual platycephalic skull. Although not pronounced enough to have been the result of Frohlich's Syndrome, this might suggest that a cranium slightly larger than the norm was a family trait. The artisans may therefore have been instructed to exaggerate this feature to emphasize royal infallibility. When Professor Harrison examined the Smenkhkare mummy in 1963, he also found evidence in certain parts of the skeleton of a trend towards femininity. Although not sufficiently marked to result in sterility, or anywhere near the extremes of the Amarna reliefs, this may suggest that the males of Akhenaten's family did appear somewhat effeminate. If so, it would

certainly have been convenient for Akhenaten's religious strata-
gem, as it seems that his god was considered an androgynous
being.

The most likely explanation for the feminine aspects of
Akhenaten's strange physiognomy is that he was being portrayed
with attributes of his god. If we examine Atenism a little more
closely it becomes apparent why the king may have wished to
have himself depicted in a bisexual fashion. The pharaohs had
always been seen as the personification of an exclusively male
god, whether Re, Re-Herakhte, or Amun-Re. The god whom
Akhenaten personified, however, had taken over from all the
gods, both male and female.

Just as there had been a chief god, there had always been a
chief goddess. In the Old Kingdom it had been Hathor, in the
Middle Kingdom it had been Isis, and in the New Kingdom, by
the time Akhenaten came to the throne, it was Amun-Re's
consort Mut. Mut was the mother, nurse and nurturer of all
living things, and the so-called 'Hymn to the Aten' makes it very
clear that Akhenaten's god had specifically appropriated this
feminine role. Something of a 'Lord's Prayer' in Akhenaten's
religion, the most fully preserved text of the hymn is found in
the tomb prepared for Ay at Amarna. In praising the works of
the Aten, it endows the god with maternal aspects previously
attributed to Mut:

> Thou it is who causest women to conceive and makest seed
> into man who givest life to the child in the womb of its
> mother, who comfortest him so that he cries not therein,
> nurse that thou art, even in the womb, who givest breath
> to quicken all that he hath made. When the child comes
> forth from the body on the day of his birth, then thou

openest his mouth completely and thou furnishest his
sustenance ... The people of the world are in your hand
just as you have created them ...

The reason why the Aten had to be seen specifically usurping
the role of the goddess Mut was that she had become as essential
to Egyptian religion as Amun-Re himself. The most important
celebration of the year was the annual rebirth of Amun-Re, in
which Mut played a vital role. Around mid-July, when the Nile
sank to its lowest level, it would mysteriously well up and spill
over the valley floor, leaving behind a rich black soil that would
support crops to feed the nation for another year. Known as the
inundation, no one knew that this life-giving phenomenon was
due to monsoon rains far to the south in tropical Africa. The
event was thus attributed to divine intervention and the annual
rebirth of the predominant god was deemed necessary for its
continuance.

As chief divinity, Amun-Re had to be the means of his own
regeneration. One of Mut's titles was 'Mother of the sun in
whom he rises', meaning that, as sun-god, Amun-Re was
considered both her spouse and her son. Mut was therefore the
means by which the god could annually re-father himself.
Temple reliefs depicting the *Opet* ceremony to mark this
occasion show the god being carried to the Temple of Luxor to
unite with the goddess and take the form of the fertility god
Min. As the details of this event are gleaned only from reliefs, it
is difficult to tell from the illustrations alone if the god was
represented by a statue, a priest or the king himself. However,
logic dictates that it must have been the latter, as the ceremony
was an occasion for oracular pronouncements by the god.
Someone obviously had to speak for Amun-Re, which rules out

a statue, and it is doubtful that any priest could talk as the god who was imagined to inhabit only the king.

This entire episode was central to contemporary Egyptian religion and, to have any chance of success, Akhenaten's new religion needed an appropriate equivalent. We can seen from the initial proclamations on the Amarna boundary stelae that the Aten is, 'he who fashions himself with his own two hands'. From this statement alone we can gather that the god was not fashioned just once, at some point in the past, but, like Amun-Re, continued to regenerate himself. Also, as the god procreates himself unaided, he had adopted the roles of both Amun-Re *and* Mut. Although often described in the masculine, the Aten is clearly imbued with both male and female characteristics. In addressing the Aten, the 'Hymn to the Aten' refers to Akhenaten as, 'your son who came forth from your body': the god is envisaged as not only siring its child, as would a man, but actually giving birth, as would a woman. The Aten has replaced all the gods, but in particular the familiar state god Amun-Re and the state goddess Mut – it is an androgynous deity.

Surely, as the personification of this hermaphrodite god, Akhenaten must himself have been considered bisexual, and as previous kings had been depicted as the masculine Amun-Re, Akhenaten would need to be depicted with both the male and female attributes of the Aten. Even the bird-like legs, the serpentine neck and the excessively long face may have been to reinforce the notion that the Aten had assumed the role of the divine mother. Mut's sacred animal and familiar image had been the vulture, a bird with a particularly long neck and an extended face.

Akhenaten being seen as the personification of an androgynous deity would certainly explain why the coffin and Canopic jars prepared for him in Tomb 55 had been adapted from female effects. The ferocity of anti-Atenist reprisals following the Amarna period clearly show that the religion was not simply dismissed as a fallacy, but was considered a heresy. Likewise, the Aten was not merely considered non-existent, but an evil entity which had possessed the king. The bizarre entombment may not simply have been designed as a punishment to imprison the king's soul; rather than destroying it, it may been an attempt to keep the evil, but nevertheless immortal, god trapped inside its human host. Only by employing both male and female paraphernalia would the interment meet the criteria for a bisexual being.

Even so, it is not Akhenaten who ended up occupying the coffin specifically adapted for him, but his successor Smenkhkare. Why? Everything discovered at Amarna has shown conclusively that it was Akhenaten who was primarily responsible for the heresy. He was firmly in control, he personally instigated the religion, and he acted as sole spokesman for the god. To resolve this enigma we must first attempt to identify whoever was responsible for the first phase of the proceedings: adapting the female burial effects to accommodate Akhenaten. A vital clue in this direction may lie with the identity of the woman for whom the coffin and Canopic jars were originally intended. She obviously played a crucial part in the strange affair. As she is clearly someone of high status, our investigation now turns to the Amarna queens, and the extraordinary influence of Nefertiti, the royal princesses and the king's secondary wife, Kiya.

SUMMARY

- Akhenaten abandoned superstition, rejected graven images, and instigated a monotheistic faith. Just one of these innovations would have been unique for the period. At face value Akhenaten would seem to have been a religious visionary, years ahead of his time.

- In all the Amarna depictions the king's physique is distinctly feminine, with heavy breasts, swelling hips and ample thighs.

- It would seem that the depiction of these curious physical characteristics was connected in some way to Akhenaten's personification as the son of the Aten, as the new god was itself considered to be both male and female.

- Akhenaten's being seen as the personification of an androgynous deity would certainly explain why the coffin and Canopic jars prepared for him in Tomb 55 had been adapted from female effects. The Aten was not merely considered non-existent, but an evil entity which had possessed the king. The bizarre entombment may not simply have been designed as a punishment to imprison the king's soul; rather than destroying it, it may been an attempt to keep the evil, but nevertheless immortal, god trapped inside its human host. Only by employing both male and female paraphernalia would the interment meet the criteria for a bisexual being.

CHAPTER FOUR

The Amarna Queens

Around the year 15 of Akhenaten's reign, the halcyon days of Amarna seem to come to an abrupt end. Gone is the ambience of euphoria and camaraderie, and in its place there is an overwhelming sense of oppression and paranoia. Within three or four years, the would-be Utopia is abandoned to the desert and most of the royal family ominously disappear. Precisely what happened is unclear, but from what we can tell it seems to begin with the death of Nefertiti.

Although, like all pharaohs, Akhenaten had a harem of secondary queens, the royal consort and heiress was the 'Chief Wife' or 'Chief Queen' Nefertiti. From her depictions, it is quite apparent that Nefertiti enjoyed far more influence than did almost any other Egyptian queen. Often she seems to have pharaonic authority equal to her husband's, and in some areas she appears to exceed him. Although, at Amarna, Nefertiti is represented as a loving mother in scenes of everyday family life, early reliefs from Thebes depict her as an authoritarian figure. One particular relief shows her grasping foreign captives by the hair and smiting them with a mace, while another shows her clubbing an enemy to death. Such militaristic postures are commonplace for Egyptian kings, but most unusual for Egyptian queens. Certain women who reigned as pharaohs in their own

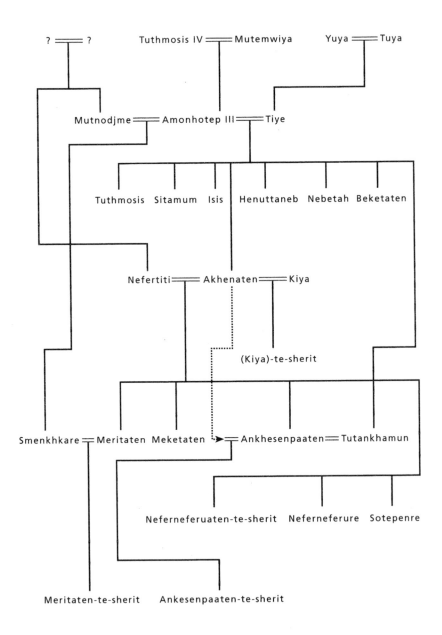

Genealogy of Amarna Royal Family

right, such as the eighteenth-dynasty queen Hatshepsut and twelfth-dynasty queen Sobeknefru, did involve themselves in military matters, but as a pharaoh's wife, Nefertiti stands virtually alone is being portrayed in such a warlike manner.

Nefertiti seems to have mellowed by the time she moved to Amarna. The title she adopted in the year 5, Neferneferuaten – 'Fair like the beauty of the Aten' – was presumably intended to demonstrate that, like her husband, she had renounced nefarious ways. Certainly her official profile is one of sweetness and light. In the tombs of Huya and the chamberlain Tutu she is described as a 'lady of graciousness', and the royal scribe Apy tells us that 'the Aten rises to multiply her love'. All the same, she is still involved in state affairs, and is even depicted wearing a king's paraphernalia. Although she usually wears her distinctive blue cap, she is often seen at official occasions wearing the double-plumed *Atef* crown, one of the sovereign crowns of a pharaoh.

However, any image of a muscle-bound macho-woman can certainly be dismissed. Her name Nefertiti, meaning 'A Beautiful Woman Comes', seems to have been aptly chosen. Together with Cleopatra and Helen of Troy, she has come to be regarded as one of history's most beautiful women, thanks to her famous head-statue discovered by Borchardt in 1911. Now on public display at the Egyptian Museum in Berlin, the bust is painted in natural colours and is so lifelike one almost expects it to move. The queen wears her unique blue crown, decorated by the cobra worn by the 'Great Royal Wife', and a typically wide Amarna necklace made of coloured beads. Around thirty years of age, Nefertiti appears both lovely and regal, gazing ahead with a serene countenance, a slight, knowing smile hovering on her lips.

Repeatedly, Akhenaten proclaims her beauty, and declares

for her his undying love. On one of the boundary stelae we read: 'The heiress, great in the palace, fair of face, adorned with the double plumes, mistress of happiness, endowed with favours, at hearing whose voice the king rejoices, the Chief Wife of the King, his beloved, the Lady of Two Lands – Nefertiti. May she live for ever and always.'

From the religious perspective, Nefertiti shares her husband's celestial role. As Akhenaten has usurped Osiris as lord of the dead, Nefertiti has taken over from the funerary goddesses as guardian of the dead. On a sarcophagus from the royal tomb at Amarna, four images of Nefertiti decorate the corners, instead of the four tutelary goddesses, Isis, Nephthys, Selkis and Neith, that usually protect the deceased. Moreover, an examination of the hieroglyphics in Nefertiti's title reveals that she may have held some special religious status all her own.

Hieroglyphics can be written to be read either from the left or right, the direction indicated by the way the characters face. If the human and animal figures, for instance, face the left, then the script is read from the left, and vice versa. In Nefertiti's title, however, we find an unusual exception. In her name, Neferneferuaten, a reed symbol at the top of her cartouche, which should uniformly point to the earlier text, is always made to face her image, even when it needs to be reversed. No one else, not even the king, enjoys such a distinction.

Akhenaten, though, is always seen to be in command. In processions Nefertiti is depicted behind him and in smaller scale, the conventional way of denoting inferior status. She may have enjoyed considerable influence, but in the end the king's word is final. In the boundary stelae proclamations concerning the location of the new city, we gather that Nefertiti is not exactly keen to set up home in the middle of nowhere. Akhenaten, however, makes it very clear that no one – not even the queen – will persuade him to build it anywhere else: only he speaks for the god.

Nefertiti's background is as enigmatic as her smile. Although we have more pictures of her in regal, religious and family life than any other queen of ancient Egypt, we have absolutely no details of her youth, birth or childhood. Her earliest representation is in the tomb of the vizier Ramose at Thebes, where she is already depicted as queen. It has been suggested that she was the daughter of the chief minister Ay, because he held the title 'Father of the God'. Queen Tiye's father, Amonhotep III's vizier Yuya, is sometimes described on commemorative scarabs as 'Father of the God', suggesting that it may have been a title meaning 'father-in-law' to the king. However, the term usually refers to a priestly office and, as chief minister, it is more likely that it alluded in some way to Ay's religious standing. In an illustration on the north wall of Tutankhamun's burial chamber Ay is actually shown acting as the *Sem* priest officiating at the last rites of the king. (Indeed, another of Akhenaten's ministers, Aper-el, also bore the title 'Father of the God' [see Chapter Eleven].) Moreover, Yuya's wife, Tuya, was described as 'Royal Mother of the King's Chief Wife', whereas the Ay's wife, Tey, is simply described as 'Governess to the King's Chief Wife'.

Nefertiti's name, 'A Beautiful Woman Comes', does not contain the noble designations normally found in the birth names of high-ranking Egyptians, such as god-names and allusions to virtues or social standing. Indeed, it seems more like a name she had acquired once she had grown up. This unconventional designation, coupled with the complete absence of family history, suggests that Nefertiti may not have been a native Egyptian. Perhaps she was a foreign princess, sent to Egypt as a child-bride to cement an alliance between Egypt and her country. Just such an arrangement seems to have been made for Akhenaten's grandfather, Tuthmosis IV, who was married to princess Mutemwiya, the daughter of the Mitannian king Artatama. Her foreign extraction did not prevent Mutemwiya from becoming the 'Chief Wife' and the mother of the next pharaoh, Amonhotep III and grandmother of Akhenaten himself.

An important indication that Nefertiti's was indeed of foreign extraction is the bust in the Berlin Museum. The fair-skinned woman it depicts is clearly not of North African origin, but markedly European. In fact, the narrow nose which follows the straight, so-called Grecian line from her brow, is a typical Aegean feature. As this was centuries before the existence of classical Greece, it may well be that she was a princess from the Minoan empire based on the Aegean island of Crete.

In the early 1900s excavations at Crete, led by the British archaeologist Sir Arthur Evans, unearthed the ruins of the ancient Minoan capital at Knossos. Dating from around 2000 BC, the heart of this remarkable city was a vast complex of royal buildings and courtyards, estimated to have housed around 40,000 people. Although not built to the enormous scale of contemporary Egyptian architecture, the city was in many ways more sophisticated. Staircases, for instance, doubled as an ingenious form of air conditioning, complex stone conduits carried running water beneath the floors, and some palace chambers even had an *en-suite* bathroom.

It soon became evident that the Minoans were a race of master shipbuilders who had dominated the Aegean for centuries, and through trade, rather than conquest, had become one of the wealthiest powers in the Mediterranean. From at least the Hyksos period they were in close commercial contact with Egypt. A circular alabaster jar, found at the palace at Knossos, was inscribed with the cartouche of the third Hyksos king, Khyan, around 1660 BC, and at the Hyksos capital Avaris (modern Tell-el-Daba), in the north-eastern Delta, archaeologists have unearthed numerous fragments of Minoan-style wall paintings. Minoan pottery, with its distinctive geometric patterns and naturalistic wildlife, turns up frequently in Egypt over the next three centuries, and by the eighteenth dynasty the two countries had strong diplomatic ties. In the tomb of Hatshepsut's chief minister Senenmut, around 1480 BC, we see scenes of foreign envoys, each in their national costume. Some are called *Keftiu* and from the goods they bear it is clear that they are Minoans. During the next fifty years or so they appear regularly as emissaries to the Egyptian court, and by the reign of Akhenaten's father, Amonhotep III, relations between the two empires have reached an all-time high. By this time the Minoans have adopted Egyptian building techniques for their new temples on Crete, while Amonhotep's new place of Malkata at Thebes is lavishly decorated with Minoan frescoes.

A special alliance between the Egyptian and the Minoan empires during Akhenaten's father's reign is very probable. By then the Egyptians had control of an empire which dominated the mainland of the eastern Mediterranean, right up to what is now northern Syria. Here, they came into contact with two neighbouring empires, the Mitanni in northern Syria and part of Iraq, and the more powerful Hittites in what is now Turkey. Treaties had been made with one side or other over the previous century, as Egypt contrived to retain its valuable province in Lebanon, from where came the hard cedar wood, essential to the Egyptian war machine. From the marriage of Amonhotep's predecessor to the Mitannian princess, it seems that a treaty of some kind already existed with the Mitanni, but the much larger Hittite empire still posed a threat. Egypt was without doubt the superior military power on land, but at sea the advantage lay with the Hittites whose major ports lay closer to Lebanon. From their seizure of the eastern seaboard around 1450 BC, the Egyptians had been relying on the swifter, more efficient Minoan ships to carry their timber supplies across the Mediterranean, and with the growing threat of the Hittites during Amonhotep's reign, a more binding pact with the Minoans would have been highly advantageous for both nations. As such, it would have been expedient to seal the treaty with the marriage of a member of the Egyptian royal family to the Minoan successor, and a Minoan princess to the Egyptian successor, Akhenaten.

Nefertiti certainly behaves like a Minoan princess. From frescoes and statues at Knossos it is clear that in cultic activities women played a far more important role than men. Priestesses, rather than priests, officiated at ceremonial events, and some scholars even believe that the throne itself was occupied by a priestess. Unlike in any other contemporary civilization, women completely dominated religious life. In Egypt, however, women, no matter how exalted, always played a subsidiary role in religion. They did not worship at the temple altar or make offerings to the principal god. Rather, they accompanied the proceedings by ringing a sistrum, a hand-held musical rattle. The moment Nefertiti appears on the scene, she immediately breaks these ancient taboos. In one of her first representations, on the pillars of the Temple of the Aten, built at Karnak early in Akhenaten's reign, Nefertiti is shown at the altar with her hands raised in worship, making an offering to Maat, the goddess of truth. Nefertiti is not merely assuming the religious role of a man, but by making an offering to Maat she is appropriating what had always been the prerogative of the king himself.

The clearest indicator to suggest that Nefertiti was of Minoan origin is the one concession Akhenaten seems to have made to the old gods – the continued veneration of the sacred bull. In the initial proclamations at Amarna, even after Akhenaten has abandoned all the traditional deities and everything associated with them, he makes specific instructions for the Mnevis bull, an animal sacred to Re, to be bought to the new city and buried in a special tomb in the eastern mountains. The Mnevis Bull, or Nemur, was a living animal worshipped at the temple of Heliopolis which, when dead, was buried with great ceremony and replaced by a new one located in the wild according to prescribed portents. Not only does Akhenaten continue to revere the sacred beast, but he even associates himself with the bull. One of the epithets used by the pharaohs of the New Kingdom was 'Mighty Bull of Horus', one which Akhenaten continues to employ: in the initial proclamations he actually refers to himself as the 'strong bull beloved of the Aten'. Even when he has abandoned wearing many of the customary pharaonic adorn-ments, he continues to wear the bull's tail appendage, while Nefertiti is often seen wearing the stylized bull horns on her headdress. Indeed this continues even after Akhenaten has outlawed the use of the Horus falcon-glyph in the full title of the Aten (see below).

It has always been a mystery why Akhenaten should have made such an uncharacteristic concession. However, if Nefertiti was a Minoan princess, her influence may well be behind it. Wherever it is found, Minoan art is dominated by the image of the bull. Its representations occur everywhere at the palace of Knossos, and there are numerous illustrations of young men jumping over the animal's back in an important religious rite. As the culture's main totem, the bull almost certainly repre-sented the chief Minoan god. Indeed, many scholars believe that the bull-cult continued on Crete well after the collapse of

Minoan civilization. It may even have been responsible for the legend of the Minotaur, which in later Greek mythology was a bull-headed man who inhabited the Labyrinth at Knossos.

Not only might the bull be explained by Minoan influence via Nefertiti, but also the flowing, naturalistic style of Amarnan art. The thrust of Minoan art, and also to some degree its subject matter, is strikingly similar to the revolutionary art at Amarna. In the luxuriant wall paintings at Knossos we see scenes of serenity and naturalistic motifs of flowers and animals, so like those favoured by Akhenaten.

Whatever her nationality, Nefertiti had enormous influence at Amarna, and once she had gone everything seems to fall apart. Some scholars have dated her death to as early as the year 11 of Akhenaten's reign, based on the cessation of wine deliveries to her estate at that time. However, she appears in scenes of a ceremony specifically dated as the year 12 in tombs of the high steward Huya and the harem overseer Meryre. In fact, she is still alive in two other scenes which must post-date this ceremony by a couple of years. All six daughters are pictured at the ceremony, and in funeral scenes from two of their tombs, Nefertiti is shown mourning their deaths. Both of these funerals can be dated after the year 14. As the Queen Mother, Tiye, is not present in the royal entourage, she must be presumed dead, and as she is recorded receiving wine in the year 14 these funerals must have occurred after that time. Nefertiti not receiving wine deliveries does not prove she is dead, but Tiye receiving such deliveries certainly suggests that she is alive. Accordingly, Nefertiti must have been alive after Tiye's death in the year 14. Nefertiti, however, appears in no scenes that can be dated after the year 14, so must, it seems, have died about that time.

Upon her death the once vigorous Akhenaten seems to have

Arthur Weigall (left), Theodore Davis (center) and Edward Ayrton (right) in 1907, the year they opened Tomb 55. Their strange behavior during the excavation of the tomb has never been satisfactorily explained. (*Birmingham City Library.*)

Tomb 55 - perhaps the most mysterious Egyptian tomb ever discovered – seems to have been constructed to keep someone or something trapped inside. (From Weigall's *The Glory of the Pharaohs.*)

The Tomb 55 entrance corridor at the time the tomb was opened, with the gilded shrine panels resting on top of the limestone rubble that filled the passage. (From Davis's *The Tomb of Queen Tiyi*.)

The Tomb 55 shrine panel which depicted Queen Tiyi and her son Akhenaten. Akhenaten's figure had been erased from the panel before the tomb was sealed. (From Davis's *The Tomb of Queen Tiyi*.)

The Tomb 55 burial chamber as it was first discovered. The shrine panels are stacked against the wall to the left of the picture and the niche containing the Canopic jars is set in the rear wall, below which lies the coffin. (From Davis's *The Tomb of Queen Tiyi*.)

The mysterious coffin lying *in situ* in Tomb 55. All evidence of the mummy's identity had been deliberately erased. (From Davis's *The Tomb of Queen Tiyi*.)

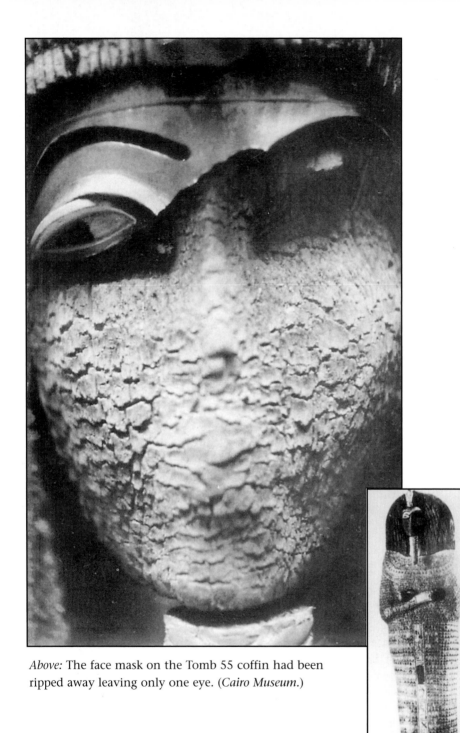

Above: The face mask on the Tomb 55 coffin had been ripped away leaving only one eye. (*Cairo Museum.*)

Right: The restored Tomb 55 coffin now on display in the Cairo Museum. The cartouche containing the occupant's name had been cut from its hieroglyphic texts. (*Cairo Museum.*)

Above: Although the Tomb 55 mummy was male, the stoppers of the accompanying Canopic jars depicted a woman. (*Metropolitan Museum, New York.*)

Right: One of the Canopic jars from Tomb 55 which contain the removed internal organs of the mummy. Inscribed panels on the jars revealed that they had been made for Akhenaten's secondary Queen Kiya, before being altered to accommodate the remains of Akhenaten himself. (*Metropolitan Museum, New York.*)

Above: The plaster-cast head of Akhenaten found during the Amarna excavations in 1911 probably depicts Akhenaten's true features. (*Berlin Museum.*)

Right: A typical profile of Akhenaten as he is depicted in the Amarna reliefs, with malformations to the skull, face and neck. The exaggerated features have long been a mystery to Egyptologists. (*Cleveland Museum of Art.*)

Above: The Nefertiti bust found at the Great Palace at Amarna in 1911. The fair-skinned woman it depicts is clearly not of North African origin, but markedly European. (*Berlin Museum.*)

Right: Like her husband, Nefertiti is often shown in the Amarna reliefs with the same exaggerated facial features. (*Petrie Museum.*)

Courtiers also emulated the 'royal deformities' in their representations. In this pair of statuettes the chief sculptor Bek and his wife are both depicted with the bodily peculiarities typical of Akhenaten reliefs. (*Berlin Museum.*)

In most Amarna depictions the king's physique is distinctly feminine, with heavy breasts, swelling hips and ample thighs. However, Akhenaten's profile is not only effeminate, it is also deformed. The legs, for instance, are fatty around the thighs but spindly below the knee. (*Cairo Museum.*)

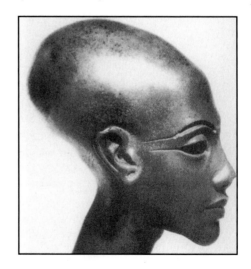

Akhenaten's daughters are often depicted with enlarged craniums and serpentine necks, such as in this bust thought to be of the Princess Meritaten. (*Berlin Museum.*)

lost all interest in expounding his precious religion and even relinquished the reins of power: artists increasingly abandon the new style of art, seemingly without reprisals, and Smenkhkare is appointed co-regent with full pharaonic power. There seems to have been no palace revolt or military coup, simply a case of chronic apathy on the part of the pharaoh. It is abundantly clear from Amarnan art that Akhenaten was an extraordinarily emotional man, who dearly loved his family and doted over his queen. The loss of his mother, two daughters and his beloved wife within a year or so must have been just too much for such a man to bear.

With Nefertiti gone, and the king's apparent withdrawal, the drama now shifts increasingly to Akhenaten's eldest daughter and ultimately to what appears to have been a bitter power struggle. The six princesses were, in descending order of age, Meritaten, Meketaten, Ankhesenpaaten, Neferneferuaten-ta-sherit, Neferneferure, and Sotepenre. Two of them, we know, had already died. A chamber in the royal tomb shows a death-bed scene of a princess lying on a couch. She is mourned by her weeping parents and two distraught attendants, while standing outside the chamber is a nursemaid holding a baby. The inference appears to be that this princess died in childbirth. A companion scene on the opposite wall identifies the deceased as the princess Mekataten, Nefertiti's second eldest daughter. As there are only four princesses in the funerary procession it appears that one of Mekataten's sisters has also died by this time.

This princess was evidently interred in a separate chamber in the royal tomb, but who she was is unclear. Two long scenes in the chamber show the king and queen accompanied by five daughters making offerings in a temple court. Other scenes show the king grieving for the princess who lies prostrate on a bier. A similar scene above shows the king and queen mourning at her death-bed. Once more, a nursemaid is seen outside the room holding a baby, suggesting that this princess also died in childbirth. As there are five living daughters illustrated here, then it is presumably not a further representation of Mekataten's funeral, at which only four daughters were present. The name of the deceased has been excised from the walls, but it would seem to have been the princess Neferneferure, as in 1984 a fragment of a funerary vessel bearing her name was discovered among rubble in the area by the Egyptian archaeologist Dr Aly el Kouly.

In order to determine the extent of the influence of the surviving princesses, we must initially try to get some idea of their ages. The first picture to show all six daughters alive is one in the so-called King's House, a series of private chambers which had been joined to the ceremonial palace by a bridge. Here, wall paintings show the king and queen seated on stools with their six daughters before them, the youngest, Sotepenre, is a babe in her mother's lap. Luckily, we can deduce the latest possible date of this scene because the name of the Aten in its earlier form.

The Aten, meaning literally 'sun disc', had originally been considered the day-time aspect, or role, played by the Middle Kingdom god Re-Herakhte. The full hieroglyphic title of the Aten was: 'Re-Herakhte, who rejoices in the horizon in his name of the light which is in the sun disc.'

An abbreviated version of this title was the glyph for Re-Horus, the falcon god, which is how the name of the Aten appears in the early years of Akhenaten's reign. From the year 9, however, Akhenaten decreed that his omnipotent god could no longer be represented in such a form, and instead could only be represented by a radiant disc or by the phonetically written word Aten – a reed followed by three other symbols one on top of the other.

As the accompanying inscriptions of the King's House illustration uses the earlier form of the god's name – i.e. the falcon glyph for the Aten, rather than the reed glyph – it must have been made before the year 9. In other words, all six daughters were living by the year 8. As she is a baby, Sotepenre cannot have been born much before the King's House was built around the year 7. This youngest daughter was therefore about eight by the time Nefertiti died around the year 15. Little Sotepenre also helps us work out the approximate age of the others.

In tombs of the high steward Huya and the harem overseer Meryre, reliefs show the royal family attending an event which is dated as the year 12. As Sotepenre is shown for the first time at an official occasion, we know that the princesses could participate in ceremonial events once they reach the age of five. Accordingly, as Ankhesenpaaten does not appear on the boundary stelae until in the year 6, but does in the year 8, she must have been around twelve or thirteen when her mother dies, and her younger sister Neferneferuaten-ta-sherit was around ten. The elder sister Meritaten already appears around the year 3 of Akhenaten's reign, officially accompanying her mother in reliefs at the Aten Temple at Karnak, so she must have been around seventeen or eighteen when Nefertiti died. Her three sisters being so young, all immediate influence must therefore have fallen to Meritaten.

Between the years 14 and 15 Meritaten is referred to in the Amarna Letters sent to Akhenaten by various correspondents, such as Burnaburiash II of Babylon and Abi-milki of Tyre. They call her by the affectionate nickname 'Mayati', and refer to her as 'the mistress of your house', implying that she assumed the duties of the 'Great Royal Wife' or 'Chief Queen'.

There is evidence that Meritaten may have been opposed in taking over from Nefertiti by Akhenaten's second wife Kiya, who seems to have enjoyed considerable influence. A toilet vessel from Amarna in the New York Metropolitan Museum of Art and a calcite vase in the British Museum are inscribed with Kiya's full title. The text includes a rectangular panel containing the early names of the Aten, and the names and titles of Akhenaten, followed by three columns of glyphs reading: 'The wife and greatly beloved of the King of Upper and Lower Egypt, Living in Truth, Lord of the Two Lands, Neferkheperure Wa'enre [Akhenaten's titles], the Goodly Child of the Living Aten, who shall be living for ever, Kiya.'

This formula, with one or two minor adjustments, is found whenever Kiya is referred to on her monuments, showing that she was far more than simply a member of Akhenaten's harem. Akhenaten had other wives, but they bear no such distinguishing titles. For example, a certain Ipy is simply called the 'Royal Ornament'. In fact, so important was Kiya that she had her own *Maru*, or 'viewing temple', discovered in the southern area of Amarna by the British archaeologist Leonard Woolley in 1921. Such temples, with their pools and gardens where the owner could sit and be rejuvenated in the sun's rays, were an exceptional privilege usually reserved for senior royalty like Nefertiti and the Queen Mother. Kiya even had a personal chapel near the entrance to the Great Temple.

There is also evidence that Kiya not only enjoyed far greater privileges than most pharaohs' secondary wives, but that her standing continued to grow. It comes from a series of decorated stone slabs found during a German excavation in 1939 at Hermopolis, near modern Ashmunein, a few kilometres down the Nile from Amarna. Called the Hermopolis Talatat (from an Arabic word), they are made from limestone which was finer and more compact than local stone. It was soon clear that they had originally come from buildings at Amarna and, about fifty years after the city was abandoned, had been ferried downstream to be used as foundation rubble in a temple built by Ramesses II. Dating from the later part of Akhenaten's reign, the talatat show Kiya functioning in an important capacity in the Great Temple itself and refer to her as the king's 'favourite'.

Meritaten clearly saw Kiya as a power rival. Kiya had obviously enjoyed Nefertiti's favour, but once the queen was gone, Meritaten had Kiya evicted from her *Maru* temple and appropriated it for herself. Inscriptions from the temple are found to have been changed to Meritaten's name, and Kiya's portraits are replaced with those of the princess. Kiya was still alive after Nefertiti's death but remained very much inferior to the princesses. One of the Hermopolis Talatat shows the royal family at a religious service, at which Akhenaten officiates at an altar. Nefertiti is absent, so it must be after her death, but the surviving daughters and Kiya are present. Kiya, however, is both behind, and on a lower level than the princesses, who are clearly of superior status.

From around the year 15, for the first time we find Meritaten accompanied by a husband – the enigmatic Smenkhkare. Various statues and reliefs, together with a scene on a box and a damaged box lid found in Tutankhamun's tomb, show them together late in Akhenaten's reign. Almost immediately Smenkhkare is elevated to co-regent, and bricks found stamped with his name at the royal apartments have suggested that a great hall was built especially for his coronation to the south of the palace.

No giant reliefs survive to commemorate the co-regency, but a number of smaller finds attest to it having occurred. In the early excavations of Amarna, Flinders Petrie found a small stone stela inscribed with two cartouches bearing Akhenaten and Smenkhkare's names, placed beside one another as co-regents are shown in other reigns. During excavations of the Great Temple of Amarna in 1933, a sculptor's model of the two kings also came to light. Carved in sunk relief, the limestone tablet shows Akhenaten and an unnamed co-regent both wearing a pharaonic *uraeus* on their foreheads. Additional evidence of the co-regency are other minor artifacts, such as the Stela of Pase from Amarna, which appear to show Akhenaten and another king sitting side by side, although the pieces lack text identifying the pair.

From the mummy in Tomb 55 we can gather that Smenkhkare was about the same age as Meritaten, but where he came from is a complete mystery as he appears nowhere before this time. The customary line of succession from early in the New Kingdom was via the eldest daughter of the king's 'Chief Wife', which had often meant an incestuous marriage to secure the throne for the king's eldest son, although, as we have seen, this seems to have been abandoned for at least three generations. Akhenaten and Tuthmosis IV seem to have married foreigners, and Amonhotep III married the daughter of a courtier. As Akhenaten apparently had no legitimate son, whoever married Meritaten would thus become successor. It stands to reason, therefore, that Smenkhkare would have been her closest legitimate male relative.

As Smenkhkare's name is often found accompanied by the title Nefernefruaten, a designation that Nefertiti used and the name given to one of her daughters, it would seem that he was related to Nefertiti in some way – perhaps the son of her sister, Mutnodjme. Reliefs from the early tombs of Akhenaten's reign often show Mutnodjme among the royal entourage acting as

Nefertiti's lady-in-waiting. She is described as: 'The sister of the Chief Queen Neferneferuaten-Nefertiti, living for ever and ever, Mutnodjme.'

On a number of occasions, for example in reliefs in Ay's tomb, she appears with two small figures, whom some have taken to be attendant dwarfs, but could equally be two young sons, one perhaps being Smenkhkare. Some scholars have dismissed her as Smenkhkare's mother as she is pictured wearing a sidelock normally associated with children, which would seemingly make her too young to have a son who was around seventeen by the fifteenth year of Akhenaten's reign. However, there are examples of older women wearing such a sidelock in the immediate pre-Amarna period, which may indicate that it was an adult fashion for a while. Mutnodjme disappears from view as the reign wears on but reappears again about fourteen years after Akhenaten's reign, married to the general Horemheb to legitimate his claim to the throne. Here she bears the titles of 'Heiress' and 'Great Queen', so it would seem that through her the line of succession was deemed to have descended.

Within a couple of years of the co-regency with Smenkhkare, Akhenaten himself disappears from the scene. Of all the scraps of pottery and inscriptions found at Amarna, nothing bears a date later than year 17 of Akhenaten's reign. We know that this must be the last year of his reign as a docket from a honey jar found at Amarna bears the date 'Year 17', which has been partly expunged and 'Year 1' written below it. This clearly demonstrates that Akhenaten has died and another pharaoh has taken over. However, this pharaoh is almost certainly Tutankhamun, as a docket from a wine jar from the same source reads, 'Year 1, wine from the estate of Smenkhkare, deceased'. The 'Year 1' therefore has to refer to Tutankhamun. The question is, did Smenkhkare and Meritaten enjoy an independent reign? The probability is that they did. In the tomb of the harem overseer Meryre, Smenkhkare and Meritaten are shown in the accoutrements of reigning royalty rewarding the owner, while Akhenaten is nowhere to be seen. Likewise, a painted slab in the Berlin Museum, found at Amarna in the early 1900s, shows them alone as king and queen.

It would appear that in the brief period of their reign, Meritaten took drastic steps against her rival Kiya, from which she had been restrained while her father was still alive. Not only did she excise Kiya's name from inscriptions, but defaced her representations in the most spiteful way. On illustrations on blocks found at Hermopolis, and on fragments of the Great Temple reliefs, we see that the eyes have been gouged from Kiya's image. Akhenaten's second wife had clearly been disgraced, and possibly killed. As the last we hear of her is in the year 16, she may not have survived long after Akhenaten's death.

Significantly, Kiya is a crucial figure in the mystery of Tomb 55, for it seems to have been for her that the burial effects in the tomb were initially made. From the feminine gender of the inscriptions, the characteristic court lady's wig on the coffin, and the female heads on the Canopic jars, we know that the original owner was a woman. Furthermore, from the inscription on the footboard of the coffin we can tell she was of exalted rank. It is an intimate address that, by its context, can only have been to Akhenaten:

Utterance by [cartouche cut out], deceased: 'May I breathe the sweet breath that comes forth from thy mouth, may I behold thy beauty daily; my prayer is that I might hear thy sweet, breezelike voice, and my limbs be rejuvenated in life through love of thee! Mayest thou extend me thine arms bearing thy spirit, that I may receive it and live by it.

Mayest thou call on my name for eternity, and it shall never cease from thy mouth, O my father [cartouche cut out] thou being [excised text] for ever and ever, living like the sun disc [excised text] the King of Upper and Lower Egypt, living on Truth, Lord of the Two Lands [cartouche cut out], thou beautiful child of the sun disc, who shall be here, living, living, for ever and ever [cut out; replaced with cartouche also cut out].

Although, at first glance, this inscription would seem to be made for a child of Akhenaten, as he is addressed as 'father', this was a common form of address used by Akhenaten's subjects, signifying that the king was their 'heavenly father'. All the same, the woman for whom the inscription was made is certainly close to the pharaoh, to have addressed him so intimately.

She was not, however, a 'Chief Queen'. The figures on both the coffin and Canopic jars show evidence of having had a *uraeus* added to the brow to make it suitable for the king for whom they were being adapted. The original female owner, therefore, had not been entitled to wear such a device, which rules out a 'Chief Queen' like Nefertiti or Meritaten who would have worn the royal serpent. Neither had the name of the original owner been contained in a cartouche, which again excludes a 'Chief Queen'. It all fits with a secondary queen like Kiya, however, who although not entitled to the *uraeus* or a cartouche, was close enough to the king to address him in an intimate manner.

When the German scholar Rolf Krauss succeeded in showing that the inscribed panels on the Canopic jars had been adapted to apply specifically to Akhenaten (see Chapter One), he also discovered that they had once contained Kiya's personal title. High-ranking Egyptians favoured the use of long titles, uniquely associating them with their king. Such a title had been on the Canopic jars and had been altered so that it applied only to Akhenaten. There had originally been a 'landscape' panel containing the early names of the Aten, together with the appellations of Akhenaten, followed by a 'portrait' panel to the right containing the name and epithets of the owner. The 'portrait' panel had been removed, but the surviving inscription in the 'landscape' panel formed a part of Kiya's unique title found elsewhere.

Closer analysis reveals that Kiya's remains had already been laid peacefully to rest in the burial effects, before her tomb was plundered to provide the trappings for the sacrilegious interment planned for Akhenaten. Although the coffin could have been prepared for Kiya at any time, the gold-sheathed footboard text would not usually be inscribed until her death. In fact, the inscription actually tells us that she is deceased. This conjecture is further supported by an inscription on the gold bands surrounding the coffin. Here a glyph for the word 'truth' was in a form of the squatting goddess Maat that was avoided after year 8 of Akhenaten's reign in favour of a phonetic spelling. This later spelling, however, was used in the prayer on the footboard and in the columns of inscriptions on the gold lining of the coffin lid. If the inscriptions had been made at the same time as the burial effects they would have been in the earlier form. The conclusion, therefore, is that the coffin was made in the early part of Akhenaten's reign but actually *used* for Kiya in the later years.

Her tomb having been plundered for her burial effects implies that Kiya had been specifically chosen as the person whose funerary items were intended to be used for Akhenaten's bizarre entombment. There must have been dozens of such funerary items lying in storage awaiting use by their owners upon their deaths. Why not commandeer any of these? Alternatively, why not simply make a coffin and Canopic jars specially for the purpose? For the perpetrators to have gone to such trouble to appropriate Kiya's coffin and Canopic jars means that the king's secondary wife was deliberately chosen to play a part in the macabre procedure. The only person we know of who had both the authority to disinter someone of Kiya's rank, and the apparent resentment of her to have done so, is Meritaten.

Indeed the state of the face mask on the coffin in Tomb 55 is a tell-tale clue which points to Meritaten. Because the addition of the uraeus to the forehead, we know that the face had been the likeness, not of the person it was adapted for, but of the original owner, Kiya. As her face was still on the Canopic jars, the removal of the mask was not intended to obscure Kiya's features, so must have been part of the macabre ritual. However, not all the face was torn away – one eye remained. What this was meant to signify is difficult to tell, but this is exactly the same peculiar manner in which Meritaten desecrated Kiya's statues – by chiselling out one of the eyes. As relief figures were always shown in profile, there was only one eye visible to excise.

If Meritaten had been responsible for planning the profane interment of Akhenaten, then she must at some point have turned against him. The same is true of her husband: a number of small artefacts, such as ring-bezels and furniture-knobs, bearing Smenkhkare's name show that he ultimately dropped the title – 'Beloved of Akhenaten' – presumably to distance himself from the king. It seems unlikely that Meritaten and Smenkhkare actually overthrew Akhenaten; rather they chose to renounce him once he had died. However, it does not seem that the couple abandoned Atenism. On the contrary, they appeared to have embraced it with fanatical zeal, persecuting those who failed to convert.

Although Akhenaten abolished the Amun priesthood and established Atenism as the state religion, there is no evidence that he oppressed those who still revered the old gods. Outside Amarna, life seems to have gone on pretty much as usual, and shrines to the traditional deities continued to be erected privately at Thebes and elsewhere. Sometime before the abandonment of Amarna, however, the Temple of Amun at Karnak suffered frenzied desecration, and monuments to Amun-Re were destroyed throughout Thebes. His obelisks were toppled, his statues were smashed to pieces, and the tallest of buildings were scaled to eradicate inscriptions bearing his name. The god's name was even proscribed from being used in personal names such as *Amon*hotep, and it is this particular edict which enables us to date the time of the destruction to the late Amarna period.

A number of inscriptions concerning Amonhotep III still employ the *Amon* (i.e. Amun) element until the very last years of Akhenaten's reign – text on the shrine from Tomb 55, for instance. As Akhenaten himself commissioned the shrine to be made around the time of Tiye's death, it shows that the violent suppression of the Amun cult had not occurred by the year 14 when the queen died. As it occurred so late in his reign it seems highly unlikely that Akhenaten himself was responsible. By this time the king had apparently all but lost interest in the world. As we have seen, artisans were virtually ignoring the official artistic decrees, seemingly without reproach. There is absolutely nothing to suggest that Akhenaten was becoming more of a hardliner. On the contrary, someone who is contemplating extreme acts of repression would hardly have relinquished much of his power to a co-regent.

It is much more feasible that it was the new king and queen who were responsible for the harsher measures, probably after

Akhenaten's death. Specifically, it would seem to have been down to Meritaten. An inscription in the tomb of a certain Pairi at Thebes, dated 'Year 3', tells us that Smenkhkare had a funerary temple in the city. This means that by the third year of his reign Smenkhkare had left Amarna and returned to Thebes, had died and was entombed, probably in the Valley of the Kings. Moreover, as the inscription also refers to divine offerings being made to Amun-Re at Smenkhkare's temple, it means that he had tried to reinstate the old religion. Abandoning Amarna and re-embracing Amun-Re very much implies that the recent anti-Amun desecrations had not been his idea, leaving Meritaten as the most likely culprit.

If this anti-Amun campaign was carried out on Meritaten's orders, then it would go some way to explaining why the peculiar entombment was originally planned for Akhenaten. As Akhenaten had evidently considered it unnecessary to wreak such havoc against Amun-Re and the other gods, he obviously did not see them as a threat. His god was the only god, so how could they be? As far as he was concerned they didn't exist. However, the desecration of Thebes implies a sudden fear of celestial opposition. Had Meritaten come to believe that her father had been demoniacally possessed by some rival god? Perhaps Akhenaten's uncharacteristic apathy, or possibly a mental breakdown following his wife's death, had ignited such fears. Indeed, such a scenario may well have led to the anti-Amun reprisals in the first place.

Smenkhkare, on the other hand, obviously considered Amun-Re to have had the upper hand and he tried to make amends. Although there is no surviving record of Meritaten's death, her husband's return to Thebes must presumably have been made once she was no longer around to stop him. However, Smenkhkare seems to have done too little, too late, for he too died within a few months to be replaced by his apparent brother Tutankhamun. However, as Tutankhamun was only about eight at the time, the real power doubtless resided with the chief minister, Ay. Tutankhamun was immediately married to the eldest surviving princess, Meritaten's teenage sister Ankhesenpaaten, and rapid attempts were made to repair the damage to the monarchy.

This new regime was responsible for the final condition of Tomb 55, which leaves us with another intriguing question. How had Smenkhkare eventually come to be buried in the grotesque burial effects originally adapted for Akhenaten? The answer may be found in two very different tombs – the defiled tomb of Akhenaten and the magnificent tomb of Tutankhamun.

SUMMARY

- In the seventeenth year of his reign, Akhenaten dies and is succeeded for a few short months by Smenkhkare and his queen Meritaten. It would appear that in the brief period of their reign, Meritaten took drastic steps against her rival Kiya, from which she had been restrained while her father was still alive. Akhenaten's second wife had clearly been disgraced, and possibly killed. As the last we hear of her is in the year 16, she may not have survived long after Akhenaten's death.

- Kiya is a crucial figure in the mystery of Tomb 55, for it seems to have been for her that the burial effects in the tomb were initially made. The one person we know of who had both the authority to disinter someone of Kiya's rank, and the apparent resentment of her to have done so, is

Meritaten. It would appear, therefore, that Meritaten and or Smenkhkare had been responsible for the original adaptation of the burial effects for the bizarre interment of Akhenaten.

• When Smenkhkare died within a year of inheriting the throne, Tutankhamun became king. As he was only about eight at the time, the real power doubtless resided with the chief minister, Ay. Tutankhamun was immediately married to the eldest surviving princess, Meritaten's teenage sister Ankhesenpaaten, and rapid attempts were made to repair the damage to the monarchy. This new regime was responsible for the final condition of Tomb 55, which means that they must have discovered Akhenaten's sacrilegious burial and decided that such an interment better suited Smenkhkare.

CHAPTER FIVE

Secrets of the Three Tombs

Well over half a century after Wilkinson's first account of the Amarna remains in 1924, Akhenaten's tomb had still not been found – at least not by the Americans or Europeans. Before the local villagers began to resent foreign intrusions and wreak havoc on the ruins in the late nineteenth century, they had been quick to realize the profitability of the ancient artefacts that still survived in the debris. Diverting their efforts from their usual subsistence toil, they had rummaged through the rubble in search of precious antiquities, particularly around the tombs in the eastern hills. Many such items were unearthed and sold to intrepid artefact hunters and so found their way into the hands of private collectors and the museums of Europe and North America. It was not until the 1880s, however, that funerary items from Akhenaten's tomb first appeared.

In 1882, pieces of jewellery, later identified as burial effects from Akhenaten's tomb, were sold to the Reverend W. J. Loftie, an English clergyman who visited Amarna in search of antiquities. He in turn sold some of them to the Royal Museum of Scotland in Edinburgh where they remained, their significance unrealized for another three decades. Unfortunately for the Scots, this was well after the villagers decided to reveal the tomb's whereabouts to a French team in the early 1890s,

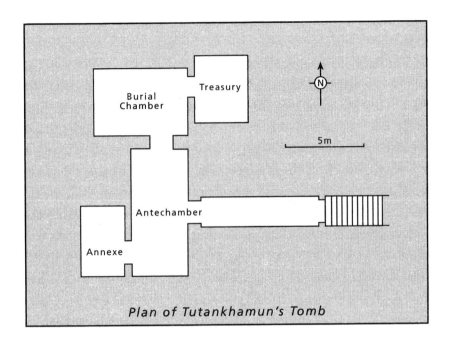

Plan of Tutankhamun's Tomb

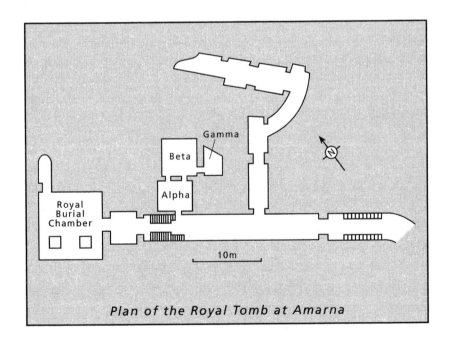

Plan of the Royal Tomb at Amarna

presumably once they considered it no longer contained anything of tradable value. The person who actually discovered the tomb of one of the most intriguing pharaohs of ancient Egypt, therefore, was no wealthy adventurer like Theodore Davis, or a world-famous Egyptologist like Howard Carter, but an uneducated, poverty-stricken peasant whose name we will probably never know.

The reason why the whereabouts of Akhenaten's tomb had remained a secret for so long is that it was situated almost six kilometres from the nobles' tombs in a remote side valley. Now called the Royal Wadi, this craggy gorge cuts its way into a barren plateau due east of what had once been the central city. As the engineer of the French expedition, Alexandre Barsanti began the official excavation of the tomb in December 1891. This painstaking sifting of rubble, that had already been rummaged through for decades, lacked all the excitement of the discovery of Tomb 55 or the glamour of the opening of Tutankhamun's tomb. In fact, Barsanti's first job was to fit iron gates to the entrance to prevent his work being hampered by further foraging by the locals.

The design of the royal tomb at Amarna departs markedly from other contemporary tombs. It is actually a series of tombs seemingly being intended to house the entire royal family. A long, wide corridor leads downward into the hillside by means of two staircases, separated by a long sloping passageway, for a distance of 28 metres to arrive at the king's burial complex. This consisted of an anteroom leading a protective well-room (a platform overlooking a shaft some 3 metres deep) giving on to the doorway of the burial hall itself. Some 10 metres square in all, the left third of the chamber was a dais with two columns to support the roof, while the remaining area contained a slightly raised emplacement for a sarcophagus. Nothing of the burial remained; even the wall decorations had been virtually obliterated by what must surely have been the anti-Atenist desecrators. Fortunately, there were one or two faint traces of inscriptions near the ceiling which revealed that the chamber had been prepared for Akhenaten and Nefertiti.

Most Egyptologists believe that when Amarna was abandoned, within a year or two of Akhenaten's demise, the tombs had been emptied by the families of the deceased and the mummies and burial goods were taken away for reinterment at Thebes. Anything that remained would have been looted during the anti-Atenist desecrations that occurred about fifteen years later. Where the majority of the mummies ended up is unknown. Some may have been ransacked during the reprisals, others may have escaped destruction by being well hidden. Whether or not these included Akhenaten himself is at present impossible to say, as his remains or alternative tomb have never been found.

The royal burial chamber at Amarna had certainly been used before the city was abandoned. Not only are there the remains of the limestone wall that once sealed the chamber, but there is the protective well which would not have been dug until the mummy and burial goods were in place. Such a well, or pit, immediately outside the burial chamber, is a common feature of New Kingdom tombs and was intended to make it difficult for thieves to remove the funerary furniture. This one had been refilled with rubble in antiquity so that the deposits could transported elsewhere.

Evidence that both Akhenaten and Nefertiti were once interred here comes in the form of a number of discarded items left behind when the tomb was evacuated, such as *ushabti* figures (small funerary statues) of the king and queen, together with fragments of Akhenaten's sarcophagus and his alabaster

Canopic chest. Recently, modern enhancement of the damaged reliefs in the burial chamber have revealed faded scenes of the pharaoh's funeral with mourning attendants similar to that in Huya's tomb, a scene that was almost certainly carved as the mummy was being laid to rest. From this assorted evidence we can tell that Akhenaten had initially been buried in the Amarna royal tomb in the usual fashion. However, whether he remained here peacefully until Amarna was abandoned, and like the other mummies removed to Thebes, or whether his body had been desecrated by Meritaten prior to the evacuation, is the all-important question. Had his remains ever been deposited in Kiya's coffin and Canopic jars as his daughter apparently intended? A strong indication that they were can be found in other chambers in the royal tomb.

Immediately to the right of the antechamber, at the end of the entrance passageway, is a suite of three rooms, designated as chambers Alpha, Beta and Gamma. Chamber Alpha is around 5.5 metres square and nearly 3 metres high and decorated with scenes showing the death and burial of a princess whose name has been excised, but may have been Neferneferure (see Chapter Four). Chamber Beta, which divides the two, is undecorated but Chamber Gamma, roughly 3.5 metres square and 1.8 in height, is decorated in a similar fashion to Chamber Alpha and inscriptions identify it as having belonged to the princess Meketaten.

Unlike the king's burial chamber, where reliefs had been thoroughly defaced by the anti-Atenists, these chambers were left virtually untouched. However, although the name of Princess Meketaten had been left intact, someone had taken the trouble to erase the name of the woman who is shown outside the death-bed room holding a baby. The same woman is found depicted in the reliefs in Chamber Alpha, and here too her name has been excised. As this is clearly not the work of the anti-Atenists, who had not considered the chambers worth violating, it means that someone else with a different motive had been responsible. The prime suspect is Meritaten, as the baby-carrying woman would, once again, seem to have been her arch-rival Kiya.

As we have seen, the royal family chose only those of the most exalted position to act as their close attendants. Nefertiti's governess, for example, had been the chief minister's wife, and her lady-in-waiting, her sister, eventually became chief queen herself (see Chapter Four). This in itself would strongly suggest that the woman was someone of Kiya's standing, but there is further evidence pointing exclusively to her. In both scenes the baby-holding woman is accompanied by fan-bearers, a sign of high rank. As even the highest-ranking courtiers in the entourage are not depicted in this way, the woman is superior to them and must therefore be either a princess or a queen. She cannot be Nefertiti or one of her daughters, all of whom are present in the Chamber Alpha scenes, albeit one of them as a corpse, and she cannot be Queen Tiye who, apart from evidently being deceased, would have had her name in a cartouche, which the intact limestone surrounding the excised name reveals not to have been the case. The only other person we know of who appears to fit this picture is the number two queen, Kiya.

Although it has been propounded that the fan-bearers are attending the child, the argument does not stand up to scrutiny. The suggested scenario is that both princesses had died in childbirth and the woman is a nursemaid leaving with the baby who would therefore itself be a prince or princess. However, this cannot possibly have been the case in one of the scenes. Although Mekataten, in Chamber Gamma, being around fourteen, could have died in childbirth, the occupant of Chamber

Alpha was far too young. As the elder sisters Meritaten and Ankhesenpaaten outlived Akhenaten and Nefertiti, and are both shown in the reliefs, the princess in question can only have been either Neferneferure, Neferneferuaten-ta-sherit or Sotepenre. Sotepenre, as we have seen, was no older than eight and, as they do not appear in reliefs until after the year 8, the other two could have been no older than ten – all too young to have conceived (see Chapter Four).

As Meritaten had been responsible for excising Kiya's name from monuments throughout Amarna, it must surely also have been she who was responsible for excising Kiya's name in the royal tomb. It is most unlikely that she would have desecrated the tomb during her father's burial. Before his death, Meritaten may have appropriated Kiya's *Maru* temple and in its inscriptions replaced Kiya's name with her own, but it was only after he died that she was free to deface her rival's monuments so savagely. It seems highly improbable that, before the priests and high officials, the princess would expunge the name of the woman who was still being described as the 'king's favourite' and 'greatly beloved' right till the end of his reign. As she had died, or had been disgraced, by the time Amarna was abandoned, she would not have been around to desecrate the chamber at that time. Consequently, if Meritaten excised Kiya's name from the burial chambers, it means that she must have ordered the tomb to be opened at some point between Akhenaten's interment and the abandonment of the city.

As no further burials appear to have been made in the royal tomb after Akhenaten's demise, the opening of the tomb by Meritaten must have been for another purpose, presumably to acquire Akhenaten's mummy for its re-burial in Kiya's effects. There is indeed evidence that Chamber Alpha was adapted for this very purpose, in the form of four niches cut into its walls to contain the 'magic bricks'. Egyptologist Geoffrey Martin of London University reasoned that such amulets were only to be found in the tombs of sovereigns or royal consorts, and proposed that the chamber was ultimately adapted for someone other than a princess. Although Professor Martin suggested that it may have been prepared for one of the secondary queens, it seems unlikely that one of the beloved princesses would have been removed from her own tomb while Akhenaten was still alive, and even less likely during Meritaten's time as queen for the benefit of one of her rivals. It would seem to fit more into the emerging picture, in view of the preparations made for Akhenaten's macabre reinterment, that it was adapted for the king himself. We know from Tomb 55 that Akhenaten had 'magic bricks' specifically made for him, yet his own burial chamber has no niches for such amulets. They must therefore have been used elsewhere, possibly in Chamber Alpha, before being appropriated, along with the other equipment, for Smenkhkare's peculiar burial. In all probability, Meritaten, not wishing to disturb her mother's remains in the royal chamber, and restrained from removing the body from the tomb complex by cultic considerations or by the need for secrecy, chose to move Akhenaten's mummy into Alpha Chamber for its profane reinterment. As for the 'magic bricks': as they employ the form of the king's name only used in the earlier part of his reign, they may have been items he ultimately considered unnecessary, and had been discarded until others deemed them an essential element in the their strange burial ritual.

The first act of the scenario of the Tomb 55 mystery would therefore seem to be this: after his death, Akhenaten is renounced by Meritaten and Smenkhkare, possibly because of his uncharacteristic behaviour following the death of his wife. The tomb of Meritaten's enemy, Kiya, is opened, her mummy defiled, her burial equipment stolen, and her coffin mask defaced to leave one eye. Akhenaten is then reinterred in Kiya's effects, in the belief that it will restrain his, or some invading demon's, spirit. For the purpose, he is moved into Chamber Alpha where the 'magic bricks' are set in place, presumably in the conviction that they would serve to prevent anyone from finding or disturbing him. At this time Kiya's name is expunged from the reliefs in this and Chamber Delta.

We now come to the second act: Smenkhkare's original burial. After Meritaten is either disgraced or dies, Smenkhkare tries to make amends by returning to Thebes and realigning himself with the cult of Amun-Re. There he dies and is interred conventionally in the Valley of the Kings, as evidenced by his burial equipment found in Tutankhamun's tomb and the reference to his funerary temple in the tomb of Parisi. In ascertaining if this initial interment was originally in Tomb 55, we need firstly to examine the traditional explanation for the condition of the tomb.

According to the orthodox theory, found in the official guide books to the Valley of the Kings and in many modern textbooks, Tomb 55 served as nothing more than a temporary storage place for the funeral equipment removed from the Amarna tombs when the city was abandoned. It was in the process of being constructed for someone of lower rank, so the argument goes, when it was requisitioned temporarily to house the mummies and burial goods of the royal family, principally those of Akhenaten, Queen Tiye and Smenkhkare (as some of their items had been left behind). When new tombs were made ready elsewhere in the Valley of the Kings the mummies had been removed, all except the defiled remains of discredited Atenist, Smenkhkare. Much of the funerary equipment, however, was appropriated by Ay and Tutankhamun and some of it was used to furnish their own tombs and those of their followers. Incredibly, this hypothesis sees no relevance at all in the final condition of the tomb, totally ignoring the bizarre circumstances of Smenkhkare's peculiar interment. It fails completely to address the following mysteries:

- Why was the mummy of a disgraced heretic left completely intact in its priceless coffin?

- Why, when he was the chief Atenist, had Akhenaten not also been left behind?

- Why were Kiya's coffin and Canopic jars modified for Akhenaten and then for Smenkhkare?

- Why had the face been removed from the coffin but not from the jar stoppers?

- Why had Akhenaten's name been removed from the burial equipment but not from the 'magic bricks'?

- Why had the valuable shrine been abandoned and the tomb hurriedly evacuated?

- Why was the male body mummified in the attitude of a woman?

We have already found answers to some of these mysteries by logical consideration of the known historical evidence. Indeed, the paradoxical nature of many aspects of the Tomb 55 enigma is beginning to make sense for the very first time. Why, therefore, has no one figured any of this out before? The answer is simple: Egyptologists don't like speculation – they need hard facts. Generally, this is a sound perspective – there is no point jumping to conclusions before sufficient archaeological evidence has come to light. However, the problem sometimes arising from such a restrained approach is to overlook the evidence which is already at hand. This would very much seem to have been the case with Tomb 55. It is very possible, therefore, that the orthodox theory of Tomb 55 is wrong about it having been used as a storage facility. Although the theory is probably correct about the tomb having been requisitioned – it was an unfinished tomb, the walls bare and the recess which contained the Canopic jars jagged and incomplete – it may have been used *exclusively* for the burial of Smenkhkare, who had died suddenly after recently returning to Thebes.

We know from the seals from treasure boxes and other broken artefacts found there, that Tomb 55 must once have contained many splendid burial goods, and because of Tutankhamun's name on the seals we know that they were removed during his reign. As the orthodox theory suggests, it seems likely that the spoils were divided among Ay, Tutankhamun and possibly other leading officials and used to supplement their own funerary trappings. Did they, however, include items from a number of royal persons or only one – Smenkhkare? As Ay's tomb, like most others of the period, was found to have been emptied in antiquity (see Chapter Six), we only have Tutankhamun's tomb from which to judge. If Akhenaten's, Tiye's and Smenkhkare's effects had all been stored in Tomb 55, as the orthodox theory propounds, we should expect to find an approximately equal cross-section of them represented in Tutankhamun's tomb.

Although some items belonging to Akhenaten were found in Tutankhamun's tomb, they were only minor artefacts such as bracelets, boxes and a fan, which were not specifically burial effects and could have been heirlooms obtained from anywhere. In fact, some items in Tutankhamun's tomb had belonged to

Tuthmosis III, such as a scarab and a number of calcite vessels, and he, having died over a century earlier, had certainly never been stored in Tomb 55. (Tuthmosis III's tomb was discovered in the Valley of the Kings by the French Egyptologist Victor Loret in 1898.) Although the objects belonging to Smenkhkare found in Tutankhamun's tomb also included similar trinkets, they also included much more important artefacts that could only have come from his tomb, as they were essential elements used in his burial. What, therefore, do we know of these?

Several finds made during the early years of the twentieth century led Howard Carter to believe that the tomb of Tutankhamun was still to be found in the Valley of the Kings. After many years of frustrating work, his venture at last succeeded on 4 November 1922, when a flight of stone steps was uncovered leading downwards to a blocked entrance, its seal intact. Beyond this there was a descending passageway, some 2 metres high, leading downwards for around 9 metres to a second doorway bearing the seal of Tutankhamun. On the evening of 28 November, his hand trembling, Carter made a small breach in the upper left-hand corner of the brickwork that blocked the entrance. In his three-volume book, *The Tomb of Tutankhamun*, he describes what he was the first to see in over three thousand years:

> I inserted the candle and peered in, Lord Carnarvon, Lady Evelyn and Callender standing anxiously behind me to hear the verdict. At first I could see nothing, the hot air escaping from the chamber causing the candle flame to flicker, but presently, as my eyes grew accustomed to the light, details of the room within emerged slowly from the mist, strange animals, statues and gold – everywhere the glint of gold.

When his patron Lord Carnavon asked him if he could see anything through the hole in the wall, all he could gasp was, 'Yes, wonderful things'. An apt description: there were literally hundreds of priceless historical treasures. Carter had made the archaeological discovery of the century.

Beyond the entrance to the tomb, and at right angles, was a large chamber, dubbed the Antechamber, and off it, to the back left, was a smaller room – the Annex. To the right was another blocked doorway guarded by two larger-than-life statues of the king, beyond which lay the burial chamber itself. The burial chamber was the only decorated room in the tomb. Its four walls were painted with scenes of Tutankhamun's funeral and his journey to the afterlife. Those on the east wall depicted the king's mummy being drawn on a sledge to the tomb; on the north wall Ay, dressed in a priest's panther skin, officiated at the last rites; the west wall represented the king's journey to the next world; and the south wall showed him being welcomed into the afterlife by the deities Hathor, Isis and Anubis. Within this chamber, filling it almost entirely, was a series of four shrines, one inside the other, the outermost measuring 5.08 metres long by 3.28 wide and 2.75 metres in height. Inside was a quartzite sarcophagus containing the nest of three coffins. The outer coffin, constructed of wood overlaid with gold, was made in the image of the dead king – a male in his late teens wearing *Rishi* (feathered-style) apparel. The inner coffin was made of solid gold, and the image of the king, although also decorated in *Rishi* style, was of a younger and thinner person – a boy of around ten. Carter concluded, as have subsequent scholars, that the inner coffin was made in the likeness of Tutankhamun while he was still a child, shortly after becoming king, and the outer coffin was made near to, or upon, his death.

The mummy itself was decorated in an astonishingly lavish way: gold bands and straps around the bandages, 170 separate pieces of exquisite jewellery adorning the body and, most incredible of all, a solid gold funerary mask weighing over ten kilograms placed over the face. Carter described it in its full glory:

> The beaten golden mask, a beautiful and unique specimen of ancient portraiture ... Upon its forehead, wrought in massive gold, were the royal insignia – the Nekhebet vulture and Buto serpent – emblems of the two kingdoms over which he had reigned. To the chin was attached the conventional Osiride beard, wrought in gold and lapis-lazuli-coloured glass; around the throat was a triple neck-lace of yellow and red gold and blue faience disk-shaped beads.

Despite its aesthetic appeal and its extraordinary value, it was not the death mask which preoccupied Carter's enquiring mind, but the middle coffin. Although the image it bore was that of a king – it wore the pharaonic appendages – it was clearly not Tutankhamun. The facial features were very different from those on the other two coffins or the death mask: the cheekbones were more pronounced, the jaw was firmer and broader, the lips were less full, and the nose was not so long. The style of headdress further revealed that this could not be Tutankhamun. The outer coffin showed Tutankhamun around the time of his death, which examination of the mummy has shown to have been around seventeen. Here he is shown in a *Khat* (bag-shaped) headdress, fashionable in the later years of his reign, whereas the middle coffin figure, like that figure on the inner coffin and the death mask, is shown in a *Nemes* (towel-like) headdress, fashionable in the early years of Tutankhamun's reign. This means that for the middle coffin figure to have been Tutankhamun it would have needed to represent a young boy, yet the face it depicted is someone of around twenty. It was clear, right from the beginning, that this piece of equipment had been appropriated from someone else.

The identity of this mysterious individual was to be revealed in the next room. Beyond the painted burial chamber, through an open doorway guarded by a large recumbent wooden figure of the jackal-god Anubis, lay the Treasury. Here stood the great wooden Canopic shrine enclosing the calcite Canopic chest, inside which were jars containing the four golden coffinettes to accommodate the king's removed organs. These coffinettes were identical miniatures of the middle coffin and clearly belonged to the same set. On the coffinettes the interior gold linings had had the owner's cartouches altered from those of the original owner. Still possible to read, it bore the title Ankhkheperure – the throne name of Smenkhkare. (Tutankhamun's throne name, found elsewhere in the tomb, was Nebkheperure.)

Today, there can be little doubt that Smenkhkare was indeed the person represented on the middle coffin in Tutankhamun's tomb, as the analysis of the Tomb 55 mummy has shown him to have been around twenty when he died. The middle coffin shows a king of this age, depicted in the style associated with the time Tutankhamun came to the throne. He must therefore have been Tutankhamun's predecessor, Smenkhkare.

Although the middle coffin is of less material value than the burial mask, not being made of solid gold, it is *its* image that the world has come to recognize as Tutankhamun. We find it reproduced in photographs to promote all manner of Egypt-related material: posters to publicize books, brochures to advertise Egyptian holidays, and literature to support Egyptian exhibitions. The reason is that the image on the middle coffin is a far more lifelike and flattering likeness than the other coffins, and shows more of the king's body than the death mask. Carter himself describes it as 'a masterpiece of superior construction'. It is altogether a more marketable face – far more handsome and regal than the chubby youth depicted on the outer coffin, or the innocent child depicted on the inner coffin and the death mask. However, it is *not* Tutankhamun – but his predecessor Smenkhkare.

The reason why this is almost unknown outside academic circles is that for four decades the world lost interest in Tutankhamun. After the initial excitement surrounding the tomb's opening, the subsequent years of the great depression, global conflict and the birth of the atomic age smothered the appeal of Egypt's ancient past. Aside from his book, written for the casual reader, Carter never published a serious study on the treasures. Most of his notes, catalogue cards and drawings, although preserved in the Griffith Institute at Oxford University, were unpublished; and so was his journal of the excavation, which was left to gather dust in the Egyptian Museum of Antiquities, along with most of the treasures. Until the *Treasures of Tutankhamun* exhibition travelled the world in the 1960s and 70s, even these lay in disorder in filthy glass cases, identified only with tattered labels, brown with age and virtually unreadable. Until the exhibition, not even a simple guide book existed for the collection.

When the exhibition visited countries all over the world, local promoters chose what they considered to be the most stunning image to publicize the event, which was often the face on the middle coffin. As there was nothing available in print, they had no way of knowing that the person they portrayed as Tutankhamun was in fact his predecessor Smenkhkare. The exhibition was a phenomenal success and Tutankhamun again became the focus of world attention. However, the erroneous image stuck in the public mind. Although much serious work has now been done on the treasures, and Egyptologists are aware that the image on the middle coffin is not that of Tutankhamun, it never seems to have occurred to anyone to draw attention to the fact.

As Carter continued to investigate Tutankhamun's tomb, more and more intimate and essential burial effects were found to have been appropriated from Smenkhkare. Some of the gold straps around the mummy had been inscribed with sacred burial texts from the Egyptian *Book of the Dead*, wherein Smenkhkare's names had been inserted in the appropriate place for the deceased, and many of the 170 pieces of jewellery that intimately adorned the mummy were also found to have belonged to Smenkhkare.

We return now to the question of Tomb 55. All these appropriated funerary effects belonging to Smenkhkare would have been essential for his burial, and so must certainly have come from his tomb. We know for sure that Smenkhkare had been in Tomb 55 – after all, he was still there when the tomb was opened. Surely, therefore, if Akhenaten's effects had been stored there too and similarly appropriated, as the orthodox theory dictates, we should expect to find similar essential burial effects belonging to him in Tutankhamun's tomb. We do not, however – we only find smaller items which could have come from anywhere.

The only essential burial effect belonging to anyone other than Smenkhkare known to have been in Tomb 55 was the shrine of Queen Tiye, part of which was destined for Tutankhamun's tomb (see Chapter One). However, this may not mean that she was ever interred in Tomb 55. On the contrary, there is evidence to suggest that the shrine had previously been appropriated by Smenkhkare and had formed part of *his* equipment. This is found in alterations made to inscriptions on the shrine panels. As discussed, the original inscription included the name of Tiye's husband Amonhotep III, still employing the *Amun* element which was proscribed by the time of Smenkhkare's coregency. At some point, however, the *Amun* element had been scratched off the panels. As Tiye had apparently died and was buried somewhere at Amarna before the *Amun* element was proscribed, it must have been after her interment that this was done. As the Ay/Tutankhamun regime had reinstated Amun-Re by the time the tombs were officially evacuated, it must, though, have been before that time. Tiye's tomb, therefore, must have been opened at some point between the two dates – a period which coincides with Smenkhkare's reign, when he may have appropriated the shrine for himself. The fact that Akhenaten's name had additionally been excised from the panels also supports this conjecture (see Chapter One). The shrine must have been tampered with after Tiye's burial – as she died when Akhenaten was still alive – but before the Ay/Tutankhamun regime removed her from Amarna: because, as we have seen, they had absolutely no reason to excise Akhenaten's name. (His name being removed from the coffin and gold bands was not intended as a desecration, but so as to adapt them for Smenkhkare.)

With an alternative explanation for Queen Tiye's shrine being in Tomb 55, and no evidence that anything essential to Akhenaten's burial was ever there, apart from the 'magic bricks', which had evidently been imported for the bizarre interment of Smenkhkare, there is no reason to believe that anyone other than Smenkhkare was ever interred in Tomb 55.

We therefore come to the last act in the drama of Tomb 55:

its final condition. When Smenkhkare dies, having recently returned to Thebes, there is no tomb prepared for him, so his followers requisition Tomb 55. Shortly afterwards the Ay/ Tutankhamum regime ordered the tomb reopened and cleared, dividing the spoils between them. All decorations were removed and the walls re-plastered. While this was happening, Akhenaten's sacrilegious interment must have been discovered.

Interestingly, there is a final desecration in the Amarna royal tomb that must have occurred at this time, namely the excising of Meritaten's image. Halfway down the entrance passageway there is a series of six additional chambers that may have been intended for other members of the royal family. In one of these rooms, a limestone relief was found showing Akhenaten and Nefertiti making floral offerings at an altar. Immediately behind her mother, Princess Meritaten is in attendance shaking a sistrum. This relief, which is now on display at the Cairo Museum, was overlooked by the anti-Atenist desecrators, as the names and faces of Akhenaten and Nefertiti, together with the image of the Aten, remain intact. Meritaten's image, however, has been damaged, having had the face cut out. As her body and the accompanying text, immediately above her head, are completely intact, this is clearly selective destruction directed exclusively at her.

Finally, Akhenaten is removed from Kiya's burial effects and they are adapted for the reinterment of Smenkhkare in Tomb 55. Tomb 55 is obviously still in the last phase of being emptied, as something occurs which causes the perpetrators to leave hastily before Tiye's shrine has been fully removed. The place is then sealed with its strange double wall, and remains unopened for over three thousand years.

The key players and series of events of this ancient drama are now beginning to fit into place. However, the greatest secret of all remains elusive. What was the nature of the evil that the perpetrators of this strange and unique burial so feared? There are still one or two peculiar anomalies concerning the adaptation of the burial effects yet to be explained, which may give us some idea of how they regarded this menace.

We have seen that in ancient Egyptian belief, if someone's name was wiped from memory, so also was their influence on this world from the afterlife. Yet despite the ritual interment to contain Akhenaten's influence, Kiya's burial effects had deliberately been adapted to include his titles, and his name had been left intact on the 'magic bricks'. This implies that Meritaten and Smenkhkare had not actually considered Akhenaten personally responsible for whatever imagined evil necessitated the strange desecration of his body. Exactly the same reasoning seems to have prevailed for the Ay/Tutankhamun regime when they reinterred Smenkhkare. In Tutankhamun's tomb, Smenkhkare's name had only been removed from the equipment where it was necessary to reinsert Tutankhamun's name, and not from the smaller heirlooms (see Chapter Four). Moreover, Smenkhkare's likeness even remained on the coffin and coffinettes that intimately surrounded Tutankhamun's mummified body and organs. These would hardly have been used, unaltered, if Smenkhkare himself was considered malevolent. It is quite clear from the actions of both perpetrators that neither considered the kings themselves to have been the malevolence, rather something that had inhabited their bodies. This sits with the evidence examined earlier, namely the need for a transsexual burial, indicating a belief that the kings had been possessed by some evil god or demon.

However, although when adapting the burial effects for Smenkhkare the Ay/Tutankhamun regime had removed Akhenaten's names, they had not reinserted those of Smenkhkare.

Although both perpetrators seem to have had the same motive, there would appear to have been a slight change of procedure. The precise thinking we can only guess at, as no text describing the strange ritual has so far been found. We can only assume that the first perpetrators – Smenkhkare and Meritaten – considered that the imprisoning ritual required leaving the body named, whereas the second perpetrators – the Ay/Tutankhamun regime – had decided, as the procedure had apparently so far been ineffective, that they should not include the inscribed name of the body which the spirit was thought to have possessed. (This also explains why there was no reason for them to remove Akhenaten's name from the 'magic bricks' – it was no longer his remains in which the malevolent influence now resided.)

Although we now have some idea of what took place to result in the strange condition of Tomb 55 as it was discovered in 1907, we still have no idea why such a unique and bizarre form of burial was thought necessary. From the transsexual nature of both burials, we can presume that whatever malevolence Meritaten had imagined to have influenced Akhenaten, the new regime also imagined it to have influenced Smenkhkare. But what was it? We have seen how the Aten was considered a transsexual deity, but it cannot have been this. Ay and Tutankhamun certainly did not consider the Aten itself to be evil, as its image was not even removed from Tutankhamun's throne. Neither did Meritaten, who actually embraced the Aten with greater zeal. So what was it they had both taken unprecedented steps to contain – something so terrible it needed to be imprisoned for eternity? Meritaten may have considered that it was responsible for her father's condition or his change of attitude, and Ay may have considered it responsible for Smenkhkare's desecration of the Temple of Karnak, yet surely, for such an unusual procedure, there must have been more involved than we have so far encountered. Apathy on Akhenaten's part, or even strange behaviour following a mental breakdown, cannot be the full story. Surely many in-bred pharaohs had acted strangely, although it never warranted such action before. Suppression of the Amun cult by Smenkhkare, equally, cannot have been the full story. After all, he did take the first steps to re-establish the old gods. Whatever it was, it must have been seen as a considerable threat to the future well-being of all Egypt.

In order to gain a better perspective on the era, we must more closely examine the figure who seems to be at the very centre of the mystery – Tutankhamun himself. Judging by the seal on the door, we can see that it was in his name that the desecration of Tomb 55 was carried out. What exactly was the relationship between Tutankhamun, Akhenaten and Smenkhkare?

SUMMARY

- We know from the seals from treasure boxes and other broken artefacts found there, that Tomb 55 must once have contained many splendid burial goods, and because of Tutankhamun's name on the seals we know that they were removed during his reign. Many of these items, it seems, had later been used for Tutankhamun's own burial.
- Egyptian mummies of the period were interred in a nest of three coffins, like a set of Russian dolls, one inside the other. In Tutankhamun's tomb, one of these, the middle coffin, had been made for, and still bore the image of, Smenkhkare.
- We find it reproduced in photographs to promote all manner of Egypt-related material: posters to publicize books,

brochures to advertise Egyptian holidays, and literature to support Egyptian exhibitions. However, it is *not* Tutankhamun – but his predecessor Smenkhkare.

- In Tutankhamun's tomb, Smenkhkare's likeness remained on the coffin. This would hardly have been used, unaltered, if Smenkhkare himself was considered malevolent. It is quite clear from the actions of the perpetrators that Smenkhkare had not been considered the malevolence, rather something that was believed to have inhabited his body.

CHAPTER SIX

The Mystery of Tutankhamun

When Tutankhamun came to the throne after the brief reign of Smenkhkare he was merely a child. Forensic analysis of his mummy has shown him to have been around seventeen when he died, and the highest recorded date of his reign, found on wine jar dockets in his tomb, is the year 9. This means that he was only about eight on his accession. The true reins of power must therefore have fallen to the chief minister Ay. To legitimate his rule, Tutankhamun was married to Akhenaten's eldest surviving daughter Ankhesenpaaten, who was considerably older, around seventeen or eighteen by this time. To what degree Ankhesenpaaten was actively involved in state affairs is difficult to say. Was she, like her elder sister, an active element in her husband's reign, or was she simply a pawn of Ay? As we have no real evidence of her activities during Tutankhamun's reign, as we do with Meritaten during the Smenkhkare period, we can only assume that she was a passive player in the events that followed.

The first important decree made during Tutankhamun's reign was a proclamation known from the so-called Restoration Stela from Karnak. This purports to describe the situation facing the king at his accession, with the temples throughout the country ruined and desecrated. The new king promises to

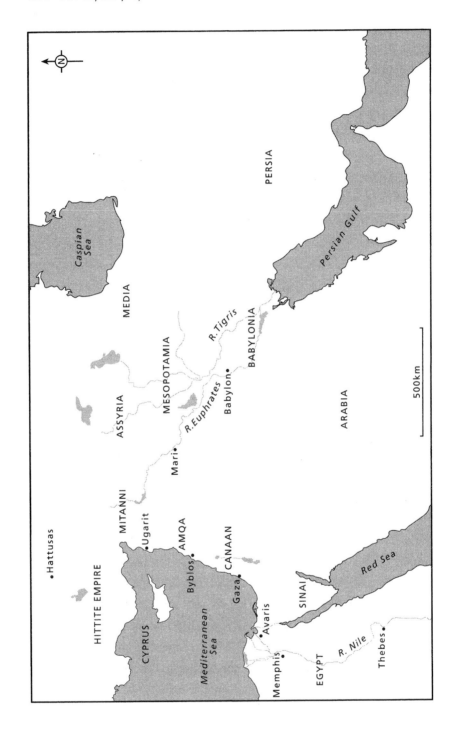

reopen and rebuild temples to Amun-Re, repair shrines and erect new statues. This he certainly seems to have done, as one of the epithets applied to him on a seal from his tomb describes Tutankhamun as: 'He who spent his life in making images of the gods'.

However, this proclamation was not made until the year 2 of Tutankhamun's reign. Before this time his government appears to have continued to adhere to Akhenaten's new religion. This conjecture is suggested by two pieces of evidence: a change in the king's and queen's names and the throne found in Tutankhamun's tomb. We know from the Restoration Stela that by the year 2 Tutankhamun had dropped the *Aten* element from his original name. His birth name had been Tutankh*aten*, meaning 'Living image of the Aten', but after the second year his name appears as the now familiar Tutankh*amun*, 'Living image of Amun'. His queen also changed the *Aten* element in her name and became Ankhesen*amun* (pronounced Ank-es-en-amun). These original names provide us with an important indication that the first two years had seen a continuation of Atenism as the chief religion. The gold-covered back panel of Tutankhamun's throne shows the king and queen beneath the Aten disc, with their names still in the original form. In the early part of the reign, therefore, the Aten must still have been the principal god. There is much debate about whether or not the new government continued to rule from Amarna. However, as Smenkhkare had himself already returned to Thebes (as evidenced by the inscription in the tomb of Pairi concerning the king's funerary temple), it would seem that at least part of the machinery of government had already been relocated there. Although Tutankhamun does seem to have remained in Amarna for a short while, as one of the Amarna letters addresses him as king, there is considerable evidence, we shall examine later, which indicates that the evacuation of Amarna was begun fairly soon after his accession.

Whatever the original intentions, events soon impelled the new administration to reinstate Amun-Re as the principle deity, albeit seemingly as a token gesture to appease opposition. There was no re-establishment of the once mighty Amun priesthood and Atenism was not only tolerated but, considering the number of items in his tomb that still bore the image of the new god, the king himself continued privately to venerate it. Even the skull cap worn by Tutankhamun as he was embalmed bore a cartouche of the Aten. Ay also seems to have continued his allegiance to the Aten, judging by the savage destruction of his monuments by the anti-Atenists a few years later.

In fact, it seems that much of the court continued to venerate the Aten. Even the person with the great responsibility for erecting the Canopic shrine in Tutankhamun's tomb seems unfamiliar with the old gods. The internal organs – the viscera – were separately preserved in four receptacles representing the four genii – or spirits – with which they were associated: the *Imsety* for the liver, the *Hepy* for the lungs, the *Duamutef* for the stomach and the *Qebehsnewef* for the intestines. Each of them was in turn under the special protection of one of the funerary goddesses: Isis guarded the liver, Nephthys guarded the lungs, Neith guarded the stomach and Selkit guarded the intestines. These four goddesses were represented by a figurine on the Canopic shrine, each of which had a specific position, prescribed for centuries in ancient texts. As Howard Carter observed, the workman responsible for assembling the shrine seems to have been completely unaware of this:

> They must have known better than we do now, that the
> goddess Nephthys should be on the south side of the chest,

and that her charge was the genius Hepy. And that Selkit should be on the east side, and her charge was the genius Qebehsnewef. Yet in erecting this Canopic equipment, even though it bears distinct marks as well as distinguishing inscriptions upon each side, they placed Selkit south in the place of Nephthys, and Nephthys east where Selkit should have been.

Not only was the workman unfamiliar with the old religious customs, but presumably so was everyone else who had been in the tomb. Surely they could not have failed to notice one of the most important effects in the entire burial procedure. We know from the reconstructed sarcophagus of Akhenaten in the royal tomb at Amarna that these goddesses had been proscribed in Amarna to be replaced by the images of Nefertiti. The priests and courtiers who had been appointed during the seventeen years of Akhenaten's reign, and a further nine of Tutankhamun's, were presumably not old enough to remember the old ways and, judging by this unnoticed error, they had not been re-versed in them. This strongly suggests that although there was an attempt to reconcile the country by reinstating the old gods, monotheistic Atenism was still being widely practised.

Tutankhamun and his chief minister certainly seem to have been unpopular in Thebes, so much so that they moved their seat from this heartland of the Amun cult to the ancient capital at Memphis in Lower Egypt. The Restoration Stela tells us that Tutankhamun was residing at Memphis by the year 2, probably in the great palace complex founded by Tuthmosis I, and from other sources we learn that Thebes was left in the hands of the chief physician Pentu, who had been appointed – perhaps reluctantly – as southern vizier.

Other important figures in the administration were Akhenaten's old treasurer and master of works, Maya, who seems to have acted as Ay's right-hand man in civil matters, and two important army officers: General Minnakht, who probably commanded the armies of southern Egypt, and General Horemheb, who was evidently in charge of the northern armies. The army was no longer the mighty imperial war machine it had been a couple of decades earlier, having been reduced to the role of a domestic police force. However, all this was to change as Tutankhamun's reign wore on. Horemheb rose to become the king's deputy, and at the end of Ay's reign he was strong enough to seize power for himself and establish what has all the signs of a military junta.

One of the greatest mysteries surrounding Tutankhamun is his origins: he seems to appear from nowhere. When Tutankhamun's tomb was found virtually intact, it was hoped that there would be preserved inside some important literature to throw new light on this enigmatic period and reveal who Tutankhamun really was. Unfortunately no historical documentation was found. As he had reached the age of eight when he came to power, we should expect, like the young princesses, to see something of this second-in-line to the throne in the last two or three years of Akhenaten's reign, yet he appears nowhere. There is not one statue or relief known to have been made of him before his accession, and only one early reference to him survives. So who exactly was he?

We know, as Akhenaten is only ever shown with daughters, that Tutankhamun was not the late king's legitimate son from Nefertiti, though a popular theory would have him as Akhenaten's son by his secondary wife Kiya. This would seem unlikely, however. Although Kiya certainly had a child, the Hermopolis Talatat identify her as a daughter, and in the Amarna reliefs Kiya is only ever shown being followed by a girl. Interestingly, *no one* in the immediate royal family is known to have given birth to a boy during the Amarna period.

Tutankhamun's marriage to Ankhesenpaaten certainly legitimated his claim to the throne, as she appears to have been Akhenaten's only surviving daughter. Along with Tiye, Meketaten, Nefertiti, Kiya and Meritaten, all three younger princesses disappear from the scene by Tutankhamun's reign. Both Meritaten and Ankhesenpaaten seem to have had daughters of their own before this time, as two children are recorded in the late Amarna years with the names Ankesenpaaten-te-sherit, and Meritaten-te-sherit – Ankhesenpaaten and Meritaten junior. Who the fathers were is unknown, but the general consensus is that the former was Smenkhkare's daughter and the latter had been the issue of an incestuous coupling with Akhenaten, perhaps still desperate for a son after his chief wife's death. However, they too disappear before Tutankhamun is made king.

Unlike Smenkhkare, we do have one reference predating Tutankhamun's reign which seemingly reveals his father's identity – or at least his occupation. Although he is not pictured, he is referred to in an inscription on one of the Hermopolis Talatat, made around the year 14 of Akhenaten's reign: 'The king's son of his loins, Tutankhaten' (Tutankhamun's birth name). Although this reference to him as a king's son has led some scholars to speculate that Tutankhamun was an illegitimate son of Akhenaten, Tutankhamun himself tells us that he is the son of another king. In an inscription on one of the huge granite lions erected at the temple of Sulb in the Sudan, Tutankhamun refers to his father as Amonhotep III. This statue, which is now in the British Museum, has led to a bitter debate about Tutankhamun's parentage. If this it is a true statement, and not just metaphorical, then it would mean that Tutankhamun was Akhenaten's younger brother. Yet at first glance this seems impossible. If Tutankhamun was only seven or eight when Akhenaten died, then he would not have been born until around the year 9 or 10 of Akhenaten's reign, seemingly a decade after Amonhotep's death. The only way Tutankhamun could have been Amonhotep's son, therefore, is if Amonhotep had not died when Akhenaten had come to the throne, and there had been a co-regency – and an exceptionally long one – between Akhenaten and his father.

Although there are no official records concerning Amonhotep III after Akhenaten's accession, or any specific account of a co-regency with his son, there are a number of archaeological clues that do hint at such an arrangement having occurred well into the Amarna years.

The first piece of evidence uncovered to suggest the co-regency hypothesis was a damaged stela found at Amarna by Flinders Petrie's associate Francis Llewelyn Griffith in the 1890s, during excavations near the chief servitor Pinhasy's mansion. It showed a royal couple seated before an altar loaded with food and flowers, above which shone the Aten. The relief, however, differed from many similar scenes found at Amarna in that it did not depict Nefertiti and Akhenaten, but Queen Tiye and her husband Amonhotep III. As the name of the Aten was in its later form, introduced after the year 9 of Akhenaten's reign (see Chapter Four), it seems to show Amonhotep alive and well a decade after his son became king.

In the 1920s, another clue indicating that Amonhotep still survived as co-regent during the Amarna period was unearthed at the site by the British archaeologist John Pendlebury. This was in the form of fragments of a carved tray bearing the name of Amonhotep III. Various tomb reliefs at Amarna depicted temple precincts in which stood statues of Akhenaten carrying such a tray to make offering to the Aten. Pendlebury's colleague,

Herbert Fairman, reasoned that if the tray they had found had come from a similar statue, it could only mean that, to have been depicted making offerings to the Aten, Amonhotep must have been alive and living in Amarna. Once again the Aten was in its later form, dating the artefact to after the ninth year.

The Akhenaten/Amonhotep co-regency also appears to be supported in a relief found outside Amarna. Carved on a giant granite boulder below what is now the Cataract Hotel on the eastern bank of the Nile at Aswan, it shows the chief sculptor Bek making offerings before Akhenaten and another sculptor Men making offerings before Amonhotep III. Once more it would imply that both kings were alive at that time it was carved, around the year 9 of Akhenaten's reign.

These three pieces of evidence, though tantalizing, are not conclusive. The reliefs on Griffith's stela and the Aswan boulder may both be depicting Amonhotep as a statue and not a living man, whereas, without the actual statue to accompany it, nothing can be determined with certainty regarding Pendlebury's tray.

Egyptologists seem to be divided equally as to whether or not such finds evidence that Amonhotep was alive for so long. Two of the leading authorities on the Amarna period, for example, Donald Redford, Professor of Near Eastern Studies at the University of Toronto, and Cyril Aldred, one-time Curator of the Department of Egyptian Art at the Metropolitan Museum, New York, come down on opposite sides of the fence, Aldred in favour of a long co-regency, Redford against.

Those who dispute the long co-regency explain such depictions of Amonhotep dating from the Amarna period as being venerations of a dead predecessor, which, they argue, were not intended to represent a living person. Such a debate could easily be settled concerning the pre-Amarna period, as the term *maet kheru* – 'deceased' – usually accompanied depictions of someone who was no longer alive. Unfortunately, Akhenaten's new religion dropped this term, and everyone of importance was described by the term *ankh er neheh* – 'living for ever' – whether they were alive or dead.

There are two reliefs, however, which certainly do appear to be showing Amonhotep very much alive, well into the Amarna period. One, in the tomb of the steward Kheruef, shows Akhenaten paying homage to his father, and the other, in the tomb of the high steward Huya, shows Akhenaten and Amonhotep together with their respective queens. In the first scene Amonhotep's wrist is held affectionately by his wife, and in the second he is blessing his wife and daughter, Beketaten. In these scenes Amonhotep is certainly no statue, nor is he being venerated as a dead ancestor, as there is clearly an interaction between him and the other figures. Once again, as the Aten is in its later form, both must show scenes at Amarna after the year 9 of Akhenaten's reign.

Perhaps the firmest indication that Amonhotep was alive and living in Amarna for many years after Akhenaten's reign began are the Amarna Letters, as a number are addressed to him personally. With one or two exceptions, only the kings of Mitanni, Babylon and Assyria name the pharaoh with whom they are corresponding. Others simply use, 'My Lord', 'My God', 'Great King' and so forth. Of the nearly 350 letters, in less than a couple of dozen do we know to whom they were sent. However, ten of them were sent to Amonhotep, which appears to evidence that he was not only acting as co-regent but was actually present in the city to receive them. It seems most unlikely that these letters had been sent to Amonhotep before the Amarna period and had been brought from Thebes. The reason is that official records were kept on papyrus – which have sadly disintegrated with time – but the clay tablets on which the Amarna letters were written were sturdier items meant only for messengers to carry with less risk of damage. Once they were received they would have been copied onto papyrus for the record and then discarded. Indeed, they were ultimately considered of no value and left behind when the city was abandoned. Accordingly, they were not an official archive, of which there would have been papyrus copies, and so there was no reason for them to have been brought to Amarna when the move was made from Thebes. Accordingly, those addressed to Amonhotep must have been sent to him while he was in Amarna.

We can further gather from the letters that Amonhotep must have been in Amarna for much of Akhenaten's reign. We know, from correspondences sent by Kadashman-Enlil I of Babylonia, that some of the letters were received in the early Amarna period, as Kadashman-Enlil I was succeeded by Burna-buriash II by the later period. We also know that the letters were being received until the very end of Akhenaten's reign, as one of them is addressed to Tutankhamun. Consequently, they are a good cross-section, if not a complete dossier, of the dispatches received. As the letters identifying the pharaoh to whom they are written include ten addressing Akhenaten, exactly the same number as address Amonhotep, it would statistically suggest that the unaddressed letters could equally be divided between them, from which we can infer that Amonhotep was in the city for many years.

With the balance of evidence on the side of a long co-regency, the remaining question is how long did Amonhotep live? Evidence for this was actually found at Amarna as early as the 1920s, when Pendlebury uncovered two fragments of pottery wine jars with dockets dated as the years 28 and 30. The dockets, he reasoned, must have been written in the reign of Amonhotep III who is the only king of the period to have enjoyed such a long rule. He concluded that, as wine is presumed not to keep much longer than around four years in permeable pottery in such a hot climate, the earliest that the year 28 could have been was the year 2 of Akhenaten's reign, four years before Amarna began to be occupied by the official classes. As the highest known dating of Amonhotep's reign, found on inscribed clay dockets from Amonhotep's Malakata palace at Thebes, is the year 38, it is generally accepted that he died in this his thirty-eighth year as king. If Pendlebury is right, and the year 28 of Amonhotep's reign corresponds within the year 2 of Akhenaten's reign, then the year 38 – the year Amonhotep died – is the year 12 of Akhenaten's reign.

Cyril Aldred sees evidence of Amonhotep's death around the year 12 of Akhenaten's reign in scenes in the tombs of Huya and the harem overseer Meryre. In both these tombs there are scenes which appear nowhere else during the reign, and so evidently depict a one-off event. Dated as the year 12, they show a large concourse of representatives from vassal states and the great powers in Asia and Africa coming to Amarna bearing gifts for the pharaoh and receiving his blessing. The uniqueness of the episode suggests more than a simple jubilee, rather, Aldred suggests, a ceremonial event to mark Akhenaten's sole accession to the throne after the recent death of his father.

As Amonhotep would seem to have been alive when Tutankhamun was born, around the year 9 or 10 of Akhenaten's reign, Amonhotep could well have been his father as the young king claimed. Amonhotep certainly seems to have been young enough. When he came to power Akhenaten must have been of adult age, as he was almost immediately capable of establishing his new religion. Going by a number of colossal statues of him excavated from the site of the Aten temple at East Karnak between 1926 and 1932 (now in the Cairo Museum), which were made in the earliest years of his reign, he seems to have been about twenty at the time. If Amonhotep sired Akhenaten when he was in his teens (as is generally thought), then he would have been somewhere between thirty-five and forty when Akhenaten came to the throne, and so between forty-five and fifty in the year 12 when he may have died. Accordingly, he was still capable of fathering Tutankhamun a couple of years earlier.

If Tutankhamun was Amonhotep's son – and there now seems little reason to doubt it – the next question concerns his mother. We have already seen how forensic analysis has revealed that Tutankhamun was almost certainly Smenkhkare's brother. If Tutankhamun was Amonhotep's son, it would follow that Smenkhkare was too, or he would presumably not have been made pharaoh ahead of Tutankhamun. It is possible, therefore, that Tutankhamun was a younger son of Nefertiti's sister Mutnodjme, the suggested mother of Smenkhkare. Amonhotep had a large, and ever increasing number of women in his harem, including two of his own daughters – Isis and Sitamun – and a number of foreign princesses, one of whom could have been Mutnodjme. As we have seen, she certainly had at least one child, and the identity of the father is unknown. However, the most likely candidate for Tutankhamun's mother is Amonhotep's chief wife, Queen Tiye.

Like his predecessor Akhenaten, Tutankhamun seems to have been an emotional young man with strong affections for his family. His tomb is filled with keepsakes and heirlooms to 'remind' him of his relations, including such items as shawls, fans, trinket boxes, sequins and scarabs. There are a number belonging to Akhenaten and Amonhotep III, and on the female side, to Meritaten, Nefernefruaten and Meketaten. Items belonging to Nefertiti, Kiya and Mutnodjme, however, are almost completely absent, except where they have been re-inscribed with someone else's name, such as Meritaten. This would seem very strange if one of them was his mother. In fact, the most personal of all the heirlooms belonged to Queen Tiye: a miniature coffin-shaped box, inscribed with her name and containing a plaited lock of her auburn hair. As Meritaten, Meketaten and Nefernefruaten were all seemingly too young to have been his mother, and from the contents of the tomb alone, this only leaves Tiye as a possible contender. We know she lived until after his birth; but was she too old for Tutankhamun to have been her son?

The mummy thought to be Queen Tiye was found in the tomb of Amonhotep II in 1898, as part of the cache stored there for safety around 1000 BC (see Chapter One). When Elliot Smith (the professor of anatomy who examined the Tomb 55 mummy) was called in to examine the remains he dubbed her 'the elder woman', to distinguish her from a younger woman found in the same tomb. She appeared to be middle aged, although she had long, lustrous brown hair with no traces of grey. She was tentatively identified as Queen Tiye because of cranial similarities with the mummy of Tiye's mother Tuya, after her tomb was discovered in 1905 by the English Egyptologist James Quibell. The identification was apparently verified in the 1980s by a team of specialists from the Universities of Alexandria and Michigan employing modern scientific techniques. An electron probe was used to compare a clipping of the mummy's hair with a sample of Tiye's hair from Tutankhamun's tomb, the results indicating that the mummy was indeed Queen Tiye. Such probes are said to provide an exact analysis of the chemical constituents in hair which are as unique as fingerprints. However, the accuracy of these findings has more recently been questioned, and at present the case remains open. The Alexandria-Michigan team assign an age of around thirty-five to the mummy, which would seem to have been too young for a woman who had a son – Akhenaten – who was around thirty-four when she died. The identity of the 'elder woman' aside, however, Tiye may have been as young as forty-eight when she died, which would mean that she could have conceived Tutankhamun five or six years earlier.

What, therefore, was Tutankhamun's precise relationship to Smenkhkare? Who was Smenkhkare's mother? Was it Mutnodjme, as we have theorized? Of one thing we can be fairly sure: it was not Queen Tiye. As we have seen, the royal children do not seem to accompany their parents at official functions until the age of around five. As Tiye appears to have been dead by the year 14 of Akhenaten's reign, we should not expect to see Tutankhamun pictured with her as he would only just have reached that age. However, the same cannot be said of Smenkhkare. Unlike Mutnodjme, who is not pictured officially attending important celebrations, Tiye does appear in the tomb reliefs at important events which take place between the years 9 and 12. For example, we see her at the induction to her personal *Maru* temple (shown in Huya's tomb) and in the great festival of the year 12 (shown in the tombs of Huya and Meryre). Here she is shown accompanied by her daughter Beketaten, so if she had a son of Smenkhkare's age – around fifteen – he would surely also have been in attendance. For this reason we must find another mother for Smenkhkare. As Kiya is also only shown with a daughter, but Mutnodjme appears to be accompanied by sons – and at the right time for one of them to have been Smenkhkare (see Chapter Four) – Mutnodjme is still by far the best bet.

Until there is positive evidence one way or the other, therefore, the most likely identity of Tutankhamun is that he was Smenkhkare's half-brother, both being sons of Amonhotep III, and that his mother was Queen Tiye, making him the full brother of Akhenaten.

Tutankhamun's death in the ninth year of his reign is yet another of the mysteries surrounding the young king. Forensic analysis of the mummy has shown there to have been a small sliver of bone within the upper cranial cavity, suggesting that he died as a result of a blow to the head, but whether this was due to a fall, perhaps from a chariot, or evidence of assassination, is difficult to say. There is certainly evidence that the clouds were gathering for the followers of the Aten religion.

Tutankhamun died without an heir, leaving the country in a precarious situation. How his queen tried to remedy the predicament is unprecedented in the history of Egypt. What happened is known not from Egyptian sources but from Hittite records excavated from their capital city at Hattusas – modern Boghazkoy – in Turkey. Here we are told of a remarkable incident. Evidently, once Tutankhamun was dead, a queen, presumably Ankhesenpaaten, wrote to the Hittite king, Suppiluliumas I, asking him to send one of his sons to Egypt so that she could marry him and make him the next pharaoh. This was an extraordinary request and aroused the suspicion of the Hittite king. He dispatched a chamberlain to the court at Memphis, and when he returned, satisfied that the request was genuine, the king sent his son Prince Zannanza to marry the queen. However, on their way the party were ambushed and the prince was murdered. In revenge, Suppiluliumas attacked the Egyptians in the Lebanon, and hostilities continued between the two empires for some years.

What prompted the queen to side with Egypt's long-standing enemy is a complete mystery, but clearly shows that she was more afraid of opposition within her own country than she was of foreign aggression. The Hittites were probably her only hope, for Egypt's old allies the Mittani had been invaded by the Hittites during Akhenaten's reign, while the Minoan empire had seemingly collapsed in circumstances we shall investigate later. Was Ankhesenpaaten acting alone, or was she acting under the guidance of Ay? Was he or someone else responsible for Zannanza's murder?

We know, from Tutankhamun's tomb, that by the time of the young king's burial Ay had appointed himself heir apparent. He is depicted wearing the blue crown of a king and, officiating at the funeral, had adopted the traditional role of the heir. We also know that Ay married Ankhesenpaaten to legitimate his rule, as evidenced by the bezel of a blue glass finger-ring, now in the Berlin Museum, which carried the cartouches of Ankhes-enpaaten and Ay side by side: the usual way of indicating wedlock. (His previous wife Tey was seemingly dead by this time.)

As we have a period of seventy days, the prescribed time for the funerary arrangements to have been completed, for Ay to have been appointed as the next pharaoh, then Ankhesenpaaten must have written to the Hittite king almost immediately. Perhaps by the time the prince was sent, Ay had seized the throne and ordered the assassination. However, this would seem unlikely. Firstly, Ay was an old man who had been loyal to Akhenaten's family for years. It seems unthinkable that he would have turned against Akhenaten's daughter. Secondly, he had been Tutankhamun's right-hand man, virtually running the county, and so would almost certainly have been aware of a visit from the Hittite delegation to investigate the queen's story. The fact that they returned happy that everything was in order would suggest that it was Ay himself who had sanctioned the arrangement. The decision to make himself king, therefore, would seemingly have been made after the Hittite prince had been murdered. If this was the true scenario then it shows that by this time, to have been desperate enough to try to forge an alliance with the Hittites, the Atenist faction was living in fear of a *coup d'état*. Ay only lived for a further four years and when he died the general Horemheb seized power. His authority having grown steadily for a decade, it is far more likely that it was on Horemheb's orders that the young prince was killed. Judging by his conduct when he became king, it was Horemheb that Ankhesenpaaten feared. The only other possibility to account for the Zannanza murder is that it was part of a clever scheme to occupy Horemheb and the army. Perhaps Ay set the whole thing up to provoke a war to keep Horemheb out of the way fighting the Hittites in the Asiatic provinces. This was certainly the outcome of the affair, which left Ay free to rule Egypt for another four years.

Apart from the return to Memphis and the re-establishment of the old religion, few events in Tutankhamun's reign have been found documented. The military situation is fairly clear from foreign sources, however. During the nine years of Tutankhamun's rule, the imperial army had been rejuvenated. It had apparently been restructured and enlarged and dispatched to restore control over the territories that Egypt still retained. A painting in the tomb of the viceroy Huy shows that raids were mounted in his province of Nubia, while Palestine and Syria probably suffered similar incursions from the northern army. Two scenes from a brightly painted gesso box from Tutankhamun's tomb shows the young king personally leading his troops, but this would seem unlikely for someone so young, and scenes from Horemheb's own tomb in Saqqara show *him* as commander-in-chief of the northern army.

By the time Ay died Horemheb had further established his

credentials for power with a series of victories over the Hittites, and, as the old king died without an heir, Horemheb was able to seize the throne for himself. To legitimate his claim he married Nefertiti's sister, Mutnodjme, and we hear no more of Ankhesenpaaten. The last of Akhenaten's daughters, it seems, was dead.

Horemheb's background is virtually unknown, except that he came from Heracleopolis, about half way between Heliopolis and Amarna, in Middle Egypt, and was obviously a career officer whose abilities were recognized early. Immediately on becoming pharaoh, he allied himself with the cult of Amun-Re, outlawed Atenism and re-established the Amun priesthood, appointing as priests loyal officers from his army. This was no nominal reversion to the old ways, as had been the policy of Ay, but a complete revival of the old gods. Whatever unique set of circumstances had brought about the rise of Atenism and led every element in the country to play along, if not actually embrace it, was now three decades in the past. Horemheb wanted to eradicate all evidence of Atenism and all those who had sanctioned it. Throughout the country, images of the Aten were defaced, Amarna was ransacked, and the temple of the Aten in Karnak was taken apart brick by brick. Although there is no textual reference to it, we can assume that the populace were subjected to a similar purge and thousands must have been persecuted and killed.

The Amarna kings became non-persons: the names of Akhenaten, Smenkhkare, Tutankhamun and Ay were struck off all monuments, save a few that were overlooked or out of the way. Horemheb even erased their names from the list of kings, beginning his own reign at the end of the reign of Amonhotep III. Consequently, none of them appeared in the king lists at Abydos and Karnak. Within a generation or two, the general population seem unaware that the Amarna kings ever existed: just half a century later, in the tomb of a certain Amenmosi at Thebes, for example, a number of New Kingdom pharaohs are depicted in their order of succession. Here, Horemheb is placed between Amonhotep III and his successor Ramesses I, as if the owner had never heard of Akhenaten, Smenkhkare, Tutankhamun and Ay.

The wrath vented against Ay's monuments knew no bounds. Statues in his mortuary temple at Medinet Habu, near Thebes, were defaced and his tomb in the Valley of the Kings was ransacked. Ay's tomb was found by Giovanni Belzoni (working for the British Museum) as early as 1816, but it was not until 1972 that a proper excavation took place. Not only was the sarcophagus found to have been smashed in antiquity, but Ay's figure was hacked out of wall paintings and his name excised from texts; there was even evidence that the mummy had been torn to sheds. This act of furious desecration was judged to have occurred during the reign of Horemheb and was almost certainly carried out on his orders. The same fate probably befell the mummies of Akhenaten, Ankhesenpaaten, Nefertiti, Meritaten and many more. The fascinating question, however, is how Tutankhamun's tomb managed to escape the carnage. It is, perhaps, understandable that Horemheb left Smenkhkare as he was, his remains desecrated and unnamed, but for Tutankhamun – a king whose statues he was toppling all over Egypt – to have been left alone surrounded by his fabulous treasures and kilogram upon kilogram of gold, is bewildering.

There can be little doubt that Horemheb knew exactly were Tutankhamun's tomb was situated. The reliefs in his burial chamber show that Tutankhamun's burial was attended by all the important dignitaries. The east wall shows a dozen of the top courtiers pulling the coffin on a sledge to the tomb, including two who can be identified by their distinctive shaven heads as the chief ministers, Pentu and Usermont. The inscription over the figures actually identify the others as 'high officials of the palace'. It is inconceivable that as king's deputy, Horemheb would not have been among them. Even if he wasn't it seems most unlikely that a man of his resources would not have been able to exert pressure to get someone in the court to reveal the tomb's whereabouts.

All this is irrelevant, however, as the location of Tutankhamun's tomb was a matter of public knowledge. Contrary to popular belief, the tomb was not completely intact when Carter found it. It had been robbed twice in antiquity, soon after it had been sealed. The first robbery was for small pieces of gold and precious jewellery, most of which the robbers got away with except for a few gold rings found still wrapped in a rag and stuffed into a box in the Annex. After the priests had resealed the tomb, it was broken into again, this time to steal the precious oils and unguents which had been stored in large alabaster jars. For such robberies to have occurred and repairs made, implies a guarded tomb of the old mastaba variety, rather than one with a concealed entrance. Moreover, if it had been buried deep underground, as it was when Carter found it, the robbers would have had to burrow down and consequently have made their way into the tomb by way of a small opening. Only this would need to have been resealed, and there would have been no point in re-exposing the entire stairwell. However, as the whole doorway had been resealed after the robbery, it means that when the theft was discovered the entrance must have been exposed.

Incredibly, Horemheb not only refrained from desecrating Tutankhamun's tomb, he seems to have protected it. It was evidently on his orders that it was resealed for the second time.

When it was finally closed, the seals used were those of the royal necropolis which bore no royal names. These were exactly the same seals that were used in the tomb of Tuthmosis IV when Horemheb ordered it to be restored after *its* violation by robbers. An inscription in the tomb of Tuthmosis IV reveals that the necropolis scribe Djehutymose had assisted in the restoration, and his name is also found scribbled on a jar-stand in Tutankhamun's tomb.

All of this implies that there was something very special about Tutankhamun's tomb. Why did Horemheb make sure it remained intact when he had no love for Tutankhamun? The first thing that springs to mind whenever most people hear the name Tutankhamun is the so-called curse that surrounded the opening of his tomb. Is this the answer? Was Horemheb afraid to disturb the tomb because he believed it was cursed?

The story of the curse of Tutankhamun's tomb began with the strange circumstances surrounding the death of Carter's patron Lord Carnarvon. On 28 February 1922, shortly after the tomb was opened, Carnarvon departed for Aswan for a few days' rest. About the same time he was bitten on the cheek by a mosquito. While shaving with his cut-throat razor, he inadvertently opened the bite which quickly became infected. A fever set in and, although he seemed to recover and two days later he was up and about and eager to revisit the tomb, he suffered a relapse and died. Soon after, the author Arthur Conan Doyle, who was fascinated by the supernatural, attributed Carnarvon's death to a curse left by Tutankhamun's priests to guard the tomb. The idea caught the imagination of the world's press. Reports included all manner of other preternatural events. Apparently, at the precise moment of Carnarvon's death the lights went out all over Cairo, while at the exact same time his dog back in England howled and dropped dead. It was also said that on the day the tomb was opened Carter's pet canary was swallowed by a cobra – the very creature depicted on pharaoh's brow. Evidently, the expedition had ignored the warning inscribed over the entrance to the tomb: 'Death shall come on swift wings to him that toucheth the tomb of the Pharaoh'. Other deaths were indeed to follow, and today they form an integral part of the curse legend.

No one who was associated with the tomb or the investigation of the mummy was apparently safe. One of the X-ray specialists invited to examine the mummy died of a stroke while on his way to Egypt. Carnarvon's younger brother, Aubrey Herbert, died suddenly the year after the tomb was opened, and Carter's right-hand men, Arthur Mace and Richard Bethell, both died under mysterious circumstances before the tomb was cleared. Others died, seemingly as a consequence of merely visiting the tomb. The American railroad magnate Jay Gould died of pneumonia as a result of a cold he caught there, and the French Egyptologist Georges Benedte died from a fall after being shown round the tomb. A more violent demise was in store for the Egyptian official Ali Kemel Fahmy Bey, whose wife decided to shoot him soon after he had viewed the discovery.

Was it fear of such a curse that evidently persuaded Horemheb to leave the tomb alone? It seems most unlikely, as the curse of Tutankhamun's tomb is a complete myth. Apart from the fact that many aspects of the story cannot be verified, such as the canary, the dog and lights going out, there never was any inscription over the door, or anywhere else in the tomb, which threatened death to those who disturbed the pharaoh. Where the story came from, God only knows! There were what the Egyptians believed to have been magic defences in place to keep the mummy safe. These Carter himself described:

Beside this traditional paraphernalia necessary to meet and vanquish the dark powers of the Nether World, there were magical figures placed in small recesses in the walls, facing north, south, east and west, covered with plaster, conforming with the ritual laid down in the *Book of the Dead* for the defence of the tomb and its owner. Associated with these magical figures are incantations to repel the enemy of Osiris [the deceased], in whatever form he may come. Magic, for once, seems to have prevailed. For of twenty-seven monarchs of the Imperial Age of Egypt buried in this valley, who have suffered every type of depravation, Tutankhamun alone has lain unscathed.

Perhaps such a statement had been misconstrued. As for the mysterious deaths: although true, they did take place before the clearance of the tomb, for the painstaking operation actually took seven years. Consequently, the deaths had not all occurred at once as the now-familiar story relates. Bethell, for instance, did not die until 1929. In fact, only Lord Carnarvon's death is in any way synchronic. Indeed, most of the chief culprits got away scot-free: Lord Carnarvon's daughter, Lady Evelyn, one of the first to enter the tomb, lived for another fifty-eight years; Douglas Derry, the doctor who actually performed the autopsy on the mummy, lived for another forty-seven years; even Howard Carter – the man responsible for the entire thing – did not die until 1939, at the age of sixty-four.

We can tell from the strange condition and signs of hurried evacuation of Smenkhkare's tomb that the perpetrators of the desecration seemed to have feared some unseen menace in Tomb 55, but there is no such evidence in the case of Tutankhamun's tomb. The protective amulets in his tomb were no different from any tomb of the period, and such things never stopped other pharaohs from plundering the tomb of a former rival. After all, they considered themselves gods and could do whatever they wanted. There must therefore have been something most unusual at stake to restrain Horemheb. The reason appears to be linked in some way with Tomb 55, as Horemheb went to peculiar lengths to protect both of them.

When Carter discovered Tutankhamun's tomb, its entrance was buried deep underground. Although the burial of many tombs occurred naturally over time, Tutankhamun's tomb had been deliberately buried a few years after its final sealing. Evidence for this was found in the tons of debris that Carter removed from the stairwell when he dug down to its entrance. Among the rubble were dozens of pieces of pottery and broken clay seals dating from the late eighteenth dynasty. For such remains to be present, the tomb must have been buried before the end of Horemheb's reign as he was the last eighteenth-dynasty king. Because the final sealing of the tomb seems to have occurred during Horemheb's reign, this means its burial must have occurred while he was pharaoh. Exactly the same seems to have happened to Tomb 55, as Ayrton also found contemporary artefacts in the rubble that covered its entrance.

The fact that, of all the royal tombs of the period, only the tombs of these two brothers survived intact surely cannot be coincidence. (Indeed, of all the royal tombs of ancient Egypt – from Giza, Saqqara and the Valley of the Kings – only a handful have ever been found as they were left.) Rather it would suggests that the steps taken to hide them from future generations may have been unique. We can understand why such a procedure may have been considered necessary for Tomb 55, but why Tutankhamun? – unless his burial was somehow linked with the condition of Tomb 55. Yet from the perspective of Egyptian magic, there is nothing unusual about Tutankhamun's tomb.

Indeed, it is the complete opposite of Tomb 55. Smenkhkare was left in a state of desecration, stripped of his belongings; Tutankhamun was left in state of splendour, surrounded by the most fabulous treasures. Is there perhaps some relevance here?

We shall return to the possible link between the two tombs later. Before we can proceed, however, we must examine the thinking behind the actions of these contemporary pharaohs. The entire mystery of Tomb 55 – and every subsequent mystery it leads on to – will ultimately remain a mystery unless we can get into the minds of those who lived during the Amarna period. We need to appreciate their reasoning, which seems almost exclusively driven by their reaction to Atenism – either pro or anti. The new god seems to have dominated the entire era. Exactly how, then, did this most unusual religion get started?

SUMMARY

- Events soon impelled Tutankhamun's regime to reinstate Amun-Re as the principle deity, albeit seemingly as a token gesture to appease opposition.
- On the balance of evidence it would seem that Tutankhamun was the son of Amonhotep III and his chief wife Tiye. As Smenkhkare seems to have been Amonhotep's son by his secondary wife Mutnodjme, this would make Tutankhamun Smenkhkare's half-brother and full brother of Akhenaten.
- We know from Tutankhamun's tomb that by the time of the young king's burial Ay had appointed himself heir apparent, and inscriptions from his own tomb suggest he reigned for four years. When Ay died the leading general Horemheb became pharaoh. Throughout the country

images of the Aten were defaced, Amarna was ransacked, and the temple of the Aten in Karnak was taken apart brick by brick.

- The Amarna kings became non-persons: the names of Akhenaten, Smenkhkare, Tutankhamun and Ay were struck off all monuments, save a few that were overlooked or isolated.

- It has long remained a mystery how Tutankhamun's tomb managed to escape the destruction. It is, perhaps, understandable that Horemheb left Smenkhkare as he was, his remains desecrated and unnamed, but for Tutankhamun – a king whose statues he was toppling all over Egypt – also to have been left alone is bewildering. Incredibly, Horemheb not only refrained from desecrating Tutankhamun's tomb; he seems to have safeguarded it.

CHAPTER SEVEN

The One God

The most remarkable aspect of Akhenaten's revolution in religious thought is that it apparently springs into existence – seemingly from nowhere – the moment Akhenaten becomes king. Apart from passing allusions, there is only a handful of references predating Akhenaten's reign which seem to give the Aten any real significance:

- At the beginning of twelfth dynasty, around 2000 BC, the deceased pharaoh Amenemhet I is referred to as having flown to heaven to unite with the Aten; as is the eighteenth-dynasty pharaoh Amonhotep I.

- Tuthmosis I, around 1525 BC, chose as one of his titles, 'Horus-Re who comes from the Aten'.

- From the reign of Akhenaten's grandfather, Tuthmosis IV, around 1400 BC, a large commemorative scarab bears an inscription in which the peoples under the dominion of the pharaoh are described as, 'his subjects under the sway of the Aten'. (Scarabs such as this, sacred to the god Khepri, represent a dung beetle rolling the sun across the sky.)

- Akhenaten's father, Amonhotep III, named his state
  barge *Radiance of the Aten*.

Although the Aten existed as a divinity before Akhenaten came
to power, there was apparently no such thing as Atenism. No
one, as far as we can tell, had ever considered worshipping it
exclusively, or indeed giving it any importance in its own right:
it was merely an aspect of Re-Herakhte. As solar deity, Re-
Herakhte had many different roles and being the Aten – namely
the sun disc itself – was just one of them. Consequently, Atenism
is even stranger than it first appears: before Akhenaten's reign
this new supreme deity was not really considered a god at all. In
order to ascertain how this extraordinary situation came about,
we must examine Akhenaten's earliest years as king, before his
move to Amarna.

It was once thought that outside Amarna no references to
Akhenaten had survived, as no monuments had been found
bearing is name. Eventually, however, it was realized that the
pharaoh had not always been known by the name Akhenaten.
He was actually born with his father's name, Amonhotep
('Amun is Pleased'), and began his reign as Amonhotep IV,
taking the name Akhenaten ('Living spirit of the Aten') in his
fifth regnal year. Under the name Amonhotep IV, references to
Akhenaten do appear in a few Theban tombs that managed to
escape desecration. But they are few and far between, and it was
only thanks to a remarkable quirk of fate that we have any real
knowledge of Akhenaten's early years in Thebes. When Horemheb attempted to destroy all evidence of Akhenaten's existence
by dismantling his Aten temple at Karnak, stone by stone, he
used the masonry to repair the nearby temple of Amun-Re.
Here reliefs from Akhenaten's temple were preserved unscathed
for over 3,000 years.

Between the wars, two of the pylons (pyramid-shaped gate towers) at the Temple of Karnak were dismantled for structural repairs by the Egyptian Antiquities Service. Inside, the two directors, Maurice Pillet and Henri Chevriery, discovered over 40,000 sculptured blocks which Horemheb had used for filling when he erected the pylons shortly after his accession. Now called the Karnak Talatat, nearly all of them came from the Aten temple and many are sculptured in sunk relief showing scenes from Akhenaten's early years as king. Reconstruction of this gargantuan jigsaw puzzle seemed almost impossible, however, until 1965, when Ray Wingfield Smith, a retired US foreign service officer and amateur art historian, initiated the so-called Akhenaten Temple Project to undertake the task. The project took years: it even ran out of money and had to be taken over by a Canadian team in 1975, under the directorship of Professor Donald Redford of Toronto University. Aided by modern computer technology, Redford was eventually able to reassemble many of the ancient scenes.

From the Karnak Talatat, together with the reliefs from early tombs that managed to escape desecration, we learn that Akhenaten had seemingly proclaimed the Aten supreme deity the moment he became pharaoh, and immediately ordered a temple to be erected to his god. Called the *Gempaaten* ('The Aten is Found in the Estate of the Aten'), it was built to the same unique plan as those that were to follow in Amarna, with its special feature – 'The Window of Appearance' – like a papal balcony were the pharaoh could appear before his followers.

From the very beginning Akhenaten sees himself as a prophet. His father's epithet, like all the preceding eighteenth-dynasty pharaohs, had been 'Ruler of Thebes', but Akhenaten described himself as 'Divine Ruler of Thebes'. To have himself depicted as an androgynous being was also his intention from early in his reign. In 1925, while digging a drainage ditch at the Temple of Karnak, workmen uncovered a row of fallen statues bearing the name Amonhotep IV. The huge colossi, of which fragments of twenty-five were eventually found, were of a startling, almost grotesque character, unlike any statues previously found in Egypt. Now reassembled in the Cairo Museum, they are extraordinary, three-dimensional representations of Akhenaten, showing the same exaggerated physiology as depicted in the Amarna reliefs. These, however, date from before the move to Amarna, and had originally adorned the *Gempaaten* temple.

Although the Aten is supreme god and Akhenaten is its only prophet from the outset of the reign, there appears to have been no suppression of the old religion for the first four or five years. In fact, the high priest of Amun was still active in the year 4, overseeing the cutting of stone for a royal statue. However, by the year 5 Akhenaten proscribed the cult of Amun-Re, closed the god's temples, and made a complete break from the past by founding his new city on a virgin site not previously sacred to any god.

Throughout the first half of his reign, Akhenaten seems to have been struggling to find a conventional Egyptian context with which to convey his new religious concept. In the Old Kingdom the Aten had been seen as the visible manifestation of Re, and when Re became assimilated with Horus as Re-Herakhte by the Middle Kingdom, the Aten became an aspect of this composite deity. It was, in fact, as Re-Herakhte that the Aten was first represented at Thebes: a falcon-headed man wearing a solar disc, the *uraeus* and the *Atef* crown (the crown of Osiris). The full title by which Akhenaten refers to his god in his early regnal years is: 'Re-Herakhte, who rejoices in the horizon in his aspect of the light which is in the sun-disc'.

However, Akhenaten clearly does not see his god as Re-Herakhte, but something which had previously been considered an aspect of Re-Herakhte. Namely, 'the light which is in the sun-disc' – in other words, sunlight. In an attempt to distinguish his deity from any previous god, however, Akhenaten had its name contained in a double cartouche. All the same, it appears that his subjects still found it difficult to grasp the idea that the Aten was something other than Re-Herakhte. On the Boundary Stelae proclamations of the year 5 at Amarna, we find Akhenaten desperately, and garrulously, attempting to explain his god to his people:

> May the good god live who delights in truth, lord of heaven and lord of earth, the Aten, the living, the great, illuminating the two lands. May the father live, divine and royal, Re-Herakhte, rejoicing in the horizon in his aspect of the light which is in the sun-disc, who lives for ever and ever, the Aten, the great, who is jubilee within the temple of the Aten in Akhetaten.

Here we learn of a very different deity from either Re-Herakhte or the Aten, as they had previously been perceived. Indeed, it is unlike any Egyptian god: an all powerful, heavenly father who demands that his children live in 'truth'. Precisely what this reference to truth implies is hard to say. One can only assume that Akhenaten's followers were encouraged to behave candidly and live an honest life. The word *Mat*, 'Truth', appears again and again at Amarna, and the phrase, 'living in truth', seems almost to have been a motto of the new religion.

The same struggle to convey his religious thought is also evident on the Boundary Stelae, when Akhenaten describes his personal relationship with the Aten:

> And may the Horus [the king] live, strong bull beloved of
> the Aten; he of the two ladies, great of kingship in
> Akhetaten; Horus of gold, upholding the name of the Aten;
> the king of Upper and Lower Egypt, living in truth, lord of
> the two lands, god like the forms of Re, the only one of Re;
> the son of Re, living in truth, lord of crowns, Akhenaten,
> great in his duration, living for ever and always. The good
> god, unique one of Re, whose beauty the Aten created,
> truly excellent in mind to his maker, contenting him with
> what his spirit desires, doing service to him who begot him,
> administering the land for him who put him upon his
> throne, provisioning his eternal home with very many
> things, upholding the Aten and magnifying his name,
> causing the earth to belong to its maker. . . .

Here it is Horus with whom Akhenaten associates himself. He
has gone back to the gods of a much younger Egypt, before the
cult of Amun-Re, when Re was the supreme deity in his own
right and the pharaoh was seen as Horus, Re's incarnation on
earth. It is quite evident from everything we know about
Atenism that Akhenaten did not personally regard Re as his god
or himself as Horus. Indeed, within a few years he proscribed
all reference to Re, Horus or any other god. It would appear,
therefore, that Akhenaten is appealing to the religious sym-
pathies of the ancient cult of Re. It still survived in northern
Egypt, principally at Heliopolis, and it may have been from here
that many of Akhenaten's devotees originated.

During the Old Kingdom the myth developed that Re
once ruled Egypt personally but, wearied by the affairs of
mankind, retired to the heavens, leaving his son the pharaoh to
rule in his stead. This notion had been initiated and nurtured
by the priesthood in Heliopolis, who had remained the primary

influence in Egyptian religious affairs until the conquest of northern Egypt by the Hyksos at the end of the Middle Kingdom. During the Hyksos period, though, the cult of the Theban god Amun, in unoccupied southern Egypt, rose to prominence.

When he expelled the Hyksos, the first New Kingdom pharaoh Amosis, thinking himself especially favoured by the god of Thebes, heaped vast wealth upon the Temple at Karnak and appointed Amun priests as his four chief prophets – the most important religious officials. The institution of the Chief Wife began at this time too, when Amosis married Ahmose-Nefertari, the chief priestess of Amun, in the belief that Amun would thereafter incarnate in him. Of course, after one and a half thousand years of existence, the Heliopolis Re cult had not died out, so to appease them and unify the country, Re had been assimilated with Amun. However, an independent cult of Re continued to exist at Heliopolis, no doubt resenting the wealth and power of the Amun priests in Thebes. It was to them that Akhenaten seems to have been appealing. Indeed, he seems actually to have been influenced by the cult of Re, as there are a number of uniquely Heliopolitan traits in Atenism:

- The Aten temple at Karnak was built in the *ben-ben* style (a truncated pyramid on a square base), which had been unique to the solar temples at Heliopolis.

- The chief priest of the Aten, Meryre, was given same title as the high priest of Heliopolis – 'Greatest of Seers'.

- Akhenaten ordered that the Mnevis bull, the sacred animal of Heliopolis, should be moved to Amarna so that its worship could continue there.

It seems very likely, therfore, that Akhenaten's ideas were formulated in Heliopolis before he became king. However, as we have seen, it is not the Heliopolitan god Re that he is exalting. Akhenaten's god – despite all the early references to Horus, Re and Re-Herakhte – is something so different from any former Egyptian deity that Akhenaten invented a new symbol to represent it: the sun disc from which shone rays holding the glyph for life, the *ankh*. The sun had previously been represented by a winged disc, but from the very begining of Akhenaten's reign, the Aten is represented as the rayed disc. A scene in the Theban tomb of the steward and king's cup-bearer, Parennefer, for instance (which must date from the first regnal years, as the king and queen are unaccompanied by children), shows the royal couple standing below this new symbol.

Akhenaten seems to have abandoned his attempt to fit his god into an orthodox context by his ninth year, when he prohibited any further association of his god with Re-Herakhte. Moreover, he ordered the removal of the plural form of the word 'god' from all inscriptions. Akhenaten's god was the *only* god, as the pharaoh had spent years trying to convey. Presumably his belief in a 'good god' – as he describes both himself and the Aten – had made him reluctant to resort to such coercion previously.

One of the chief difficulties Akhenaten must have encountered in expounding his religion is that a nation used to visible gods – in the form of idols – could not grasp the idea of an invisible god: Akhenaten forbade the making of any image of his god. If the Aten had simply been the sun disc, as it had previously been, and Atenism had merely been sun worship – as the first visitors to Amarna had thought – then it would have been a very simple concept to convey. Akhenaten could have continued to use the winged disc symbol to represent his god. However, he chose a glyph that represented sun*light*, just as he had initially chosen the sunlight aspect of Re-Herakhte to represent his god. It seems clear that sunshine – which brings warmth, light and life, yet cannot be seen in its own right – was the nearest Akhenaten could come to comprehending and conveying the idea of an invisible, omnipresent, all-providing god. The Aten – a word that simply means 'sun disc' – does not actually, therefore, appear to be the god's name, rather the nearest written word that previously existed for life-giving sunlight. In conclusion, Akhenaten seems to have been inspired by the idea of a universal god – something which was impossible to fit into an established Egyptian context. Accordingly, this would seem to imply that the thinking behind Atenism was a foreign concept.

There are three essential aspects of Akhenaten's god which sets it apart from all other Egyptian deities:

- It is the one and only universal god.

- It appears to have had no name.

- It cannot be represented by a graven image.

How did Akhenaten conceive these innovative ideas? As there is only one brief reference to Akhenaten before he becomes pharaoh – a wine-jar seal from Malkata referring to 'the estate of the true king's son Amonhotep' – there are no records to go by. However, to help us solve this ancient riddle, perhaps we should rephrase the question: *Where* did Akhenaten conceive these innovative ideas? What are normally seen as political or religious innovations are usually concepts that have been around for years before being adopted as anyone's state policy. Marxism had already existed for half a century before the Bolsheviks seized power in Russia; Christianity had existed for almost three hundred years before the Roman Empire embraced it as the state religion; and the political ideal of a written constitution had been around for two thousand years before it was implemented during the French Revolution. Could Atenism really have sprung into existence overnight? Or did Akhenaten take his religion from others?

If we look at the above list again, we see an exact description of another god – the God of the Hebrews. Like the Aten, God, as represented in the Old Testament, is the only god; he cannot be addressed by name, and cannot be represented by a graven image. Could there be a connection? Each one of these unique characteristics it shares with Atenism:

- Repeatedly, the Old Testament makes it abundantly clear that God was the sole universal creator: the Bible actually starts with the words, 'In the beginning God created the heaven and the earth.' He is the only god that the Hebrews can worship. In Exodus: 20.3, God commands the Hebrews: 'Thou shalt have no other gods before me.'

- The name of God is written in Hebrew as *Yhwh* (pronounced 'yahveh' and later rendered as Jahweh or Jehovah) and is understood to mean 'I AM', coming from the biblical account of Moses speaking to God within the burning bush. When Moses asks God his name, God replies, 'I AM THAT I AM ... Thus shall thou say unto the children of Israel, I AM hath sent me unto you'. (Exodus: 3.14.) The biblical Hebrews do not even use *this* term when addressing God; rather they use the word *Adonai,* meaning 'Lord', or *Elohim,* meaning simply 'God'.

- When Moses returns from Mount Sinai with the Ten Commandments, he tells his people that God has forbidden them to make, 'any graven image, or any likeness of anything that is in heaven above'. (Exodus: 20.4.)

There is another remarkable similarity between the two religions: Both the Hebrew God and the Aten are regarded as heavenly kings. The Aten's titles are enclosed in a royal cartouche and a pharaonic serpent hangs from its sun disc symbol. The God of Israel is also spoken of as a king. For example, in Isaiah: 44. 6 – 'Thus saith the Lord the King of Israel' – and Psalm 47 which tells us that, 'God is the King of all the earth'.

Is there a link between Atenism and the Hebrews? The Hebrews are certainly the only people on earth who are known to have conceived of monotheism so early. In fact, as the other two great monotheistic religions – Christianity and Islam – did not develop until well over a millennium later, the Hebrews were years ahead of their time. They were also apparently in Egypt, perhaps during Akhenaten's reign. The Bible does not provide dates, but it does tell us that the Hebrews were held captive in Egypt before they escaped in the Exodus. Although no historical record has been found outside the Old Testament concerning the bondage in Egypt, most biblical scholars consider that the Hebrews were in the country some time prior to the tenth century BC. It would therefore seem to have been possible for Akhenaten to have been influenced by the early Israelites. But is there hard evidence?

The surest way to tell if there was a connection between the two religions would be to compare their religious texts. Although we have plenty of Hebrew texts, as the faith has survived to the present day, no such works of long-forgotten Atenism remain. Its religious texts, if there were any, would have been preserved on papyrus and would long ago have perished. The nearest thing, however, is a prayer, surviving in fragmented form in a number of Amarna reliefs, which seems to be the Atenist equivalent of a 'Lord's Prayer'. Known as 'The Hymn to the Aten', it was seen by the American Egyptologist James Breasted in 1909 as strikingly similar to Psalm 104 in the Old Testament. The longest extract appears in the tomb prepared for Ay at Amarna:

> Thou arisest fair in the horizon of heaven, O living Aten, beginner of life. When thou dawnest in the East, thou fillest every land with thy beauty. Thou art indeed comely, great, radiant and high over every land. Thy rays embrace the lands to the full extent of all that thou hast made, for thou art Re and thou attainest their limits and subduest them for thy beloved son (Akhenaten). Thou art remote yet thy rays are upon the earth. Thou art in the sight of men, yet thy ways are not known.
>
> When thou setest in the western horizon, the earth is in darkness after the manner of death. Men spend the night indoors with the head covered, the eye not seeing its fellow. Their possessions might be stolen, even when under their heads, and they would be unaware of it. Every lion comes forth from its lair and all snakes bite. Darkness lurks, and the earth is silent when their creator rests in his habitation.
>
> The earth brightens when thou arisest in the eastern horizon and shinest forth as Aten in the daytime. Thou drivest away the night when thou givest forth thy beams.

The Two Lands are in festival. They awake and stand upon their feet for thou hast raised them up. They wash their limbs, they put on raiment and raise their arms in adoration at thy appearance. The entire earth performs its labours. All cattle are at peace in their pastures. The trees and herbage grow green. The birds fly from their nests, their wings raised in praise of thy spirit. All animals gambol on their feet, all the winged creation live when thou hast risen for them. The boats sail upstream, and likewise downstream. All ways open at thy dawning. The fish in the river leap in thy presence. Thy rays are in the midst of the sea.

Thou it is who causest women to conceive and makest seed into man who givest life to the child in the womb of its mother, who comfortest him so that he cries not therein, nurse that thou art, even in the womb, who givest breath to quicken all that he hath made. When the child comes forth from the body on the day of his birth, then thou openest his mouth completely and thou furnishest his sustenance. When the chick in the egg chirps within the shell thou givest him the breath within it to sustain him. Thou createst for him his proper term within the egg, so that he shall break it and come forth from it to testify to his completion as he runs about on his two feet when he emergeth.

How manifold are thy works! They are hidden from the sight of men, O Sole God, like unto whom there is no other! Thou didst fashion the earth according to thy desire when thou wast alone – all men, all cattle great and small, all that are upon the earth that run upon their feet or rise up on high flying with their wings. And the lands of Syria and Kush and Egypt – thou appointest every man to his place and satisfiest his needs. Everyone receives his sustenance and his days are numbered. Their tongues are diverse in speech and their qualities are likewise, and their colour is differentiated for thou hast distinguished the nations.

Thou makest waters under the earth and thou bringest them forth at thy pleasure to sustain the people of Egypt even as thou hast made them live for thee, O Divine Lord of them all, toiling for them, the Lord of every land, shining forth for them, the Aten Disc of the daytime, great in majesty!

All distant foreign lands also, thou createst their life. Thou hast placed a Nile in heaven to come forth for them and make a flood upon the mountains like the sea in order to water the fields of their villages. How excellent are thy plans, O Lord of Eternity! A Nile in the sky is thy gift to foreigners and to the beasts of their lands; but the true Nile flows from under the earth for Egypt.

Thy beams nourish every field and when thou shinest they live and grow for thee. Thou makest the seasons in order to sustain all that thou hast made, the winter to cool them, the summer heat that they may taste thy glory. Thou hast made heaven afar off that thou mayest behold all that thou hast made when thou wast alone, appearing in thy aspect of the Living Aten, rising and shining forth. Thou makest millions of forms out of thyself, towns, villages, fields, roads, the river. All eyes behold thee before them, for thou art the Aten of the daytime, above all that thou hast created.

Thou art in my heart, but there is none other who knows thee save thy son Akhenaten. Thou hast made him wise in thy plans and thy power.

Psalm 104, although obviously not concerning Akhenaten or the Aten, does appear to have a number of correlations suggesting a common source:

> Bless the Lord, O my soul. O Lord my God, thou art very great; thou art clothed with thy honour and majesty. Who coverest thyself with light as with a garment; who stretchest out the heavens like a curtain; who layeth the beams of his chambers in the waters; who maketh the clouds his chariot; who walketh upon the wings of the wind; who maketh his angels spirits; his ministers a flaming fire. Who laid the foundations of the earth, that it should not be removed for ever. Thou coveredst it with the deep as with a garment; the waters stood above the mountains. At thy rebuke they fled; at the voice of thy thunder they hasted away. They go up by the mountains; they go down by the valleys unto the place which thou hast founded for them. Thou hast set a bound that they must not pass over; that they should turn not again to cover the earth.
>
> He sendeth the springs into the valleys, which run among the hills. They give drink to every beast of the field; the wild asses quench their thirst. By them shall the fowls of the heaven have their habitation, which sing among the branches. He watereth the hills from his chambers: the earth is satisfied with the fruit of thy works. He causeth the grass to grow for the cattle, and herb for the service of man: that he may bring forth food out of the earth; and wine that maketh glad the heart of man, and oil to make his face to shine, and bread which strengtheneth man's heart. The trees of the Lord are full of sap; the cedars of Lebanon that he has planted; where the birds make their nests; as for the stork, the fir trees are her house. The high

hills are a refuge for the wild goats; and the rocks for the conies. He appointed the moon for seasons; the sun knoweth his going down.

Thou makest darkness, and it is night: wherein all beasts of the forest do creep forth. The young lions roar after their prey, and seek their meat from God. The sun ariseth, they gather themselves together, and lay them down in their dens. Man goeth forth unto his work and to his labour until the evening. O Lord how manifold are thy works! In wisdom hast thou made them all: the earth is full of thy riches. So is the great and wide sea, wherein are things creeping innumerable, both small and great beasts. There go the ships; there is that leviathan, whom thou hast made to play therein. These wait all upon thee; that thou mayest give them their meat in due season. That thou givest them they gather; thou openest thy hand, they are filled with good. Thou hidest thy face, they are troubled; thou takest away their breath, they die, and return to their dust. Thou sendest forth thy spirit, they are created; and thou renewest the face of the earth. The glory of the Lord shall endure for ever; the Lord shall rejoice in his works. He looketh on the earth, and it trembleth; he toucheth the hills, and they smoke. I will sing unto the Lord as long as I live; I will sing praise to my god while I have my being. My meditation of him shall be sweet; I will be glad in the Lord. Let the sinners be consumed out of the earth, and let the wicked be no more. Bless thou the Lord O my soul. Praise ye the Lord.

Although both 'The Hymn to the Aten' and Psalm 104 describe in a similar way how their gods are seen as creators, nurturers and prime movers of all phenomena on earth, and show that the deities were regarded in a like manner, we only have this isolated example from which to make a comparison. There is, however, other evidence which actually associates two of the Hebrews' most important figures with what seems to have been the birthplace of Atenism – the city of Heliopolis.

Heliopolis was the name the Greeks eventually gave to the city; in ancient times it was called On. According to Genesis Chapter 41: Verse 45, the Hebrew patriarch Joseph married the daughter of the high priest of On. A story survived in Egypt during Roman times which also linked Moses with the city. The scholar Apion, who taught in Rome under the emperors Tiberius, Caligula and Claudius, wrote in the third volume of his *History of Egypt* that, 'Moses, as I have heard from the elders in Egypt, was a native of Heliopolis'.

Sigmund Freud, the father of psychoanalysis, even considered that Moses may have been inspired by Akhenaten. In his book *Moses and Monotheism*, published in 1939, he argued that the Hebrews had been followers of Akhenaten's religion, and that their God was actually the Aten. Much of Freud's evidence rested on the similarity between the Hebrew word for God – *Adonai* – and the word Aten. The Hebrew letter D was a transliteration of the Egyptian letter T, he argued, and likewise E and O. Accordingly, the Egyptian pronunciation of the Hebrew word for God would be *Atenai* – which sounds very similar to Aten. However, linguists have since pointed out a flaw in the argument. The word *Adonai*, meaning 'Lord', was not an exclusive term for God; it was used just as the English word Lord is used, either to address God or as a title of nobility. The Egyptian word for Lord is *Neb*. Consequently, if the Hebrews had adopted the custom of addressing God by the title Lord from the Egyptians, their term would not have been derived from the word Aten at all.

For another more fundamental reason it seems unlikely that the Hebrews took their faith from Atenism: there is no evidence of Atenism as a cult anywhere in Egypt before the accession of Akhenaten. Logic dictates, therefore, that if there is a connection between the two religions, Akhenaten took his ideas from the Hebrews.

However, there is compelling evidence to link the two faiths which does suggest that some Atenists later merged with the Hebrews and contaminated their religious practices. There is one pagan practice that both religions seem to have retained. We have seen in Chapter Four how the sole concession Akhenaten seems to have made to the old ways was the continued veneration of the bull. Just such an animal seems to have been revered by the early Hebrews.

A sacred bull is echoed in the biblical story of the golden calf. According to Chapter 32 of Exodus, when Moses is absent communing with God on Mount Sinai, his people, fearing some ill has befallen him, ask his deputy Aaron to make images of the gods to protect them. Agreeing, Aaron collects golden jewellery from the people and makes a 'molten calf'. In fact, contrary to the popular Hollywood image, it is not one calf they make but many, as the others are said to follow Aaron's lead (Verses 31 and 35). Aaron declares that these calves are, 'thy gods, O Israel, which brought thee up out of the land of Egypt' (Verse 4). Furthermore, they do not seem to be life-size representations either. We are not told how big they are, but Verse 4 seems to suggest that they are small enough to be held in the hands. When the people gave Aaron their golden earrings to make the idol, 'he received them at their hand and fashioned it with a graving tool'.

That the early Israelites historically did venerate such idols is supported by archaeological evidence. A number of hand-size carved bulls have been found at early sites throughout Palestine. Perhaps the most interesting was a bronze bull, some 200 centimetres (8 inches) long, found at a site excavated by Israeli archaeologist Dr Amihay Mazor (of Hebrew University, Jerusalem) in the Samarian Mountains just to the north of Nablus. This was the biblical Shechem, one of the holiest sites in ancient Israel where Abraham and Joshua both raised altars to God. The artefact dates from the twelfth century BC, a time after the period that Moses apparently lived, and consequently a time when the Hebrew faith was said to have been fully established. This can be gathered from an inscription on a large granite stela found by Flinders Petrie in 1896. It came from the funerary temple of the nineteenth-dynasty pharaoh Merenptah near Thebes and is dated as the fifth year of his reign. Now in the Cairo Museum, it has become known as the Israel Stela because it includes the first and only known mention of Israel in an Egyptian text. (See Chapter Eight.) Its unique importance is that it shows that Israel already existed during Merenptah's reign in the late thirteenth century BC (*circa* 1212 to 1202 BC) – a time before the date of the bronze bull (the 1100s BC).

If the Old Testament story of the Israelite conquest of Canaan is remotely true, then the site of Shechem was the *most* sacred Hebrew site of the period. According to the Book of Joshua, after Canaan is conquered by Joshua he erects an altar to give thanks to God:

> So Joshua made a covenant with the people that day, and set them a statute and an ordinance in Shechem. And Joshua wrote these words in the book of the law of God, and took a great stone, and set it up there under an oak, that was by the sanctuary of the Lord. And Joshua said unto all the people, Behold this stone shall be a witness

unto us; for it hath heard all the words of the Lord which he spake unto us: it shall be therefore a witness unto you, lest you deny your God. (Joshua: 24. 25–27.)

If the Bible is right then Shechem is the religious heartland of the Israelites in their earliest days in Canaan. The bronze bull – coming from a contemporary site in this very area – is clear evidence of the continued veneration of the pagan bull, certainly by some Hebrews, well after they had apparently settled in the 'Promised Land'.

Of all the hundreds of pagan religious practices that there were in the world, that both the Atenist and Hebrew religions should seemingly be tainted by one that is exactly the same, is surely more than coincidence.

Standing alone, the story of the golden calf is a mystery: why should a people, who had recently witnessed the awesome power of their God free them from captivity in Egypt, lose faith so easily and revert to idolatry? More importantly, why should they have chosen a calf to venerate? If there is any historicity reflected in the story – and the archaeological evidence suggests that there is – then the answer to both questions must be that they had only recently abandoned the calf as an object of veneration. As the biblical narrative provides no prior evidence of such a practice among the Hebrews, we can only construe that it was an external influence, and judging by the reference in Exodus 32:28, which tells us that the idolaters were only a faction (3000 individuals that the tribe of Levi were ordered to kill), then they also seem to have been a Gentile (non-Hebrew) element among the Israelites. The only Gentiles we know of during this early era who would have had enough in common with a monotheistic religion to embrace the Hebrew God are the Atenists. The very people that also venerated the bull.

Why the Atenists might have been among the Hebrews after their flight from Egypt. we shall return to later. Firstly, we must see if there is any firm historical evidence to place the Hebrews in Egypt during, or just prior to, Akhenaten's time.

SUMMARY

- Akhenaten's revolution in religious thought springs into existence seemingly from nowhere. Although the Aten existed as a divinity before Akhenaten came to power, there was apparently no such thing as Atenism.
- Akhenaten seems to have been struggling to find a conventional Egyptian context with which to convey his new religious ideas. In an attempt to distinguish his deity from any previous god Akhenaten represented it by a new glyph: a disc from which emanated rays. Akhenaten, therefore, seems to have been inspired by an idea which was impossible to fit into an established Egyptian context, implying that the thinking behind Atenism was a foreign concept.
- There are three essential aspects of Akhenaten's god which set it apart from all other Egyptian deities: it is the one and only universal god; it appears to have had no name; and it cannot be represented by a graven image. This is also an exact description of another god – the God of the Hebrews. Like the Aten, God, as represented in the Old Testament, is the only god, he cannot be addressed by name, and cannot be represented by a graven image. The Hebrews are certainly the only other people on earth who are known to have conceived of monotheism so early.
- The Bible does not provide dates, but it does tell us that the

Hebrews were held captive in Egypt before they escaped during the Exodus. It consequently may have been possible for Akhenaten to have been influenced by the early Israelites.

- The sole concession Akhenaten seems to have made to the old ways was the continued veneration of the sacred bull of Re. Just such an animal seems to have been revered by the early Hebrews. A sacred bull is echoed in the biblical story of the golden calf.

- As the biblical narrative provides no prior evidence of such a practice among the Hebrews, we can only construe that the bull-worship was an external influence. Judging by the reference in Exodus 32:28, which tells us that the idolaters were only a faction, then they may also have been a Gentile (non-Hebrew) element among the Israelites. The only Gentiles we know of during this early era who would have had enough in common with a monotheistic religion to embrace the Hebrew God are the Atenists. It is possible, therefore, that a number of Atenists joined the Hebrews when they too were persecuted around fifteen years after Akhenaten's reign.

CHAPTER EIGHT

The Children of Israel

In the biblical account, the Israelites spend 430 years in Egypt before the Exodus. They are originally made welcome by a pharaoh during Joseph's time, but later, concerned by their growing numbers, the Egyptians enslave them. Eventually, Moses is called by God to lead them out of Egypt and, after the country is beset by a series of plagues and terrible deaths, the pharaoh begrudgingly lets them leave. Suffering a change of heart, he then pursues the Israelites, who manage to escape when the waters of the Red Sea miraculously part. Finally, after wandering for forty years in the wilderness, they are led by Joshua into the 'Promised Land' of Canaan.

Although the narrative concerns what are purported to be monumental historical events, the Bible gives us no idea when they were supposed to have occurred: it provides no dates and fails to name the pharaohs in question. Despite the mass of contemporary records that survive from ancient Egypt, not one historical reference to the presence of the Israelites in that country has yet been found. Not a word about Joseph, whom the Bible tells us was the pharaoh's 'grand vizier' – his chief minister. Not a single mention of Moses, whom the Bible tells us was raised as an Egyptian prince. Nothing concerning the plagues, which included the day turning to night and the Nile turning to

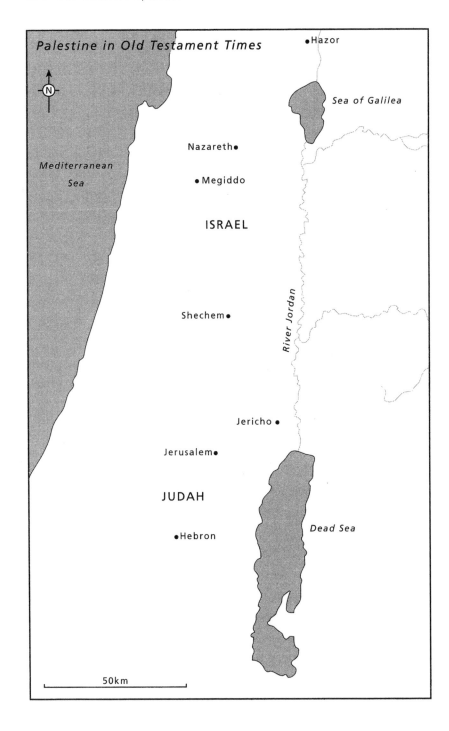

blood. And nothing regarding the spectacular flight from Egypt by a people which, we are told, number over half a million. In fact, there is no ancient evidence independent of the Bible – from anywhere – which directly corroborates any of these events. From the purely historical perspective, there would seem to be no real evidence that the Israelites were ever in Egypt at all.

There were certainly a people known as the Israelites who had settled in Canaan – an area which included modern Israel, Palestine and the Lebanon – by around 1200 BC, as demonstrated by the Israel Stela (see Chapter Seven) and archaeological evidence (see below); and that they were the forefathers of the Jews is not in question. Historians, however, have long debated whether or not the Israelites had really arrived there from Egypt as the Bible relates.

The Bible does not come into any known historical context until around 1000 BC, before which time the Israelites seem to have existed as separate tribes ruled by a series of chieftains called Judges. According to the First Book of Samuel, the prophet Samuel is instructed to unite the tribes of Israel under one king. He first chooses Saul, who ultimately fails to keep the country together. Saul's son-in-law David is then proclaimed king by Samuel and he succeeds were Saul has failed. He establishes the united kingdom of Israel, and captures the city of Jerusalem from the Jebusites and makes it his capital. David is succeeded by his son Solomon who builds the first temple in the holy city. After Solomon's death the southern part of the country, around Jerusalem, breaks away from the rest of Israel to form the kingdom of Judah (which the Romans later called Judea), named after one of the Hebrew tribes. It is with the kingdom of Judah that the Judaic tradition thereafter focuses, the name Jew actually coming from the Hebrew word *Yehudi* – meaning a member of the tribe of Judah.

Most modern historians accept that these particular events did occur during the tenth century BC, although there is much disagreement regarding the finer details. After this time, however, the Old Testament account becomes increasingly verifiable from external sources. Jerusalem was sacked and the temple destroyed by King Nebuchadnezzar in 586 BC, after Judah was invaded by the Babylonians and thousands of the Jews were carted off to exile in Babylon. They were eventually resettled by the Persians who conquered the failing Babylonian empire in 538 BC, although thereafter they were subjected in turn to rule by the Persians, the Greeks and ultimately the Romans. Under the Romans, Judah enjoyed enough independence for its king, Herod the Great, to rebuild the temple completely, but after the Jews later revolted it too was razed to the ground in AD 70. This effectively spelt the end of Judah, as many of its citizens were reduced to slavery and deported.

Historically, it was sometime between the building of the first temple and the exile in Babylon that Judaism as we now know it emerged. It was also during this time that most scholars believe that the account of the Israelite period in Egypt was actually written.

The first five books of the Bible, which cover the period from the Creation to the arrival of the Israelites at the Promised Land, were traditionally believed to have been written by Moses himself. Collectively called the Pentateuch (Genesis, Exodus, Leviticus, Numbers and Deuteronomy), they are now thought by biblical scholars to have been derived from various sources, as different elements in the narrative do not share the same literary character. For example, the accounts of Joseph or Joshua do not belong to the same literary class as the stories of Adam and Eve or Noah's Ark. The authors fail to identify themselves, but whoever they were it seems unlikely that they were eyewitnesses to the events they are describing. Indeed, they may not even have been remote contemporaries, as the Pentateuch contain a great many anachronisms.

According to Genesis 37:25, Joseph and his brothers encounter a company of Ishmaelite traders, 'who came from Gilead with their camels bearing spicery and balm and myrrh, going to carry it down to Egypt'. The Egyptians depicted every type of animal in their art, but never once show camels as a means of transport until the seventh century BC. Like the other contemporary works from the Asiatic, they show asses being used to carry goods. The oldest literary reference to domesticated camels is by the people of the Arabian Gulf around 850 BC, and not from Egypt for another two centuries. This was long after David's time, yet the Bible itself tells us that Joseph had lived hundreds of years *before* David.

Another example is early references to the Israelite enemies the Philistines. Genesis describes Joseph's great-grandfather, Abraham, living in the Land of the Philistines at Beersheba, in southern Canaan. According to Genesis 21:32–34, Abraham makes a treaty with the Philistine king Abimelech. The name Philistine comes from *Peleset*, an Egyptian word meaning 'Sea Peoples', and they are first recorded arriving in the Eastern Mediterranean in the reign of Ramesses III around 1180 BC. Archaeology, which has shown them to have been of Aegean origin, has produced no evidence of Philistine migration into Canaan much before the twelfth century BC. Although this is around 150 years before David's time, the Bible tells us that Abraham had lived well over 500 years before the Israelites even left Egypt.

In the 1970s Professor Donald Redford, in his *A Study of the Biblical Story of Joseph*, argued that the Egyptian elements in the story reflect the seventh century BC at the earliest. For instance, in Genesis 42:16, Joseph uses the oath, 'by the life of the pharaoh', which would not have existed in that form until the seventh century BC; and an Egyptian who appears in the Joseph story is an officer called Potiphar, a name which only occurs as an Egyptian name at the same late date. Other scholars consider that the entire Pentateuch was written as late as the seventh century BC, due to a number of tell-tale clues. For instance, money, in the form of coins, is referenced repeatedly, although the oldest known form of coinage was that used by the Lydians around 650 BC. This does not mean to say that the events were invented in the seventh century BC, only that they were committed to writing in their present form at that time.

Many biblical authorities consider that the stories were handed down verbally for generations and, like many oral accounts, were embellished or reinterpreted. Fundamentalists would disagree, of course, believing that every single word in the Bible is absolutely true. Regardless of whether or not the events were originally the result of divine intervention, the Old Testament, as it appears in the most popular English edition, is the product of a series of translations from one language to another – and even these individual languages changed over time. That certain elements in the narrative would also undergo change is almost inevitable.

These are minor problems, however, compared to actually translating a completely foreign tongue. A perfect example of a totally misleading mistranslation occurred in the Exodus account concerning the place were the sea parted to allow the Israelites to escape Egypt. In the original Hebrew it was written *Yam Suph,* which was mistranslated as 'Red Sea'. It actually means 'Sea of Reeds' and appears to have been a location in the Nile Delta (see Chapter Ten).

Then there are examples of scribal errors that have been

The entrance to Tutankhamun's tomb shortly after it was discovered in 1922.
It lay only thirteen meters across the valley floor from the mysterious Tomb 55.
(*Griffith Institute.*)

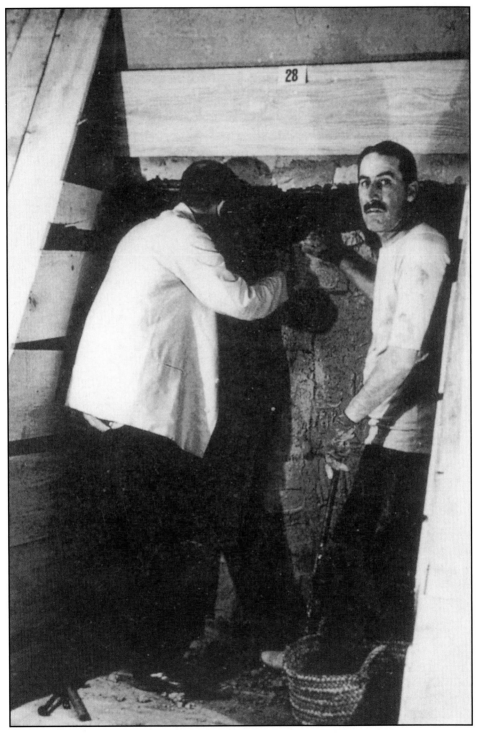

Lord Carnarvon (left) and Howard Carter (right) dismantling the entrance to Tutankhamun's burial chamber. Within a few weeks Carnarvon would be dead, some believe the victim of an ancient curse. (*Griffith Institute.*)

'Wonderful things!' The southern end of the Antechamber of Tutankhamun's tomb. This was the first glimpse of Tutankhamun's treasures seen by an ecstatic Howard Carter on the evening of 28 November 1922. (*Griffith Institute.*)

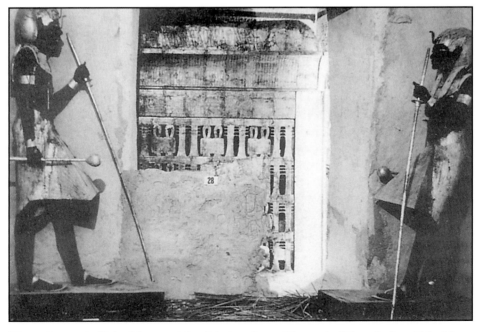

The entrance to Tutankhamun's burial chamber with most of the plastered blocking removed to reveal the outermost shrine. (*Griffith Institute.*)

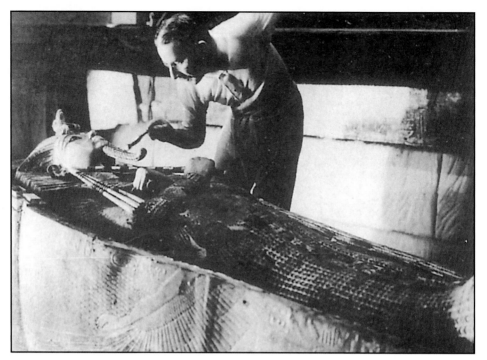

Carter examines Tutankhamun's middle coffin, at once realizing that it did not bear the image of the young king whose mummy it was supposed to contain. (*Griffith Institute.*)

When the second coffin was raised it was found to be much heavier than anyone had thought. The reason – it contained a third coffin of solid gold. (*Griffith Institute.*)

Above: Tutankhamun's inner coffin still *in situ* in the tomb. (*Griffith Institute.*)

Right: Carter carefully cleans Tutankhamun's inner golden coffin. (*Griffith Institute.*)

The outer coffin, depicting Tutankhamun around the time of his death, which forensic examination of the mummy has revealed to have been around seventeen. (*Cairo Museum.*)

The inner coffin, made of solid gold and depicting Tutankhamun while he was still a child, shortly after becoming king. (*Cairo Museum.*)

The middle coffin used for Tutankhamun's burial. Although the image it bears is that of a king it is clearly not the same person represented on the other two coffins. (*Cairo Museum.*)

copied and recopied. A good example concerns Abraham's father, Terah, in Genesis. According to Genesis 11:26, he was 70 years old by the time Abraham was born and, according to Genesis 11:32, he lived to the age of 205. However, in Genesis 12:4 – after we are told Terah has died – Abraham leaves home, aged 75. This means that Terah could have been no older than 145 when he died. Even if we attribute such an incredible age to divine intervention, we cannot accept both accounts. At some point, it seems, someone must have mistranslated what the original author had said.

Other examples reflect the multi-authorship of the Pentateuch. For instance, in Exodus, the Mount of God, where Moses communes with the Lord, is called Sinai; whereas in Deuteronomy it is called Horeb. We appear to have separate authors, at different times, independently interpreting the Mount of God's location. Even if these are different names for the same place, we must still have separate authors involved, each using the common name of their period or locale.

Such are the problems with the Pentateuch from an historian's perspective, that the more sceptical scholars question the entire Old Testament narrative prior to the time of David. To them Joseph, Moses and Joshua are just mythical Israelite heroes who were slotted into a vaguely historical framework by much later writers. Regardless of whether this is right or wrong, the Israelites had to have come from somewhere. The question that concerns us at the moment is, was this from Egypt?

In order to gain any kind of insight into the historicity of the Pentateuch account of the Israelite period in Egypt, we must start with the earliest historical reference to their existence in Canaan and work backwards. The Israel Stela, found by Petrie, gives us the first – but infuriatingly oblique – reference to Israel. It is simply included among a list of Egyptian campaigns. We are told nothing more than 'Plundered is the Canaan with every evil' and 'Israel is laid waste'. Whether this refers to Egyptian military activity or some natural catastrophe, such as famine, is difficult to tell, although we can infer from their inclusion in the list that the pharaoh had sent troops to oppose the Israelites. It certainly shows that the Israelites were in Canaan when the stone was inscribed, during the reign of the nineteenth-dynasty pharaoh Merenptah. As this was around 1220 BC, at least two centuries before David's creation of a unified kingdom, the reference must pertain to the separate tribes of Israel; presumably in the period the Bible refers to as the age of Judges, such as Samson and Gideon.

If the Israelites were in Egypt, as the Bible relates, then it has to have been before this time. They are already in Canaan around 1220 BC, and had presumably been established there long enough to pose some kind of threat to the pharaoh. It would therefore seem that the Israelites would have to have been in Canaan from at least as the middle of the thirteenth century BC. Is there archaeological evidence to support this?

In the biblical account, the Israelite entry into the Promised Land of Canaan began with Joshua's conquest of the city of Jericho, forty years after the Exodus from Egypt. According to the Book of Joshua, many further cities fell to the Israelite armies until the destruction of the last, the city of Hazor. From historical sources we know that contemporary Canaan comprised many independent city states, just as the Old Testament tells us, and of these, both the cities of Jericho and Hazor have been excavated.

In 1952 the British archaeologist Dame Kathleen Kenyon excavated a Bronze Age fortification at Tell es-Sultan near the Dead Sea, thought to be the site of ancient Jericho. She concluded that from 1900 BC the city was a prosperous walled town, just as the Bible describes, until it was destroyed by fire around 1500 BC. Many scholars took this to be evidence of Joshua's capture of the city, as Joshua 6:24 tells us that after its capture the Israelites burned Jericho. However, more recent excavations around the Dead Sea have uncovered no evidence of Israelite occupation until around 1250 BC. It is now generally agreed that Kathleen Kenyon's excavations uncovered evidence of an early conquest of the city by the Egyptians, probably by Tuthmosis III. Unfortunately, no evidence of Joshua's campaigns came to light in the area. There was more luck at Hazor, however.

Joshua 11:11 describes Joshua's destruction of Hazor: 'And they smote all the souls that were therein with the edge of the sword, utterly destroying them; there were not any left to breathe, and he burned Hazor with fire.'

In the 1950s excavations were conducted at the site of ancient Hazor, modern Tell el-Qedah, some fourteen kilometres north of the Sea of Galilee. Here the eminent Israeli archaeologist Dr Yigael Yadin unearthed the remains of a huge fortified palace which had been destroyed by fire around 1250 BC. The precise dating was made possible by broken Mycenean pottery found lying in the level of destruction. Such ceramics were popular throughout the Near East during the thirteenth century BC, but ceased to be imported into Palestine by the twelfth century. The destruction of the city had almost certainly been the work of an enemy, rather than accidental, as statues and temple decorations had been deliberately defaced. Because of the remains of hearths, tent bases and hut footings, together with a characteristic desert-style pottery, the next level of occupation was found have been by tent dwellers – a previously nomadic people. Part of the area was rebuilt again as a fortified city in the tenth century BC, and distinctive artefacts, such as beads, show this to have been the work of the Israelites.

Dr Yadin was satisfied that the discoveries at Hazor matched the biblical account of Joshua's conquest in a number of ways. The conquerors had razed the city to the ground, just as the Bible says; they had attempted to destroy the cultic practices of the Canaanites, as we are told God charged the Israelites to do; and they had been a nomadic people just as the Israelites had recently been. He was certain that the Israelites had occupied the area from the time of the burning, but had not had the power or motivation to rebuild the city until the creation of the unified kingdom after the time of David.

Although there is much difference in opinion as to how structured their civilization was, there is little doubt that the Israelites – or at least the people who would later form the kingdoms of Israel and Judah – were in Canaan as a distinct culture by around 1250 BC. According to the Old Testament, the period between Joshua's campaigns and the establishment of the united kingdom of Israel by David was the age of the Judges, when the Israelites existed as twelve tribes who were constantly fighting the Philistines. Historically this would seem to reflect the period between 1200 and 1000 BC when both the Philistines and the Israelites (among others) were struggling for possession of Canaan. This is known from Egyptian and Hittite sources to have been a time of considerable upheaval, when both the Egyptian and Hittite empires were collapsing. The golden age that linked Canaan to Egypt ended with the collapse of the trade routes, which in turn resulted in the collapse of the city states. It seems that in many ways it was a period similar to the European Dark Ages after the collapse of the Roman Empire. Britain, for instance, descended into virtual anarchy, allowing the Anglo-Saxons from Scandinavia and northern Germany gradually to take over the country. Today most archaeologists agree that after the upheavals of the twelfth and eleventh centuries BC, the kingdom of Israel emerged.

As the age of Judges – as described in the Book of Judges – seems to reflect historical events, then perhaps the same is true of Joshua. If he did exist, then, from the archaeological perspective, he would seem to have entered Canaan sometime around 1250 BC. Accordingly, if there is any historical truth reflected in the biblical account of the forty years previously spent in the wilderness, then the Israelites must have been in Egypt until around 1300 BC – the end of the eighteenth dynasty and the period of Horemheb. This is certainly interesting: Horemheb was the pharaoh who instigated the anti-Atenist reprisals. As the Bible seems to reflect some evidence of an Atenist element among the Hebrews when they left Egypt (see Chapter Seven), it may be that both groups were forced to flee Egypt at the same time, and for similar reasons: persecution under Horemheb. We shall return to this question later. For the moment, however, we still have no real historical evidence – outside the Bible – that the Israelites were ever in Egypt. We must, therefore, start at the begining. How and when does the Bible tell us the Israelites arrived in Egypt?

After the account of the Creation, the expulsion of Adam and Eve from Eden and the great flood, we come to the first of God's chosen people – Abraham. When Abraham's father dies God speaks to Abraham and tells him to move from his home at Haran, high on the Euphrates, and settle in the Promised Land of Canaan. According to Genesis 12:7, God tells Abraham: 'Unto thy seed will I give this land.' Canaan, therefore, is seen right from the beginning as the Israelites' true home. The name Israelite emerges with Abraham's grandson, Jacob, whom God renames Israel. According to Genesis 35:10, God tells Jacob, 'Thy name shall not be called any more Jacob, but Israel shall be thy name.' It was from Jacob that all the Hebrews later held captive in Egypt are said to descend. Hence the term children of Israel or the Israelites.

The Genesis account of how the Israelites came to be in Egypt begins with the famous story of Joseph and his 'coat of many colours'. Joseph is a younger son of Jacob, whose ten elder brothers grow jealous of him because he becomes their father's favourite. Eventually they come to detest him when he develops prophetic powers and tells them of a dream in which he sees them paying him homage. One day the brothers seize Joseph, stripped him of his 'coat of many colours', with which Jacob has honoured him, and sell him for twenty pieces of silver to a caravan of traders heading for Egypt.

In Egypt, Joseph is sold to an official who soon promotes him to the position of overseer of his household. Eventually, when the official's wife tries to seduce Joseph and he refuses her, she falsely accuses him of trying to seduce *her* and he is thrown into prison. In prison he developed a reputation as an interpreter of dreams, and when the pharaoh himself is disturbed by a series of strange dreams, Joseph is summoned to tell him what they mean. Joseph tells the pharaoh that his dreams predict a period of seven years of abundance in Egypt, followed by seven years of famine. He therefore advises the pharaoh to appoint someone to oversee the gathering of stockpiles of food to tide the country over the lean years that are to follow. The grateful pharaoh accepts Joseph's interpretation and appoints him as the grand vizier, or chief minister, to supervise the seven-year plan.

Eventually, when the famine occurs as predicted, it affects Canaan too, and Jacob sends his sons down to Egypt to buy corn. When they appear before the chief minister to beg for help, they do not recognize him as their grown brother Joseph. He, however, recognizes them and makes them humble themselves before him – just as his dream had once foretold. Ultimately, he reveals his true identity, forgives them and sends for his father. The entire family then settles in Egypt and are raised to high estate. Over the following centuries the descendants of Jacob – the children of Israel – remain in Egypt, their numbers continuing to grow until they are thousands.

Historically, the Israelites belonged to a large group of Asiatic people collectively called Semites, and Semite trading journeys into Egypt, as described in the Joseph story, did occur as early as early as the nineteenth century BC. A wall painting in the tomb of the nobleman Khnumhotep, at Beni-Hassan 322 kilometres south of Cairo, shows a group of thirty-seven Semites with laden donkeys entering Egypt at a border post where they are met by frontier officials. Described as traders, they are depicted wearing colourful striped garments which some biblical commentators once associated with Joseph's 'coat of many colours', as described in Genesis 37:3. More recent textual studies, however, have shown that this familiar phrase from the King James version of the Bible is another example of a mistranslation – the original Hebrew phrase seems to have meant 'a long, sleeved robe'. In any event, it would seem unlikely that these first Semite traders had any link with the Joseph story. There is no evidence of these early Semites ever having settled in Egypt: certainly not in any great numbers. Besides which, as the painting dates from around 1890 BC, it seems to be far too early for the Genesis account of Joseph.

Exodus 12:40 tells us that the Sojourn – the period that the children of Israel spent in Egypt before the Exodus – was 430 years. As we have seen, if the Exodus did occur it must have been somewhere around 1300 BC – about half a century before the destruction of Hazor and the first archaeological appearance of the Israelites in Canaan. If the Joseph story in any way reflects historical events, it would therefore need to be set around the eighteenth century BC. The peoples who occupied much of Canaan at this time were the Hyksos, a people who seem originally to have come from the Mesopotamian kingdom of Mari. The site of the city of Mari lies on the west bank of the Euphrates, just inside Syria on a hill called Tell Hariri (about twenty kilometres north of what is now the Iraq boarder). In 1933 a team of French archaeologists, led by Professor André Parrot, began excavating the site. Here they discovered a splendid royal palace dating from around 2000 BC, which had more than 300 rooms, richly furbished with statues and frescoes. Since 1933, the Mari excavations have unearthed thousands of inscribed clay tablets which provide valuable information about the history of the Mari kingdom and its vassal states.

The Mari kingdom was invaded by the Babylonians around 1750 BC, and its capital taken and destroyed. With the overthrow of the kingdom, many of the various peoples previously under its sway migrated south into Canaan, and within about a hundred years they had formed themselves into an effective alliance of tribes with considerable military muscle – enough, in fact, to invade northern Egypt. The Egyptians at the time refer to the tribal chiefs of these people as *Hikau khasut* – 'rulers of the desert uplands' – a term which the Graeco-Egyptian historian Manetho later rendered as Hyksos – 'desert princes'. *Hikau khasut* seems to have been the term the Egyptians used for the chieftains of the city states which the migrant Mari people had established in Canaan. City states is actually a misleading term – they were in fact fortified Bronze Age hilltop enclosures, from where a regional warlord could dominate the

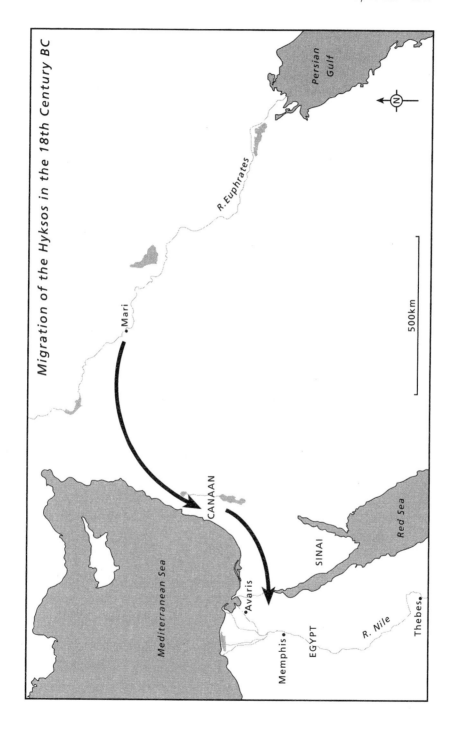

Migration of the Hyksos in the 18th Century BC

immediate countryside. To save confusion, the word Hyksos is now generally used to describe all these peoples, but what they actually called themselves is unknown. It is doubtful whether they had any one name, as they existed as separate tribal groups.

The first of the Hyksos in Egyptian records appear shortly after the collapse of the Mari kingdom. Unlike the previous Semitic traders, these people seem to have been settling in the country. A text dating from around 1745 BC, for instance, in the reign of the pharaoh Sobekhotep III (now in the Brooklyn Museum), contains a list of seventy-nine household servants, of which forty-five seem to be Hyksos. Over the next half century, increasing numbers of Hyksos continued to settle in the Nile Delta, where the authority of the ailing Middle Kingdom pharaohs was weak, and within a further fifty years they had set up their own rival kingdom in the area. For the next century, the Hyksos would rule northern Egypt. According to Manetho, writing in the late fourth century BC, the Hyksos came to power through a fierce and bloody invasion, but modern scholars tend to discount the invasion theory in favour of a steady build-up of power from within.

Were the Hebrews the Hyksos? Or at least one of the tribes which the Hyksos comprised? It certainly appears to sit with the story of Jacob's family settling in Egypt, attaining an exalted position and ultimately growing in number. According to Exodus 1:7, 'The children of Israel were fruitful and increased abundantly, and multiplied, and waxed exceedingly mighty; and the land was filled with them.' Then in verse 9, the pharaoh says to his people: 'Behold, the people of the children of Israel are more and mightier than we.' There is only one historical period when any Semites were so mighty and numerous within the boarders of ancient Egypt, and that was during the Hyksos era. Perhaps the family of Jacob represent an influential Hyksos tribe of this time. The words used by the pharaoh in verse 9 appear to suggest just this: he refers to the threat coming from the *people* of the children of Israel, seemingly implying that the Israelites were part of a larger group over which they held sway.

The Bible tells us that Joseph was appointed the pharaoh's grand vizier. It is certainly feasible, indeed almost certain, that the Hyksos rulers of northern Egypt appointed as their chief ministers those of Canaanite extraction – after all, they were from Canaan themselves. It is also a period from which few records survive, meaning that someone like Joseph could have gone unrecorded. The story would further sit with the Genesis account, as the Hyksos rulers did see themselves as pharaohs. (Although the term pharaoh did not emerge until the New Kingdom, the word is generally used to refer to a specifically Egyptian style of king.) According to Manetho, the Hyksos not only ruled Lower Egypt, they emulated the Egyptians and established their own pharaonic dynasty. This is demonstrated by archaeological evidence which has unearthed their royal palace.

The Hyksos kings established their capital in the Nile Delta at the city of Avaris where, Manetho tells us, they installed a garrison of 240,000 men. Until recently Avaris was thought to have been the Egyptian city of Tanis, near the modern fishing village of San el-Hagar. Today, however, Egyptologists have identified it as a site thirty kilometres to the south, at Tell-el-Daba. Recent excavations by the Austrian archaeologist Dr Manfred Bietak, of Vienna University, have revealed four distinct levels, three of them certainly levels of occupation: a Middle Kingdom layer; a layer that is distinctly Semitic and culturally associated with Canaan, dating from around 1650 to 1550 BC; a period of abandonment and relative inactivity; and a level of extensive rebuilding from around 1300 BC. The ruins and artefacts unearthed at Tell-el-Daba clearly demonstrate that the Hyksos rulers lived as Egyptian-style kings and not as the 'desert princes' they had once been. These must have been the five so-called fifteenth-dynasty kings of Lower Egypt mentioned by Manetho, and the two mysterious sixteenth-dynasty pharaohs, also seemingly of Hyksos origin, whose names have been found on scarabs discovered in both Egypt and Palestine. These dynasties co-existed with the seventeenth dynasty of the Egyptians proper in Thebes: the Theban princes who continued to rule unoccupied Upper Egypt.

If there is any truth in the biblical account of the Descent (the Israelite arrival in Egypt), it must have been one of the Hyksos pharaohs who raised the family of Jacob to high status and appointed Joseph as his chief minister. Not only are the Hyksos the only pharaohs of the time who would actually have done such a thing, but Avaris is precisely where the Bible places the Israelites. It was in a region later known as Goshen, and it is in the 'Land of Goshen' that the Bible tells us the Israelites had settled. Moreover, Avaris was later reconstructed as the city of Pi-Ramesses – the very city that the Hebrews are said to have been used as slaves to help build (see Chapter Eleven).

Remarkably, one of the sixteenth-dynasty Hyksos pharaohs was called Yakob-aam, a name in which a number of biblical scholars have seen a striking similarity to the Hebrew name Jacob, which Israelites, certainly later, had used. (The English J represents a Y-sound in Hebrew). As Yakob-aam seems to have been one of the last Hyksos kings, it may be that by the time that the Egyptians retook the north, the Israelites were actually the ruling faction among the Hyksos. This might explain the pharaoh's remark, 'the people of the children of Israel are more and mightier than we'. It might also explain why, according to the Bible, they were so harshly treated – they were the Hyksos' leaders.

If the Joseph story is in any way true, and he did arrive during the period of a Hyksos king, it would make it a little later than the period derived from the 430-year-Sojourn reference in Exodus 12:40. However, one has to be careful when it come to precise biblical numbers, as we have already seen with the references to Abraham's father's age. On balance, however, there is certainly enough evidence to accept that the early Israelites did settle in Egypt during the Hyksos era.

We now come to the enslavement of the Israelites. According to Exodus 1:8–11:

> Now there arose a new king over Egypt which knew not Joseph. And he said unto his people, Behold, the people of the children of Israel are more and mightier than we. Come on, let us deal wisely with them; lest they multiply, and it come to pass that, when there falleth out any war, they join also unto our enemies, and fight against us, and so get them up out of the land. Therefore they did set over them taskmasters to afflict them with their burdens. And they built for Pharaoh treasure cities, Pithom and Raamses [the historical Pi-Ramesses, previously Avaris].

This is clearly many generations after Joseph's time, as we can infer from the immediately preceding verse: 'And the children of Israel were fruitful, and increased abundantly, and multiplied, and waxed exceedingly mighty; and the land was filled with them.' (Exodus 1:7.) It is very possible that the biblical enslavement of the Israelites reflects the historical period when the Egyptian pharaohs of the south – the seventeenth-dynasty

Theban kings – eventually overcame the Hyksos pharaohs of the north.

During the Hyksos period Upper Egypt had been governed by a line of native Egyptian princes from the ancient capital of Thebes. For well over a century Upper Egypt, although a free state, had been a vassal state of the Hyksos. This was due to the superior military might of the Hyksos. While the Egyptians had old-fashioned solid wood bows, and had been somewhat backward in metallurgy for the manufacture of such weapons as swords, shields and battleaxes, the Hyksos had the much more powerful composite bow and weapons of a superior construction. Most of all they had employed the revolutionary innovation of the horse-drawn chariot.

In Thebes the Egyptian monarchy ultimately devised plans for reconquest of the north, by adapting and even improving the very weaponry by which they were being held in submission. The composite bow was a difficult weapon to make. Many of its raw materials – such as wood from birch trees and the tendons from a certain breed of bull – were not to be found in the south of Egypt. Even when these were obtained, and the techniques mastered to construct the weapon, considerable time would need to be spent practising the skills to use the new bow. Chariot warfare, on the other hand, was a completely new concept. It required numerous horses, the main supply coming from the north-east of Canaan. Some had to be captured, brought back, then bred and their offspring ultimately trained, while the soldiery had to be taught to drive and fight from chariots. Somehow, and quite remarkably, the Theban kings managed to organize all of this – and right under the noses of the Hyksos. Relatively speaking, the espionage missions and covert activities involved must surely have been as complex and elaborate as anything dreamed up by the modern CIA. The result of the Egyptian effort was a new, professional army, the likes of which Egypt had never known before.

The first Theban king to lead the offensive against the Hyksos was Seqenenre II, around 1570 BC, who apparently revolted against a provocative command from Avaris. Although the Hyksos suffered, the revolt failed to defeat them and Seqenenre was killed. His mummified body, found in 1881, shows that he had five sword wounds on the neck and head, indicating that he had literally been hacked to death. His son and successor, Kamose, launched a full-scale attack on the Hyksos king Apophis, and drove him back to the walls of Avaris. The account of his campaign was discovered in 1954, on a limestone stela from the Temple of Amon-Re at Karnak. Kamose's mother Queen Ahhotep, we are told, took an active part in rallying the people in the struggle and was awarded military honours. According to an account of the struggle found in the tomb of a ship's captain named Ahmose at el-Kab, just to the north of Aswan, Kamose's younger brother and successor, Amosis, kept up the pressure; he laid siege to Avaris itself, which fell sometime around 1550 BC, and pursued the defeated Hyksos into Canaan. Under Amosis, as Amosis I, Egypt was reunified under Egyptian rule – the start of the eighteenth dynasty and the beginning of the New Kingdom.

That many of the Hyksos were enslaved there can be no doubt. The inscriptions in the tomb of Ahmose make this very clear. Indeed, many of the Hyksos that retreated into Canaan were ultimately pursued and taken prisoner. Under a series of eighteenth-dynasty pharaohs, Egyptian armies repeatedly swept through Canaan, laying waste the city states. Tuthmosis III, the most formidable campaigner, finally crushed the dispossessed Hyksos at the decisive battle of Megiddo, a strongly fortified town overlooking the Plain of Esdraelon, and completely invaded Canaan. The account of this crucial campaign, which brought Egypt to the zenith of her power, was discovered on the one of the pylons (the so-called Seventh Pylon) erected in the Temple of Amun-Re at Karnak.

Let us return to the Biblical account of the enslavement of the Israelites: in the popular misconception, portrayed by Hollywood, the Israelites, unlike the Hyksos, never fight against the Egyptians. However, Exodus 1:10 suggests that they did. The pharaoh is concerned that, 'they join also unto our enemies, and fight against us'. Historically, the Hyksos made an alliance with the Nubians of Kush, to the south of Thebes, in order to contain the kings of Upper Egypt. The account of the king who 'knew not Joseph' , therefore, and decided to do something about the Israelites, could well refer to Kamose and his attack on Avaris.

Precisely when the Israelites themselves might have been enslaved is difficult to answer, but it may have been once the Hyksos city states had been overrun. Although biblical scholars have tended to think of the 'king over Egypt, which knew not Joseph' of Exodus 1:8 as the same character as the 'Pharaoh' who sets taskmasters over them in Exodus 1:11, this is not made clear in the narrative itself. The Pentateuch were religious texts and long periods of history, being considered irrelevant, are forever being condensed into a few verses or even words.

From various eighteenth-dynasty tomb illustrations, it is clear that the number of Hyksos slaves rose dramatically by the reign of Tuthmosis III. In the tomb of Tuthmosis III's vizier Rekhmire at Thebes, for instance, there is a scene showing Hyksos slaves making bricks, while taskmasters stand over them, beating rods in hand. According to Exodus, this is precisely the fate of the Israelites. In Exodus 1:11: 'So they were made to work in gangs, with officers set over them, to break their spirit with heavy labour.' And in Exodus 1: 14: 'And they made their lives bitter with hard bondage, in mortar, and in brick.' (A number of bodies from Egyptian graves of the era have been found with a broken left forearm, prompting speculation that the individuals sustained such fractures when they tried to protect themselves against a blow from a weapon such as the beating rods shown in the tomb illustrations.)

There is even evidence of a people who may actually have been the Israelites being prominent among the Hyksos slaves. They are specifically referred to as *Apiru* – also rendered as *Hapiru* or *Habiru* by some translators – a name which some scholars believe to have been the origin of the word Hebrew. There are a number of scenes and textural references which include them during and after the reign of Tuthmosis III:

- *Circa* 1500 BC: The oldest reference to the *Apiru* is on a scene from the tomb of Tuthmosis III's great herald Antef, which lists them among the prisoners of war captured during the pharaoh's campaigns.

- *Circa* 1475 BC: A scene on the tomb of the noble Puyemre at Thebes, dating from the reign of Tuthmosis III, shows four men working a wine press and accompanying hieroglyphics read 'straining out wine by the *Apiru*'. It is accompanied by another inscription telling us of the location: 'wine of the vineyard of War-Hor'. This was in the very area which was later called Goshen.

- *Circa* 1430 BC: A list of foreign captives found on an inscribed stela discovered at Memphis, dating from the reign of Amonhotep II, includes 3600 *Apiru*.

- *Circa* 1305 BC: In the reign of Seti I, the *Apiru* are referenced in connection with a revolt at Beisham in Palestine.

- *Circa* 1270 BC: The Leyde Papyrus, concerning the reign of Ramesses II, mentions the *Apiru* being used as hard labour to erect a pylon at Memphis.

- *Circa* 1270 BC: In the reign of Ramesses II the *Apiru* are recorded being used to make bricks at Miour in the province of Fayum.

- *Circa* 1180 BC: During the reign of Ramesses III the *Apiru* are listed working on land sacred to the god Atum at Heliopolis.

- *Circa* 1180 BC: The last mention of the *Apiru* is in the reign of Ramesses III when they are listed as quarrymen.

Although it has been suggested that the term *Apiru* was used to refer to a particular type of workmen, prisoner of war or class of slave, this would seem unlikely. Similar workers are shown time and time again throughout the eighteenth and nineteenth dynasties, without being referred to by any name other than captives, foreigners or slaves. The only distinctions usually made are by words such as *fa-kat* – 'workers' – or *yus* – 'builders'. In fact the word *Apiru* almost certainly refers to a specific Hyksos tribe, as a very similar name is recorded in the texts found at Mari. Here a tribe whom the Mari king Zimri-Lim had some difficulty in controlling are called the *Habiru*.

The word Hebrew actually means 'one from the other side of the river', and seems to have been derived from a word by which foreigners called the Israelites. Hebrew is very seldom a word that the ancient Israelites use to describe themselves. Apart from the fact that the very term, 'one from the other side of the river', appears to be someone else's description of them, in the Bible itself it is usually others who use the word Hebrew, or it is for their benefit that the term is employed.

In the First Book of Samuel 29:3, for example, it is the Philistines who call them by this name: 'Then said the princes of the Philistines, What do these Hebrews here?' Another example is in Exodus 1:19. Here the Israelite midwives are talking to a foreigner when they explain their actions to the pharaoh: 'And the midwives said unto Pharaoh, Because the Hebrew women are not as Egyptian women.'

Perhaps the most telling example is found in Exodus 5 :1–3, where the pharaoh would seem to be unfamiliar with the term Israel:

> And afterwards Moses and Aaron went in, and told the pharaoh, Thus saith the Lord God of Israel, Let my people go, that they may hold a feast unto me in the wilderness. And the pharaoh said, Who is the Lord, that I should obey his voice to let Israel go? I know not the Lord, neither will I let Israel go. And they said, The God of the Hebrews hath met with us.

Here it is for pharaoh's benefit that God is being referred to as the 'God of the Hebrews', as he seems to have no understanding of the term 'God of Israel'. In other words, to themselves they are the children of Israel, to others they are the Hebrews.

The only problem in connecting the *Apiru* with the Hebrews is that they are still in Egypt around 1180 BC, which seems to have been over a century after the most likely period of the Exodus. However, the later references may refer to new captives. From the reference on the Israel Stela, we learn that Merenptah had recently sent troops to fight the Israelites around 1220 BC, and was seemingly victorious. If so, he would presumably have returned with a fresh supply of Hebrew slaves. The last mention of the *Apiru* pre-dating Merenptah's reign is around 1270, when they are recorded making bricks during the reign of Ramesses II. This is precisely the time that most biblical scholars actually place the Exodus (see Chapter Eleven).

The biblical account itself certainly does not contradict the theory that the Exodus took place in the early thirteenth century BC. The story of the Exodus proper begins with the birth of Moses who, according to the account, is born at a time when the pharaoh, in an attempt to check the population of Israelite slaves, ordered that every male child born to them should be killed. Moses' mother, to save him from his fate, hides Moses in a basket in the reeds of the river bank, where the infant is found by the pharaoh's daughter and brought up as her son at the royal court. Although the popular Hollywood image has the pharaoh of Moses' time being the same pharaoh who enslaved the Israelites, it seems clear from the Biblical account that a period of at least a generation, probably far more, separates the two. According to Exodus 1:12, the following separates the original enslavement of the Israelites from the birth of Moses: 'But the more that they [the Egyptians] afflicted them [the children of Israel] the more they multiplied and grew...' This is clearly a considerable period of time. The enslavement could therefore first have occurred during the time of Tuthmosis III (*circa* 1500 BC), and the Exodus from Egypt occurred much later in the reign of Ramesses II (*circa* 1270 BC) – shortly after the anti-Atenist persecutions of Horemheb.

We will return to the question of the Exodus later. For the moment we must reach a conclusion regarding the Israelite presence in Egypt. From the assorted evidence we have examined, it would seem that the Biblical account of the Israelite period in Egypt is probably correct – certainly in outline. In other words, the direct ancestors of the Israelites who historically appeared in Canaan in the thirteenth century BC had for many years been used as slaves in Egypt. In conclusion, it would seem that they were a tribal group known as the *Apiru*, or Hebrews, who were an influential people among the Hyksos who settled in Egypt around 1700 BC. They could certainly have reached high office during the Hyksos era, have been appointed chief ministers, and may even have been pharaohs themselves – namely the sixteenth dynasty. They were ousted from power along with the Hyksos around 1570 BC, and had been enslaved by the reign of Tuthmosis III around 1500 BC. Thereafter, they had been used as hard labour, principally in northern Egypt, by a successor of pharaohs until the early thirteenth century BC. (Nearly all the above references to the *Apiru* are from northern Egypt.)

Just prior to Akhenaten's reign (*circa* 1360 BC), therefore, the Israelites certainly seem to have been present in Egypt to have influenced the young king. Moreover, they seem to have been in northern Egypt, around the area of Heliopolis – precisely the location from where Akhenaten seems to have been influenced (see Chapter Seven). The big question, however, is why? Why should the most powerful man in Egypt, and seemingly thousands of others like him, abandon their centuries-old beliefs in favour of a foreign religious concept? How could they have been influenced by the religion of enemy slaves?

SUMMARY

- In the biblical account, the Israelites spend 430 years in Egypt before the Exodus. They are originally made welcome by a pharaoh during Joseph's time, but later, concerned by their growing numbers, the Egyptians enslave them. Eventually, Moses is called by God to lead them out of Egypt and, after the country is beset by a series of plagues and terrible deaths, the pharaoh begrudgingly lets them leave. Suffering a change of heart, he then pursues the Israelites, who manage to escape when the waters of the Red Sea miraculously part. Finally, after wandering for forty years in the wilderness, they are led by Joshua into the 'Promised Land' of Canaan.

- The Bible provides no dates and fails to name the pharaohs in question. However, archaeological evidence has shown that the Israelites did exist and had settled in Canaan – an area which included modern Israel, Palestine and the Lebanon – by around 1250 BC.

- According to the Book of Genesis the Israelites first arrive in Egypt from Canaan when the Patriarch Joseph is made chief minister by the pharaoh and he settles his family in the kingdom. Over the following centuries their descendants remain in Egypt, their numbers continuing to grow until they are thousands. If the Joseph story in any way reflects historical events, it would need to be set around 1750 BC.

- The peoples who occupied much of Canaan at this time were called the Hyksos. Around 1750 BC they began to settle in northern Egypt and within fifty years they had set up their own rival kingdom in the area with their capital at Avaris. It is certainly feasible, indeed almost certain, that the Hyksos rulers of northern Egypt appointed as their chief ministers those of Canaanite extraction. The story would further sit with the Genesis account, as the Hyksos rulers did see themselves as pharaohs.

- Not only are the Hyksos the only pharaohs of the time who would actually have raised an Israelite faction to high status, but Avaris is precisely where the Bible places the Israelites.

- It is very possible that the biblical enslavement of the Israelites reflects the historical period when the Egyptian pharaohs of the south – the seventeenth-dynasty Theban kings – eventually overcame the Hyksos pharaohs of the north. Many of the Hyksos were enslaved.

- There is evidence of a people who may actually have been the Israelites being prominent among the Hyksos slaves. They are specifically referred to as *Apiru* – also rendered as *Hapiru* or *Habiru* by some translators – a name which many scholars believe to have been the origin of the word Hebrew.

Cataclysm

Around 1350 BC Egypt is at the height of her power and Amonhotep III is on the throne. His great-grandfather Tuthmosis III has laid the foundations of the largest empire the world has yet seen and the land of Egypt is now filled with abundance. Amonhotep has erected great buildings and monuments in cities throughout the kingdom, all of them notable for their affluence and exceptional quality of design. In Thebes, he has built his enormous Malkata palace, as splendid as any before, and he has glorified Amun-Re in gratitude for his country's fortunes. He has embellished the already massive temple at Karnak, and at Luxor he even builds a new temple to the mighty god. As much as any pharaoh, Amonhotep is worshipped by his people. Images of him stand proud in temples at Memphis, Hierakonpolis and Thebes, and in the temple of Sulb Amonhotep is even depicted adoring his own image.

Here is an Egypt stronger and more prosperous then ever before: a land with Amun-Re firmly entrenched as supreme deity, and with a pharaoh who is immensely rich, powerful and confident. Then, all of a sudden, when he still has years of life left in him, the mighty Amonhotep relinquishes his power, retreats from public life and Akhenaten is appointed as senior co-regent. Moreover, the impeccable state religion is totally abandoned and an altogether new type of god is installed as principle deity. What on earth has happened?

One would expect such fundamental changes, particularly religious ones, to follow some terrible calamity or period of upheaval. The phenomenal spread of Christianity in the second half of the first century, for example, followed the destruction of the Jerusalem temple and the virtual annihilation of Judea, and the rise of Islam throughout the Middle East in the seventh century followed the collapse of the Roman Empire. Yet even these events did not happen overnight. The peculiar events surrounding the inception of Atenism appear to suggest some very unusual – perhaps unprecedented – set of events. It is not only that Akhenaten himself had been possessed by such radical notions, but that Egypt's population at large seems to have accepted them.

We can gather from the fact that Horemheb did not later expunge Amonhotep's name from the list of kings, and even claimed him as his predecessor, that Amonhotep had never personally sanctioned Atenism. We have also seen how Amonhotep seems to have lived on for some considerable time as co-regent. If Akhenaten had not enjoyed wide support, any dissenters could easily have rallied around Amonhotep resulting in civil strife; yet all the evidence points to the contrary. The country is actually stable enough for Akhenaten to remove himself and his court to a remote location, seemingly without any fear of revolt. All this suggests that virtually everyone was prepared to go along with Akhenaten's peculiar ideas – including the old king himself, who actually moved aside to make way for his son. Egypt shows all the signs of a country shocked into silence. Surely there must be some evidence that something quite extraordinary had recently occurred.

For someone so completely devoted to Amun-Re, Amonhotep does something very strange towards the end of his independent reign: he erects literally hundreds of statues to another deity – the goddess Sekhmet. At Asher, half a kilometre to the south of the Temple of Amun, Amonhotep was in the process of rebuilding a temple to the chief goddess Mut, when he suddenly reconsecrated it as a temple to Sekhmet. Furthermore, he decreed that Sekhmet should be assimilated with Mut, effectively making her the principal goddess. So many statues did he erect of Sekhmet, here and elsewhere, that nearly every Egyptological collection in the world can boast at least one example. The British Museum has the largest number: over thirty specimens in various states of preservation. Hundreds still remain *in situ* in Egypt, the majority being at the temple of Luxor. It has been estimated that there were around 700 at the temple of Mut alone. In fact, no other deity of ancient Egypt is represented by so many large-scale statues – and nearly all of them were erected by order of Amonhotep III. These statues of Sekhmet are a clear indication that, despite the apparent stability and wealth of the country, something was wrong. Sekhmet was the goddess of devastation!

Sekhmet was represented as a lioness or a woman with a lion's head. She was the daughter of Re who, in Egyptian mythology, had once almost annihilated mankind. They were only saved through Re's personal intervention. Called the 'mighty one', Sekhmet was a fierce goddess of war and strife who brought destruction to the enemy. In tomb scenes, she is depicted spitting flames and a fiery glow emanates from her body; the hot desert winds were even regarded as her breath. She was seen as the *udjat* – 'The Eye of Re' – representing the scorching, destructive power of the sun.

Why these monumental statues of the goddess exist in such unrivalled numbers has never been satisfactorily explained. The fact that Amonhotep erected more statues to her, by far, than he did to Amun-Re suggests that something had occurred to make him question the power of the chief god. Akhenaten acted in the same way by establishing the Aten as supreme, and ultimately the only, deity. On one of the Sekhmet statues in the British Museum Amonhotep even describes himself with the epithet 'Beloved of Sekhmet', as Akhenaten would later describe himself as 'Beloved of the Aten'. Surely something had afflicted the country: Amonhotep considering it to have been caused by Sekhmet, Akhenaten seeing it as the influence of an altogether new type of god, the Aten.

Sekhmet and the Aten have something which may be very indicative in common: they were both solar deities. Had there occurred some pernicious episode in some way associated with the sun? As both kings had chosen fairly obscure – and particularly unusual – deities to appease, it would seem to suggest a somewhat unique set of circumstances: drought, an intense heat wave, or other such solar-related conditions would be relatively commonplace in the desert belt, and there is no evidence that the ancient Egyptians had previously, or since, behaved in such an unusual manner.

There are only a limited number of things that can have happened to the sun. Most, such as solar flares and sunspot activity, would not be visible to the naked eye. Even if such phenomena did cause adverse effects on earth, there is no way the ancient Egyptians could have linked them together. If something strange had – from the earthbound perspective – happened to the sun, there is only one realistic possibility: something had obscured it. There had been a partial eclipse visible from Egypt in the 1370s BC, but it is doubtful that this would explain such drastic and long-term reactions by the Egyptians. After all, if Amonhotep had originally considered the phenomenon the work of Sekhmet, and had enough time to build the statues, then, as the eclipse had not heralded the end of the sun, he and others would have seen his actions as having been successful. The goddess would have been appeased, and there would have been no support for Akhenaten's introduction of Atenism – a cult that endured as the state religion for well over a decade. Besides, Egypt had witnessed many eclipses which, although being regarded as indicative celestial events, were not seen as omens of catastrophe. If some strange phenomenon had occurred, it would have to have been either longer-term, unprecedented, or far more spectacular.

The remaining possibility is that the sun's light had been dimmed, or its appearance altered, due to atmospheric contaminants. This could be caused by such phenomena as an intense meteorite shower, an asteroid or comet impact, or a massive volcanic eruption. Airborne debris from such events – particles of dust thrown high into the stratosphere – can in some circumstances contaminate the atmosphere of the entire globe. The asteroid collision believed to have wiped out the dinosaurs 65 million years ago is thought to have thrown up enough material to have darkened the skies the world over. Something less life-threatening, but equally dramatic, can result from volcanic activity. In 1980, for example, when the volcano of Mount St Helens erupted in America, there were green sunsets reported months afterwards as far away as Russia. Had such a rare solar phenomenon happened during Amonhotep's reign?

There is compelling evidence that a gigantic volcanic eruption did occur in the Mediterranean around the time of Amonhotep's reign. Every winter a fresh layer of ice forms on the Greenland ice cap, creating clearly defined strata, one for each year. Every layer contains trapped air, holding a sample of the earth's atmosphere as it was when the ice formed. In the

1970s Danish geophysicists began taking core samples many metres down into the ice, so as to recover a year-by-year record of the earth's atmospheric conditions going back some 100,000 years. The team, led by Drs C.U. Clausen, H.B. Hammer and W. Dansgard, soon observed that from years when there had been major volcanic eruptions, such as the one that destroyed Roman Pompeii in AD 79, the samples evidenced high levels of acidity. In an article in *Nature* magazine in November 1980, the team reported that there had been a massive eruption somewhere in the world around 1390 BC, with a margin of error of some fifty years either way. This might indeed have coincided with the reign of Amonhotep III (*circa* 1389–1352 BC).

The only eruption large enough to have resulted in the atmospheric conditions recorded by the Danes, and known by geologists to have occurred within 200 years either side of this date, was a gigantic eruption on the Aegean island of Thera. Although, at the time, this seemed to place the eruption around a hundred years after it was previously thought to have occurred, more recent radiocarbon tests from Thera have tended to support the findings (see Appendix). However, even if Thera *had* erupted during Amonhotep's reign, would it have had any significant, or observable effects in Egypt?

Thera (also called Santorini) was the southernmost of the Greek Cyclades islands, and in the fifteenth century BC it had supported an important trading port of the Minoan civilization. Today Thera is a crescent-shaped island forming a bay almost ten kilometres across, and the cliffs surrounding it are ribboned with layers of volcanic debris and once-molten rock, testifying to the island's violent past. The bay itself is actually a crater formed by the ancient eruption, and it is so deep that no ship's anchor reaches the bottom. In the 1930s, the Greek archaeologist Spyridon Marinatos was the first to propose that at some

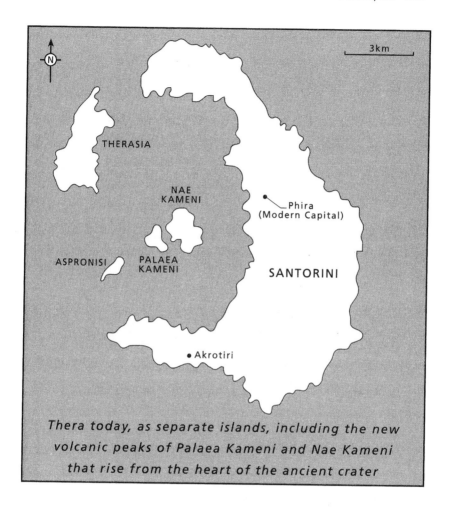

Thera today, as separate islands, including the new volcanic peaks of Palaea Kameni and Nae Kameni that rise from the heart of the ancient crater

point towards the end of the Minoan period a gigantic volcanic eruption had all but destroyed the island, and in 1956 two geologists, Dragoslav Ninkovich and Bruce Heezen of Columbia University USA, conducted a survey of the sea bed to try to determine precisely how large the eruption had been. From their survey ship, the *Vema,* they were able to determine the exact size of the volcanic crater – 51 square kilometres – and from this, they estimate the incredible magnitude of the event.

There are various types of volcanic eruption: some spew forth rivers of molten lava, others produce searing mud slides, but by far the most devastating is when the pressure of the magma causes the volcano literally to blow its top. Going by the resultant crater size, that is what happened at Thera almost three and a half thousand years ago. A similar eruption occurred at the volcano of Mount St Helens in Washington State in 1980, when the explosion blasted away the mountain side with the power of a fifty-megaton bomb.

The first sign of trouble came in the middle of March, when a series of earth tremors gradually grew more violent and frequent. Scientists were certain that an eruption was imminent after a series of rumbling explosions were heard to come from deep within the mountain, and searing-hot steam began to vent through cracks in the rocks. By April, a geological survey team was established in the area to keep a round-the-clock watch on an enormous 90-metre bulge that had appeared on the volcano's north slope. Even though they were prepared for an eruption, no one had anticipated the sheer magnitude of the event. The mountainside slid away exposing the molten core. When super-heated magma under sufficient pressure is exposed to air the result is an explosion of unimaginable proportions. At 8.32 on the morning of 18 May the whole mountain began to shake and one of the observers called excitedly over his radio: 'This is it!'

They were his last words. In that instant, he and forty-six others were vaporized. A mass of searing volcanic material blasted outwards, killing a further twenty-five people over twenty-two kilometres away. They too had thought themselves safe, and many of them had been photographing the event when they were killed. Every living thing in a 251-square-kilometre swath of land north-west of the volcano was utterly destroyed. Thousands of hectares of forest were flattened and molten debris covered everything like the surface of the moon. What had once been a bustling tourist resort over sixteen kilometres from the volcano was now covered entirely by volcanic material. Luckily it had been evacuated, but a nearby farmer had declined to leave his home. He had refused to believe that such a distant eruption – as far away from him as the outskirts of a major city are from its centre – could possibly affect him. His farm is still buried beneath solidified molten rock.

Within a few hours, a cloud of ash some eight kilometres high, containing billions of tons of volcanic material, had rolled 800 kilometres east. In three states – Washington, Idaho and Montana – the massive volcanic cloud covered the sky and day was turned to night. Throughout the whole area ash fell like rain, clogging motor engines, halting trains and blocking roads. Seven million hectares of lush farmland now looked like a grey desert, and millions of dollars'-worth of crops were flattened and destroyed. Hundreds of people, as far away as Billings in Montana (950 kilometres from the volcano), were taken to hospital with eye sores and skin rashes caused by exposure to the acidic fallout ash. For weeks afterwards, fishes in thousands of kilometres of rivers were found floating on the surface, killed by chemical pollutants in the water.

Mount St Helens was one of the most destructive volcanic eruptions in recent years, yet compared with the explosion of

Thera it was tiny. When Ninkovich and Heezen published their findings regarding the Thera explosion, they used the Krakatau eruption of 1883 as a comparison. In August 1883, Krakatau, a volcanic island in the Sunda Strait between Java and Sumatra, exploded with a force twenty times that of Mount St Helens. The eruption was heard over 4,800 kilometres away in Australia, a volcanic cloud rose eighty kilometres into the air, fallout ash covered thousands of square kilometres, and the resultant tidal wave reached a height of thirty metres. Over 36,000 people perished!

The first signs of trouble began in May: firstly a series of earthquakes, followed by a succession of minor eruptions. On 26 August the volcano exploded. Forty kilometres away, at Katimbang on the Sumatran coast, 3,000 people who had been evacuated from Krakatau thought they were safe. Over a thousand of them died, and as many more were seriously injured, as suffocating ash and flaming cinders descended around them, setting fire to buildings and trees. People fled in all directions as thunder and lightning raged above, the result of the tremendous turbulence inside the deadly fallout cloud. A series of further explosions continued on Krakatau for two days, creating gigantic *tsunami* – tidal waves – over thirty metres high which swept away 165 villages on the Sumatran coast. The cloud of ash covered thousands of square kilometres, and over 3,000 kilometres away in the Indian Ocean ships' decks were covered with ash and pumice. Krakatau continued to belch forth ash for days and for almost a week there was no daylight up to 800 kilometres down wind.

It has been estimated by the size of the resultant crater that 19 cubic kilometres of volcanic material blasted skywards from Krakatau – yet Thera's crater is six times bigger. Accordingly, the explosion would have been heard halfway round the world, volcanic debris would have been hurled over 100 kilometres high, and the ash fallout would have covered well over a million square kilometres. However, the most devastating phenomenon would have been massive tidal waves which thrashed the eastern Mediterranean.

The last nuclear weapon mankind used in warfare was the atom bomb that totally destroyed half the Japanese city of Nagasaki in 1945. It was a 20-kiloton explosion (the equivalent of 20,000 tons of conventional explosives). Mount St Helens exploded with a far greater force of 50,000 kilotons; Krakatau reached an incredible 1,000,000 kilotons; yet Thera dwarfs them all with a staggering 6,000,000 kilotons. It would take 6,000 of the most destructive modern nuclear warheads – each with the power to wipe out an entire city – to equal the explosive magnitude of Thera. Much of the estimated 114 cubic kilometres of debris ejected skywards would have fallen to earth, although smaller particles would remain in the atmosphere for years. The green sunsets caused by Mount St Helens would be nothing compared to the bizarre observations made by the ancients for months, even years, after the Thera eruption. (A year after Krakatau, the sun was seen to be blue all day long in some parts of the world.) Is this what had prompted the strange behaviour of Amonhotep III, Akhenaten and the Egyptian people in the mid-fourteenth century BC?

Actually, the Thera eruption may have had a direct, and far more dramatic, affect on the ancient Egyptians. It was such a enormous eruption that it seems to have decimated an entire civilization: the Minoans. The first evidence of this came to light in 1901, when the Boston archaeologist Harriet Boyd excavated Minoan remains at Gournia on the island of Crete. Crete had been the centre of the Minoan seafaring empire, and Gournia had been a thriving community in the late Minoan era. Ms Boyd was shocked by what she found: everywhere there was evidence that the last Minoans to have lived in the town had suddenly dropped everything and fled. Personal belongings and workmen's tools were found abandoned and cooking hearths still had their utensils in place as if in preparation for a meal. The cause of the panic was clear – a layer of charcoal revealed that the town had been razed by fire.

Gournia was not the only late Minoan community to suffer the same fate. In 1906, another American archaeologist, Richard Seager, excavated the Minoan port on the island of Mochlos, a couple of kilometres off the coast of Crete. He discovered that this community had also come to a sudden and violent end in the late Minoan period. As at Gournia, tools and other personal effects had been abandoned when fire swept the town. Here, however, the occupants seem to have been overwhelmed more quickly, as the charred remains of townsfolk had been found among the ruins.

Over the following decades many more Minoan sites discovered in eastern Crete revealed an almost identical picture of sudden catastrophe. For some time it was thought that the Minoan civilization had been overwhelmed by foreign invaders, who had sacked and plundered its cities: possibly the Greek Mycenaeans who had later established their own power base on Crete. However, in the 1920s, when the Greek archaeologist Stephanos Xanthoudidis uncovered the once magnificent villa of Nirou Khani, the invasion theory was discounted. Like the other sites, it had been destroyed by fire. However, at the time disaster struck it was crammed with valuable objects, such as jewellery and expensive ceramic ware, some of which had escaped the fire and lay exactly were they were left. Surely, if marauders had sacked the villa they would not have left such valuable items behind. Most indicative of all were the bronze

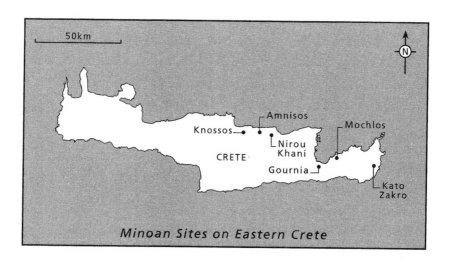

Minoan Sites on Eastern Crete

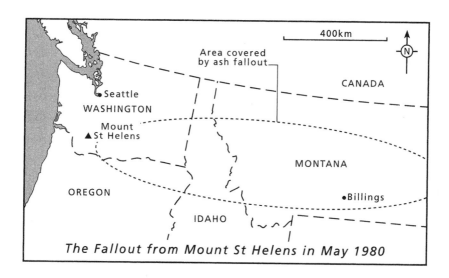

The Fallout from Mount St Helens in May 1980

battleaxes which had been left in the armoury, stacked neatly against the wall. The guards had clearly not attempted to repel a human foe.

The picture was rapidly emerging of a number of Minoan towns having been razed, simultaneously, by some type of natural disaster, and in the 1930s the respected Greek archaeologist Spyridon Marinatos found evidence for what that might have been. Excavating the site of Amnisos, once the harbour town for the capital at Knossos, he uncovered a villa whose walls had been bulged outward in a curious way. Large upright stones seemed to have been prised out of position as if by some huge external force, suggesting that they had been hit by the backwash of an enormous tidal wave. It seemed that the harbour town had been drowned by a towering wall of water, evidently the result of some tremendous seismic event.

In the 1960s another Greek archaeologist, Professor Nicholas Platon, discovered the remains of Crete's easternmost Minoan palace at Kato Zakro. Once more it had been destroyed by fire, and again precious objects had been left behind – elephant tusks, bronze ingots and exquisitely made vases, together with tools and cooking utensils – all hurriedly abandoned. Professor Platon noticed something else that was even stranger: 'Huge stones, some dressed, some not, had been hurled to a distance or had fallen and shattered, blocking passages and filling open spaces. Whole sections of the upper storey had been thrown down . . .'

Just like the evidence for a tidal wave at Amnisos, this was a clear indication of seismic upheaval. However, the disaster seemed to have been more than simply an earthquake. Professor Platon also noticed that many storage jars had been compressed and squeezed as if by the enormous pressure of an explosion, and the walls seemed to have fallen from their foundations in one piece, as if toppled by some massive external force. Moreover, the ruins were full of volcanic pumice. There could be little doubt that Kato Zakro had suffered the effects of a volcanic eruption.

As Amnisos was on the north coast of Crete, then the tidal wave that pulverized the harbour must have come from the north of the island. As Thera lay only 112 kilometres north of Crete, Spyridon Marinatos was convinced that the Thera eruption had been responsible for the ancient devastation. He turned his attentions to the island of Thera, and in 1967 discovered there the remains of Akrotiri, a Minoan town that had been completely buried beneath molten lava in the same late period as the carnage on Crete. Marinatos excavated Akrotiri for seven years, until he was tragically killed by a falling wall while working on the site in 1974. He is actually buried were he fell, and his daughter Dr Nanno Marinatos continued his work.

Akrotiri must rank as one of the most spectacular archaeological discoveries of the twentieth century. It had escaped total obliteration by the fact that it was shielded by the lower slopes of the surviving volcano. However, molten debris had smothered the town, burying it 36 metres below solid lava rock. It was only discovered because local quarrying uncovered some of its buildings. The archaeology was an enormous task; the pumice layer was ten times deeper than that which Vesuvius spewed over Roman Pompeii. As the pumice was removed slowly and laboriously, an entire Minoan town gradually came to light. It was if it had been frozen in time for three and a half thousand years. Three-storey buildings of sophisticated construction and beautifully paved streets reflected a people who were surprisingly affluent. Indeed, the distribution of wealth among the common people exceeded anything found in other contemporary civilizations, such as Egypt and Babylon. Each house even had its own water closet, which a network of clay pipes connected to a communal sewage system. It would be many centuries before the ancient Greeks would match these achievements, and even then such amenities would only be available to the privileged elite. Fresco scenes actually showed daily life in Akrotiri: the mighty Minoan ships being steered into harbour, while women and children leant from balconies, happily welcoming their menfolk home.

At first, the findings at Akrotiri seemed to contradict Marinatos' theory that the Thera eruption had been responsible for the carnage on Crete. Pottery found at Akrotiri was of a slightly earlier period than that found at the other excavations. On Crete every one of the destroyed cities had pottery classified as Late Minoan 1B, which is uniquely decorated with marine life. At Akrotiri the latest pottery found was of the period immediately proceeding it – Late Minoan 1A. From examples found all around the Aegean, it is known that Late Minoan 1B designs had been fashionable for about thirty years before disaster struck the Minoan cities on Crete. Consequently, it appeared that the Thera eruption must have occurred at least this much earlier.

Ultimately, further excavations revealed that there had been a major earthquake, or series of earthquakes, on Thera which may have led to Akrotiri being abandoned some years before the actual eruption. Collapsed walls found without pumice beneath them showed that they must have fallen during violent earth tremors before the eruption occurred. As a layer of soil had had time to build up between the earthquake debris and the first layer of pumice, the city must have been empty for some years before it was smothered by the volcano.

There was additional evidence that Akrotiri had been abandoned well before the cataclysm. At Pompeii, hundreds of people were overcome in the streets, most of them asphyxiated by searing hot ash. They still lay were they had dropped, the molten debris solidifying around them and encasing their bodies. At Akrotiri, however, no human victims of the eruption were found. Also, as the excavated houses lacked gold, silver, jewellery or anything of intrinsic value, it seems certain that the inhabitants had evacuated the city at some point between the earthquake and the eventual eruption. In 1972 Marinatos concluded that following a build-up of volcanic activity, and the resultant earthquakes, Akrotiri was abandoned. Then, some thirty years later, the massive eruption finally buried the city. Luckily for the inhabitants, it seems, by the time the volcano exploded they had long since taken to their ships and left the island.

Support for Marinatos' theory had actually emerged back in the 1950s. At this time, the geologists Ninkovich and Heezen had already concluded that the Thera eruption was responsible for the carnage on Crete. From core samples taken from the seabed, it was discovered that the layer of volcanic sediment from the Thera eruption spread across the Aegean in a south-easterly direction, bisecting Crete at the eastern end of the island. This is precisely were the burned-out towns had been uncovered. A fiery ash cloud, similar to that which rained down on Sumatra after the Krakatau eruption, must have been responsible. The affected Sumatran coast had been forty kilometres from Krakatau, and the six-fold larger eruption of Thera may have created similar conditions up to 240 kilometres away. Crete is only 112 kilometres from Thera and so must have suffered far worse – just as the archaeological evidence revealed.

The fire storm may have ravaged part of Crete and a number of other Aegean islands, but the fallout was not the greatest danger. Based on the Krakatau event, it has been estimated that a tidal wave a staggering 90 metres high would have thrashed the coast of Crete. (The *tsunami* in the immediate vicinity of the eruption would have been huge, but then it would have settled down to be only a couple of metres high, all its force deep under water. Then, when it approached shallow water, it would again have built into a mighty wave.) The towering wall of water would have lashed the densely populated north coast, sweeping through the great ports, pulverizing towns and villages – claiming countless lives.

The Minoan empire had spread throughout the Aegean islands. It had absolute supremacy over the waters of the eastern Mediterranean and as a result had grown remarkably rich. Dozens of Minoan ports must have been effected by the calamity, and hundreds of Minoan ships must have been sunk. For a civilization based on sea power, the consequences would have been disastrous. Although there is still debate as to how severely the Minoan empire was hit, there can be little doubt that the Thera cataclysm was a decisive element in the collapse of the civilization by the mid-fourteenth century BC, a time when the entire area was taken over by the Mycenaeans from mainland Greece.

One of the most dramatic and emotive discoveries to portray the last moments before disaster overwhelmed Minoan Crete was uncovered in 1979 at excavations at a temple sanctuary on Mount Euptos. Here, a ritual had been taking place before a huge statue of the chief Minoan goddess when a massive quake had collapsed the building, burying the assembly for over three thousand years. Archaeologists uncovered the remains of a young boy lying prostrate on the altar: his throat had been cut and a priest lay on the floor beside him, the offending knife still by his side. Not only does this show the ferocity of the shock waves that must have been produced by Thera – in addition to the searing fire storm and deadly *tsunami* – but it reveals that when disaster struck, the Minoans may have been attempting to appease their goddess with a human sacrifice.

Minoan writing was far less sophisticated than Egyptian hieroglyphics, and what there is of it has never been translated. Whether or not the survivors of the cataclysm ever wrote of their terrible ordeal we may never know. However, it is believed by some scholars that the story was preserved in mythology. As the single most catastrophic natural disaster in the history of civilization, the Thera eruption may have been responsible for one of antiquity's most baffling mysteries: the legend of Atlantis.

Around 400 BC, the Greek philosopher Plato wrote of Atlantis as a rich and powerful island empire. His *Dialogues* describe an ideal city state where the citizens lived in peace, obeyed their laws and prospered. As they grew richer, however, they also grew arrogant, angering their gods. In a single day and night earthquakes and tidal waves rocked the island, completely destroying the once mighty people. Could Plato's Atlantis have been more than an instructive fable? Until only a century ago, historians believed that the Greek poet Homer had invented Troy. Then, in 1870, the German archaeologist Heinrich Schliemann uncovered the city's remains at Hissarlik in Turkey. As Homer had not invented Troy, perhaps, some scholars began to speculate, Plato had not invented Atlantis?

On 19 February 1909 an article appeared in *The Times* which first suggested that there may be a connection between the Minoan civilization on Crete and the legend of Atlantis. The author, a young Belfast scholar named K.T. Frost, had based his idea on the degree of sophistication of the discoveries made by Arthur Evans at Knossos, and the apparent sudden destruction of the towns being excavated. Remarkably, this was thirty years before Marinatos' paper was published in the British archaeological journal, *Antiquity*, which first outlined his tidal-wave theory. It was the Greek seismologist Professor Angelos Galan-opoulos, however, in a series of short articles published in the 1960s, who first proposed the theory that Minoan Akrotiri and the island of Thera had been the city and island of Atlantis.

According to Plato his account came from Solon, a famous Athenian statesman and philosopher of the sixth century BC. His notes had been handed down by the Critas family, relatives Plato shared with Solon. Solon, evidently, had in turn been told the Atlantis story by priests on a trip to Egypt, sometime around 565 BC. As we have seen, the Egyptians certainly had close commercial ties with the Minoans during the time Thera seems to have erupted, and it is quite possible for the survivors of the disaster to have given a full account to the Egyptians. On the negative side, Thera does not fall outside the Pillars of Hercules – that is, in the Atlantic – where Plato tells us Atlantis was situated, and eruption had not happened 9,000 years earlier than Solon's time, the period that Atlantis was said to have been destroyed. However, as the only island city that is known to have perished in a manner anything like Plato describes, Akrotiri is so far the only truly historical contender for Atlantis.

We return now to the possibility that the Thera eruption may have had considerable effects in Egypt at the time of Amonhotep III and Akhenaten. Ninkovich and Heezen's survey of the Mediterranean seabed showed that sediment from the Thera eruption spread across the sea floor and bisected Crete at the eastern end of the island. This positively demonstrates that the prevailing wind was in the direction of Egypt. After blowing over Crete the fallout would have continued on its way to cross central and southern Egypt. On land, evidence of the ash fall would now be difficult to detect as it breaks down to produce a highly fertile soil. Apart from larger pieces of pumice, which are unlikely to have made it as far as Egypt, there was no discernible layer of volcanic ash even on Crete. Moreover, erosion of the springtime *khamsin* winds (that create huge sandstorms) in Egypt, and the annual flooding of the Nile would long ago have obliterated all evidence.

Although the volcanic fallout must certainly have reached Egypt, how significant would have been its effects? The Egyptian coast is only about 800 kilometres from Thera. The much smaller Mount St Helens eruption resulted in thick falls of ash just as far away, and after Krakatau ash was falling on ships 2,000 miles from the volcano. Thera – six times bigger than Krakatau – would certainly have plunged much of Egypt into darkness, and covered the countryside with volcanic debris. It can be estimated that the effect on parts of Egypt would have been at least what it was on Washington State after Mount St Helens erupted. Few historians now doubt that something similar had occurred in Egypt. The question is: was this really during the reign of Amonhotep III?

The precise date of the Thera eruption has been difficult to determine by scientific techniques. It is a popular misconception that science can now fix the time of any historical event by radiocarbon dating. For a start, radiocarbon dating needs organic matter. Organic matter in whatever form, animal or vegetable, contains the radioactive isotope of carbon, Carbon 14, and once the living organism has died the Carbon 14 gradually decays until some 120,000 years later it disappears altogether. The amount of Carbon 14 in dead organic material can be measured by chemical analysis, thus enabling dating. Once thought to be the answer to archaeological dating, it has often proved more trouble than it's worth. Firstly, considerable quantities of organic material, such as wood or bone, are needed for the procedure – often more than is present among the remains in question. Secondly, radiocarbon dating often has to allow for a considerable margin of error. Indeed the further back we go, the more inaccurate it becomes.

In the early 1990s a team of geologists from The National Museum of Denmark in Copenhagen attempted to date the Thera eruption by radiocarbon dating organic remains from within the ancient volcanic crater. Inside once-molten rock, they found charcoal deposits thought to be from trees that had perished in the eruption. Unfortunately, there was not enough for standard radiocarbon dating, so they tried a new approach using nuclear physics. The carbonated material was pressed into cartridges of an atomic accelerator and bombarded with electrically charged particles. On impact, the material was to shatter in such a way that a small amount of Carbon 14 could be dated. Using this procedure, the team arrived at a date two centuries earlier than anyone had previously considered Thera to have erupted – around 1650 BC. If the Danish team was right, then the archaeologists had been completely wrong.

From the archaeological perspective, the Minoan civilization was still going strong in the mid-fifteenth century BC: Egyptian records show that the great Minoan trading ships were being used regularly to carry timber from Lebanon to Egypt; distinctive Minoan pottery turns up all over the Eastern Mediterranean; and Minoan envoys are pictured in Egyptian art (see Chapter Four). It was not until the mid-fourteenth century that the Minoans would weaken sufficiently for the Mycenaeans to take over Crete.

To slot their findings into some kind of historical perspective, the Danish geological team postulated that the Thera eruption may not have been responsible for the end of Minoan civilization. In other words, they had survived the Thera eruption with little or no effect on their empire. To many historians and archaeologists alike, this hardly seemed credible. The general consensus was that the new technique needed refinement. It was fairly clear from the late style of Minoan pottery found at Akrotiri that the city was not abandoned until at least the fifteenth century BC – 150 years after the new findings indicated.

In the summer of 1996 new arguments erupted over the date of Thera, with archaeologists, scientists and historians disagreeing with each other by as much as 300 years. After analysing the pattern of tree rings from ancient wood taken from Sarikaya Palace at Acemhoyuk in Turkey, Dr Stuart Manning of Reading University estimated a date of 1628 BC for Thera. Trees have annual growth rings which are wider in warmer weather, due to more growth, and thinner when cooler, due to less growth. The Turkish samples showed that there had been a particularly dismal summer in 1628 BC, which Dr Manning and his team attributed to fallout from Thera (dust in the stratosphere having reflected much of the sun's energy back into space). Professor Colin Renfrew of the McDonald Institute for Archaeological Research, Cambridge, disagreed with this dendrochronology (tree ring dating). He was sceptical that the growth ring in question was due to the Thera eruption. He argued that another eruption may have been responsible. Hekla in Iceland, for instance, had erupted a few hundred years before Thera, and going by the size of its crater it was about twice the size of Thera. Dr Manning countered that a high latitude eruption was unlikely to have had an effect in mid-latitude Turkey. However, the year after the Krakatau eruption, which was more than 5 degrees south of the equator, the fallout caused it to snow in California, almost 40 degrees to the north. Iceland is only 25 degrees north of the site in Turkey. There were other objections besides: the whole question of whether or not the eruption of Thera would have resulted in a colder Turkish summer depends on too many unknown variables and weather patterns. The year after Krakatau, for instance, Moscow was exceptionally hot.

A date somewhat later than had previously been considered appeared in an article in the journal *Nature* in July 1996. Two scientists – Hendrik J. Bruins of the Ben-Gurion University of the Negev in Israel, and Johannes van der Plicht of the University of Groningen in Holland – had been dating ancient cereal grains from the site of Jericho (Tell es-Sultan) in Israel. They arrived at a date of 3,311 years (give or take 8 years) before the date of their writing for the destruction of Jericho. This made the central date 1315 BC. They concluded from various observations that this may have been around forty-five years after the eruption of Thera. They based their conclusions on Carbon 14 tests that had been carried out on what were considered to have been sufficient samples of organic matter found at Akrotiri, measured separately at Oxford and Copen-hagen. The first had provided a central date of 3,355 years before the time of writing, and the second a date of 3,356 years before. Respectively, these gave dates of 1359 BC and 1360 BC for the Thera eruption – with a margin of error of 32 years either side.

Even though this last example would fit with the reign of Amonhotep III, we have seen how caution is called for when it comes to radiocarbon dating. The ice core samples from Greenland would still seem to be the best indicator of the time Thera erupted. Whereas the tree rings only provide the date of a cool summer – which may or may not have been the result of a volcanic eruption – the ice core samples clearly indicate a year of high volcanic acidity. The precise year the ice core readings obtained for a large-scale eruption was 1390 BC, with a margin of error of fifty years each way. This shows that a massive volcanic eruption had happened somewhere in the world either in the second half of the fifteenth century BC or the first half of the fourteenth century BC. As they show no eruptions anywhere near the known magnitude of Thera until two and a half centuries later (way into the Mycenaean period and so much too late), or for hundreds of years earlier, it was almost certainly the Thera eruption that was evidenced.

From every excavated site on Crete there can be no doubt that the Minoan civilization suffered from a major seismic event at the very end of its period of supremacy – when palaces, villas and entire settlements were abandoned permanently. From the geological findings of Ninkovich and Heezen, together with the archaeological discoveries of Spyridon Marinatos, we know that Thera was responsible. From the late Minoan style of pottery found at Akrotiri, we also know that Thera cannot have erupted before the fifteenth century BC. The ice core samples and the latest radiocarbon tests do not contradict any of this. However, archaeologists have tended to place the eruption of Thera no later than 1450 BC, whereas the ice core and latest radiocarbon dates all provide a central date well into the 1300s BC. Although this would not contradict the archaeological evidence, it would require a certain reinterpretation of the events at the end of the Minoan era.

From the historical perspective, Thera weakened Minoan power, resulting in the empire's gradual decline over a period of around a century before being overrun by the Mycenaeans. If Thera did not erupt until the first half of the fourteenth century BC, then its affects on the Minoan civilization would have been much greater than is generally thought, causing its empire to collapse within a few decades. This, however, would seem quite plausible. The tidal wave alone could have destroyed half of the

Minoan fleet and devastated the empire's ports all over the Aegean. It had been a sea-based empire with little power on land. The Minoans were seemingly involved in a pact with Egypt against the Hittites in Turkey, who would no doubt have taken full advantage of the situation. Indeed, the Minoan decorations from Amonhotep III's Malkata palace appear to show that the Minoans were still well placed during the early fifteenth century BC (see Chapter Four). On the balance of evidence, therefore, Thera would seem to have erupted in the first half of the fourteenth century BC – *circa* 1400 to 1350 BC.

This would certainly sit within the reign of Amonhotep III. This can be dated from the Sothic Cycle discussed in Chapter Two. One particular calendar alignment occurred in the ninth year of the reign of the pharaoh Amonhotep I. It happened on the 309th day of the civil calendar, meaning that 1236 years had transpired since the beginning of the Sothic Cycle in 2781 BC, making the ninth year of Amonhotep I's reign 1545 BC. The first year of his reign was therefore 1554 BC. From various inscriptions from which the lengths of his and the subsequent eighteenth-dynasty kings' reigns can be determined, together with the calculated overlaps of co-regencies, Egyptologists generally estimate some 165 years separate the beginning of Amonhotep I's reign from the beginning of the reign of Amonhotep III. That means that Amonhotep III's reign began around 1389 BC. We know he lived for another thirty-seven years, which would place his death around 1352, the orthodox date Akhenaten came to the throne. However, as we have seen, there seems to have been an overlapping co-regency that has not been taken into consideration. If Cyril Aldred is right (see Chapter Six), Amonhotep died in Akhenaten's twelfth year, which would mean that Akhenaten came to the throne around

1364. Interestingly, this coincides almost exactly with the latest central radiocarbon dates for the Thera eruption.

The affects on Egypt of the Thera eruption would certainly account for Amonhotep's erection of the Sekhmet statues – the darkening of the skies, perhaps for days on end, and the shower of volcanic ash, would have terrified the Egyptians. They were not able to see the volcano erupting hundreds of miles away, although, if Krakatau is anything to go by, they would certainly have heard it. Witnessing something completely unprecedented, and totally outside the assumed order of things, the Egyptians would surely have thought that the world was coming to an end. In their mythology, this had almost happened once before, when Sekhmet had decided to annihilate the human race. She was the negative aspect of the sun's power, and it was the sun that was being obscured. She was also the goddess of devastation. Sekhmet would almost certainly have been considered responsible. Amonhotep may, therefore, have attempted to appease her by erecting the statues and making her supreme deity. However, the sun would continue to appear strange, its colour repeatedly turning sickly months, even years, after the ash cloud had dissipated. This may well have been taken as a sign that it could all happen again at any moment – and next time the world *would* end. Amonhotep and his policy of appeasing Sekhmet would accordingly be questioned – it clearly hadn't worked. Under such circumstances it is doubtful whether the frightened population would have opposed Akhenaten when he assumed control and installed an aspect of the god Re as chief deity.

In mythology it had been Re's intervention that had previously saved the world from the fury of Sekhmet. The priests of Heliopolis would have been quick to draw attention to this fact. Re's assimilation with Amun, they would argue, had obviously displeased the god. If he was not reinstated, individually, as supreme deity, he would no longer restrain the wrath of his heavenly daughter. We know it was the cult of Heliopolis which had principally influenced Akhenaten. Indeed, to begin with, Akhenaten sees virtually no difference between Re and the Aten: many early references refer to him as 'only one of Re' (on the Boundary Stela at Amarna, for instance [see Chapter Three]). An early scene from the tomb of the vizier Ramose, at Thebes even describes Akhenaten as 'the image of Re who loves him more than any other king'.

As for the Amun priesthood: it is unlikely that they would have had much support if they tried to oppose the new religion Their cult revolved around the daily supplications to Amun, to keep the world in order and the forces of chaos at bay. Even from their own perspective, this had clearly failed. Akhenaten's logic would seem impeccable: Amun was no longer the chief god. Within a few years, once Akhenaten installed his new religion, the dust in the atmosphere would have subsided and the sun's appearance would have returned to normal. Surely, no one, no matter how much the new regime has altered his status, is going to risk the end of the world by opposing Akhenaten.

This scenario fits perfectly with everything we have so far examined – indeed, something along these lines is just about the only scenario that makes any sense of the Amarna era. It explains Amonhotep's Sekhmet statues, Akhenaten's new religion, the apparent wholesale acceptance of Atenism, even by the Amun priesthood, and it explains why the army went along with it all even when they had so much to lose. Does it, therefore, also explain the apparent Hebrew link with Akhenaten's religion?

Remarkably, the effects of the Thera eruption on Egypt bear

a striking similarity to the plague of darkness and other ills which the Bible tells us God inflicted upon Egypt when the pharaoh refused to let the Israelites leave. Had Akhenaten come to believe that it was the God of the Hebrews who had been responsible for the terrifying phenomena, and ultimately incorporated their beliefs with his own?

SUMMARY

- It is not only Akhenaten's new religion which suggests that something very unusual had occurred just prior to his reign, but the behaviour of his father Amonhotep III. A year or two before Akhenaten comes to the throne, Amonhotep does something very strange for someone so completely devoted to the god Amun-Re: he erects literally hundreds of statues to another diety – the goddess Sekhmet. No other deity of ancient Egypt is represented by so many large-scale statues – and nearly all of them were erected by order of Amonhotep III. These statues of Sekhmet are a clear indication that, despite the apparent stability and wealth of the country, something was wrong, as Sekhmet was the goddess of devastation.

- There is compelling evidence that a gigantic volcanic eruption occurred in the eastern Mediterranean around the time of Amonhotep's reign. Every winter a fresh layer of ice forms on the Greenland ice cap, creating clearly defined strata, one for each year. Every layer contains trapped air, holding a sample of the earth's atmosphere as it was when the ice formed. In the 1970s Danish geophysicists began taking core samples many metres down into the ice, so as to recover a year-by-year record of the earth's atmospheric conditions going back some 100,000 years. The team soon observed that from years when there had been major volcanic eruptions the samples evidenced high levels of acidity. In November 1980 they eventually concluded that there had been a massive eruption somewhere in the world around 1390 BC, with a margin of error of some fifty years either way. This might indeed have coincided with the independent reign of Amonhotep III (*circa* 1389 to 1364 BC).

- The only eruption large enough to have resulted in the atmospheric conditions recorded by the Danes, and known by geologists to have occurred within 200 years either side of this date, was a gigantic eruption on the Aegean island of Thera. Although, at the time, this seemed to place the eruption around a hundred years after it was previously thought to have occurred, more recent radiocarbon tests from Thera have tended to support the findings, dating the eruption to around 1360 BC.

- In 1956 two geologists, Dragoslav Ninkovich and Bruce Heezen of Columbia University, conducted a survey of the seabed to try to determine precisely how large the eruption had been. It would take 6,000 of the most destructive modern nuclear warheads – each with the power to wipe out an entire city – to equal the explosive magnitude of Thera.

- Ninkovich and Heezen's survey of the Mediterranean seabed showed that sediment from the Thera eruption spread across the sea floor and bisected the eastern end of the island of Crete. This positively demonstrated that the prevailing wind was in the direction of Egypt. The Egyptian coast is only about 800 kilometres from Thera. The much smaller Mount St Helens eruption in the USA in 1980 resulted in thick falls of ash just as far away, and after the eruption of the Krakatau volcano near Sumatra in 1886 ash was falling on ships over 3,000 kilometres away. Thera – six times bigger than Krakatau – would certainly have plunged much of Egypt into darkness and covered the countryside with volcanic debris.

- The effects in Egypt caused by the Thera eruption would certainly account for Amonhotep's erection of the Sekhmet statues – the darkening of the skies, perhaps for days on end, and the shower of volcanic ash would have terrified the Egyptians. Witnessing something completely unprecedented, and totally outside the assumed order of things, the Egyptians would surely have thought that the world was coming to an end. In their mythology, this had almost happened once before, when Sekhmet had decided to annihilate the human race. Sekhmet would almost certainly have been considered responsible. Akhenaten, however, may have considered it to have been the work of his new god, the Aten, punishing Egypt for worshipping other gods. Under such circumstances it is doubtful whether the frightened population would have opposed Akhenaten when he installed the Aten as chief deity.

CHAPTER TEN

Exodus

According to the Exodus account, the pharaoh, concerned about the growing number of Israelites, orders that all their newborn sons should be killed. Although many are murdered, the baby Moses is saved when his mother places him in a basket made from bulrushes and hides him below the river bank. The daughter of the pharaoh then discovers the child and decides to raise him as her own son. Years later, although he has been brought up as an Egyptian prince, Moses still has compassion for his countrymen, and when he sees an Egyptian beating an Israelite slave he kills the man. When the deed is discovered, the pharaoh orders Moses to be executed. However, he manages to escape and settles in the land of Midian, east of the Gulf of Aqaba. After many years, God appears to Moses and charges him to return home and confront the new pharaoh of Egypt. Moses does as God asks and, accompanied by his brother Aaron, appears before the pharaoh with God's command: he must free the Israelites and let them return to Canaan. When the king refuses, and actually makes life harder for the Hebrews, God punishes the Egyptians by a series of plagues: bloodied water, frogs, lice, flies, cattle deaths, boils, hailstorms, locusts and darkness.

In 1985, British author Ian Wilson, in his book *The Exodus*

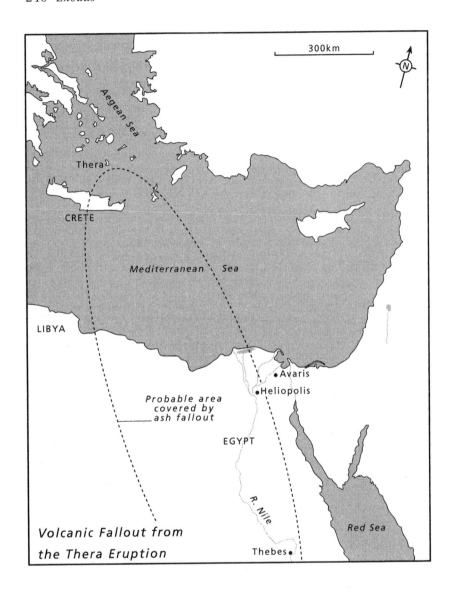

300km

Aegean sea

Thera

CRETE

Mediterranean   Sea

LIBYA

•Avaris

•Heliopolis

*Probable area
covered by
ash fallout*

EGYPT

R. Nile

Red Sea

*Volcanic Fallout from
the Thera Eruption*

Thebes•

Enigma, drew scholarly attention to the astonishing similarities between these biblical plagues and the likely effects on Egypt from the Thera eruption. At the time the eruption was thought to have occurred around the mid 1450s BC, and accordingly Wilson placed the event around the reign of Tuthmosis III. However, as we have seen, it now seems more likely that the volcano really erupted over half a century later, during the reign of Amonhotep III. Unfortunately, neither reign – nor any other from ancient Egypt – has records making direct allusions to the Thera eruption. If any records were made during Amonhotep's reign or during the time of Akhenaten, the former would probably have been destroyed during the anti-Amun desecrations of the late Amarna period, and the latter would have been destroyed during the anti-Atenist backlash during the period of Horemheb. Although we cannot make direct comparisons between biblical plagues and Egyptian reports of the Thera eruption, we can compare the Exodus account with modern reports of Thera-like eruptions. When we do, we find them to be almost identical.

When Krakatau erupted, the explosion was so loud that in the Northern Territory of Australia – 4,800 kilometres away – people were woken from their sleep by what they thought were inconsiderate quarry workers blasting rocks nearby. The Egyptian coast is only 800 kilometres from Thera and so its explosion, six times bigger, would have sounded like thunder throughout the country. In fact, its shock waves would have rattled the windows of modern Cairo. They would certainly have been felt by the ancient Egyptians. Within a day of the eruption, the fallout cloud would have drifted high over Egypt and the skies would have darkened. After Mount St Helens, the sun was obscured for hours 500 kilometres from the volcano, and after Krakatau the skies were darkened to a much greater distance –

it was actually as dark as night for days on end up to 800 kilometres away. Because of the greater magnitude of the Thera eruption, we can assume that the same must have been true for much of Egypt.

According to Exodus 10: 21–23:

> And the Lord said unto Moses, Stretch out thine hand towards heaven, that there may be darkness over the land of Egypt, even darkness that may be felt. And Moses stretched forth his hand towards heaven; and there was thick darkness in all the land of Egypt three days: They saw not one another, neither rose any from his place for three days: but all the children of Israel had light in their dwellings.

Apart from the fact that the event is being attributed to divine intervention, the account might as well be a description of the effects of Thera. That just one of the ten plagues matched the likely effects of the Thera eruption would be interesting enough: the truth is, they all do. In Exodus 9:23–26, we are told that Egypt is afflicted by a terrible fiery hailstorm:

> And Moses stretched forth his rod towards heaven: and the Lord sent thunder and hail, and fire ran along upon the ground; and the Lord rained hail upon the land of Egypt. So there was hail and fire mingled with the hail, very grievous, such as there was none like it in all the land of Egypt since it became a nation. And the hail smote all throughout the land of Egypt, all that was in the field, both man and beast, and brake every tree in the field. Only in the land of Goshen, where the children of Israel were, was there no hail.

This would be an accurate description of the terrible ordeal suffered by the people on the Sumatran coast after the eruption of Krakatau – pellet-sized volcanic debris falling like hail; fiery pumice setting fires on the ground and destroying trees and houses; lightning flashing around, generated by the tremendous turbulence inside the volcanic cloud. Even after the lesser eruption of Mount St Helens, volcanic debris fell like hailstones, flattening crops hundreds of kilometres away. Remarkably, both this and the previous account tell of something which may specifically relate to the Thera eruption. We are told that the children of Israel, in the land of Goshen, were not affected by these or any of the other plagues. Based on the ancient sea bed pumice samples taken during the *Vema* survey, the estimated destruction of the communities on Crete, and a comparison with the Mount St Helens devastation (see Chapter Nine), we can determine the approximate direction and swath – or width – of the fallout cloud. It seems that it may only have crossed over southern Egypt including Thebes, but may have missed part of the Delta region which included the land of Goshen around Avaris. Interestingly, northern Egypt, where the Aten cult seems to have persisted, is also in this unaffected area. In such circumstances, like the Hebrews, the cult of Re may have believed that *their* god had spared them from the carnage, and consequently concluded that he was punishing the Amun cult at Thebes. Here we may have another – and perhaps the original – link between the Israelites and the Atenists.

The Exodus account of another of the plagues could easily be a report given by someone living in the states of Washington, Idaho or Montana after the Mount St Helens eruption of 1980: 'And it shall become small dust in all the land of Egypt, and shall be a boil breaking forth with blains upon man, and upon beast.' (Exodus 9:9.) Fine dust causing boils and blains!

Hundreds of people were taken to hospital with skin rashes, sores and pustules after the Mount St Helens eruption, and many cattle, horses and other livestock perished, while as many again had to be destroyed due to prolonged inhalation of the acidic ash. According to Exodus 9:6: 'And all the cattle of Egypt died.'

After Mount St Helens fish also died and were found floating on the surface of hundreds of kilometres of waterways. The pungent odour of pumice permeated everything, and water supplies had to be cut off until the impurities could be filtered from reservoirs. According to Exodus 7:21: 'And the fish that was in the river died: and the river stank, and the Egyptians could not drink of the river, and there was blood throughout all the land of Egypt.'

As well as the grey pumice ash the volcano blasted skywards, Thera had another, more corrosive toxin in its bedrock – iron oxide. (This is the same red material that covers the surface of Mars.) Wilson pointed out that in the submarine eruptions that still occur at Thera, tons of iron oxide is discharged which kills fishes for miles around. As it oxidizes in contact with air, the consequent red-coloured rust stains might explain the reference to blood. It would certainly explain the mention in the preceding verse of the Nile turning to blood, as iron oxide would turn the river red. 'And all the waters that were in the river turned to blood.' (Exodus 7:20.)

The remaining plagues do not immediately suggest themselves as having anything to do with a volcanic eruption – frogs, flies, lice and locusts. However, they can be just as linked to volcanic activity as the fallout cloud itself. Those who have not suffered the dreadful effects of a volcanic eruption might imagine that once the eruption has subsided, the dead have been buried, the injured tended, and the immediate damage repaired, the survivors can begin the task of putting their lives back together, free from further volcanic horrors. This is very often far from the truth, as the entire ecosystem has been affected. Most forms of life suffer from volcanic devastation, but some, remarkably, actually thrive on it.

Geologists estimate that the asteroid or comet collision that exterminated the dinosaurs around 65 million years ago also killed around 75 per cent of life on earth. The impact resulted in a cataclysmic event similar to a volcanic eruption – but on a global scale. Those that survived the holocaust were generally the smallest creatures, including insects, frogs and even our own direct ancestors – tiny rat-like mammals. Crawling invertebrates, and insects in their larval, pupal or egg stage would be safe underground, as would burrowing snakes and rodents; so also would frog-spawn, protected under submerged ledges. Exactly the same set of circumstances prevail over the countryside buried beneath the ash of volcanic eruptions. Insects have a very short life cycle and accordingly reproduce at a frightening rate. After such a cataclysm, therefore, they have plenty of time to establish a head start on their larger predators and competitors. Moreover, compared to bigger animals, they reproduce in vast numbers.

Swarming insects are therefore commonly associated with volcanic eruptions. Having survived the calamity, the ash-cover forces them to seek out new habitations and food supplies – and heaven help anyone who gets in the way! Ian Wilson cited the flesh-crawling aftermath of the Mount Pelee eruption on the island of Martinique in the West Indies in 1902. Volcanic debris covered the nearby port of St Pierre, killing over 30,000 people, but the horrors were not to end there. The survivors were exposed to a terrifying episode. Huge swarms of flying ants descended upon the sugar plantations and attacked the workers. As they fled for their lives, the vicious creatures seared their flesh with dreadful acidic stings. It was no fluke that the insect assaults had followed the eruption: the creatures had attacked before when Mount Pelee had erupted in 1851. On this occasion they not only drove away workers and devoured entire plantations; they were even reported to have attacked and killed defenceless babies while they were still in their cots. Three types of insect infested Egypt according to the Exodus account: lice, flies and locusts.

> Aaron stretched out his hand with his rod, and smote the dust of the earth, and it became lice in man, and in beast; all the dust of the land became lice throughout all of the land of Egypt. (Exodus 8:17.)
>
> Behold I will send swarms of flies upon thee, and upon thy servants, and upon thy people, and into thy houses: and the houses of the Egyptians shall be full of swarms of flies, and also the ground whereon they are. ... And the Lord did so and there came a grievous swarm of flies ... and the land was corrupted by reason of the swarm of flies. (Exodus 8:21–24.)
>
> And the locusts went up over all the land of Egypt, and rested in all the coasts of Egypt: very grievous were they; before them there were no such locusts as they, neither after them shall be such. For they covered the face of the whole earth, so that the land was darkened; and they did eat every herb of the land and all the fruit of the trees which the hail had left: and there remained not any green thing in the trees, or in the herbs of the field, through all the land of Egypt. (Exodus 10: 14–15.)

Frogs are perhaps the most prepared of all the land-based vertebrates for such cataclysms: like insects, they produce vast numbers of offspring. Each frog lays literally thousands of eggs. Under normal circumstances this is a biological necessity, as the tiny tadpoles emerge from the eggs almost completely defenceless. The only chance the species has for survival is in numbers. When frog spawn hatches, the local fish are in for a banquet and only one or two of the tadpoles ever survive to become frogs. However, after Mount St Helens the predatory fish were decimated. The tiny would-be frogs, on the other hand, were kept safe inside their spawn. By the time they emerged, the hazardous chemicals had washed away down river, but the fish had not yet returned. The result was a plague of frogs throughout much of Washington State. In their thousands they littered the countryside – there were so many squashed on the roads that they made driving conditions hazardous: they clogged waterways, covered gardens, and infested houses.

According to Exodus 8:2–8, this is exactly what happened to the ancient Egyptians:

> Behold, I will smite all thy borders with frogs. And the river shall bring forth frogs abundantly, which shall come up and come into thine house, and into thy bedchamber, and upon thy bed, and into the house of thy servants, and upon thy people, and into thine ovens, and into thy kneadingtroughs ... And Aaron stretched out his hand over the waters of Egypt; and the frogs came up, and covered the land of Egypt.

Over the years, various scholars have individually attributed these plagues to different natural phenomena. The darkness could have been due to a particularly violent sandstorm, the hail the result of freak weather conditions. The boils could have been caused by an epidemic, and the bloodied river may have been the result of some seismic activity far to the south in tropical Africa. Swarms of locusts, flies and infestation of lice would not have been that uncommon. However, the likelihood of them all happening at the same time seems just too remote. The only real problem with attributing the plagues of Egypt to Thera is that they do not appear in the order that they would have occurred after such an event. The darkness and fiery hail would come first, followed by the sores, the bloodied river, dead cattle and fish, and some time later the frogs and insects. In Exodus they appear in a different order: blood, fish, frogs, lice, flies, cattle deaths, boils, hail, locusts and darkness. However, as we have already seen, Exodus seems to have been written many centuries after the events being described. The account of the plagues would have been handed down orally for many generations and, as in examples already cited (see Chapter Eight), certain details would have been reinterpreted.

In the story of Moses it seems that many details had been forgotten entirely: the names of the pharaohs, the location of the court, Moses' time in the Egyptian royal household, to name but a few. Surviving details would no doubt have been modified somewhat during many retellings of the story. If we look at the order of the plagues again, we see that they appear to occur in ascending order of magnitude – getting progressively worse as the pharaoh continues to refuse the Lord's demands. This is precisely how we might expect a story to develop for dramatic effect as it was told and retold. From a purely historical, or even scientific, perspective, the only explanation for the plagues known at this time is the eruption of Thera. If the eruption was responsible for the plagues, then what must have happened is that the cataclysmic details were remembered accurately, while the order of events was altered for narrative purposes.

Today, few scholars – even the most religious ones – see

anything blasphemous about suggesting that some of the biblical events were the result of natural phenomena. Concerning the life of Christ, for instance, the general consensus is that the star of Bethlehem, which heralded his birth, was a supernova or planetary alignment, while the daytime darkness during the Crucifixion was due to an eclipse. Equally, Old Testament scholars and biblical historians alike have suggested that an earthquake was responsible for the fall of Jericho. It is not the nature of the phenomena, they argue, but the remarkable timing involved which implies divine intervention. Time and time again, in the Bible, God uses nature's phenomena to fulfil His plans. He uses rain to cleanse the world and cause the great flood, for instance, rather than simply making mankind disappear in an instant. Then, on the positive side, he uses a rainbow as a sign of his promise to Noah not to do such a thing again. In fact God actually tells Noah that He will not use powers beyond His created forces of nature to harm mankind. In Genesis 8:22 he tells Noah: 'While the earth remaineth, seedtime and harvest, and cold and heat, and summer and winter, and day and night shall not cease.'

From the theological perspective, God created the forces of nature, and they are His to use as He pleases. In conclusion, therefore, there is nothing unscientific *or* irreligious about attributing the plagues of Egypt to the eruption of Thera. On the contrary, it offers scientific evidence for a biblical episode that many now regard as nothing more than myth. Yet the plagues are not the only miraculous episodes from the Exodus story which Thera may have caused. Its eruption may well have made possible the Exodus itself, by helping the Israelites to escape.

Even if northern Egypt had not suffered the same fate as the south, there would certainly have been panic and confusion.

Well before the fallout cloud reached the coast, they would have heard a colossal explosion, or series of explosions, and felt shock waves and earth tremors. Most frightening of all, within an hour of the explosion a tidal wave would have hit the Egyptian coast and made its way up the Nile Delta. Those living on the coast, on the river banks, or in ships on the Nile would have been in considerable peril. It is difficult to estimate how high the tidal wave would have been as too many variables are involved. However, a very much smaller seismic event, an earthquake in Japan in the 1940s, created a series of devastating ten-metre *tsunami* tidal waves the other side of the Pacific in California. We can be sure, therefore, that much of the Nile Delta experienced flooding, and that river-going vessels were over-turned or sunk. North-east Egypt may not have been affected directly by the fallout, but they would have seen the awesome black cloud far away on the western horizon, drifting ominously towards Upper Egypt. The resultant panic may well have afforded many foreign slaves the opportunity to escape.

According to Exodus, once the plagues have finally per-suaded the pharaoh to free the Israelites, they are led out of Egypt by following 'a pillar of cloud by day' and 'a pillar of fire by night' (Exodus 13:22). Could this be a reference to the Thera plume (the towering ash cloud over the volcano itself), which would have been visible for days – possibly weeks? It certainly matches the description of a British official in Java, over 900 kilometres from Krakatau, a week after the volcano erupted: 'a black cloud, which at night became a fiery glow above the sea'. This is about the same distance as Goshen is from Thera, and so the much larger Thera would have appeared even more spec-tacular for perhaps much longer. (Taking the earth's curvature into account, we can calculate that Thera's plume would have been visible from Lower Egypt if it rose more than 48 kilometres high. In fact, Thera's plume is estimated to have risen over a hundred kilometres into the sky.)

If the Israelites had attributed the phenomena to the intervention of their God, then they may well have made for the direction of the Thera plume in the belief that it was a beacon to lead them to safety. According to Exodus 13:18: 'God led the people round by the way of the wilderness towards the Red Sea.' We have already seen that the name 'Red Sea' comes from a mistranslation of the Hebrew words *Yam Suph*, which actually means 'Sea of Reeds'. At least a dozen different places have been put forward as possible locations of the Sea of Reeds along the line of the Suez Canal and the Bitter Lakes, but since the topography has changed much since biblical times there is no way of directly verifying any of them. In fact, there may have been a number of places described by the term 'Sea of Reeds'. In Kings 9:26, for instance, the term is used for part of the Gulf of Aqaba which, being some 300 kilometres south-east of Goshen, would make it an unlikely location for the Sea of Reeds referenced in Exodus.

The term Sea of Reeds probably applied to an expanse of water which looked exactly like it sounds: a large shallow lake or inlet covered by reeds. We find the Hebrews constantly describing lakes in terms of seas – what they called the Sea of Galilee or the Dead Sea others would call a lake. The Great Lakes of North America, for instance, could swallow both of them many times over, yet are still referred to as lakes. The Hebrew word *Yam* – 'Sea' – therefore, is probably just as misleading as the Hebrew word *Suph* was when it was mistranslated to mean 'Red'.

The first orthodox Egyptologist to propose a connection between the Thera eruption and the Exodus events was Dr Hans Goedicke, the Chairman of the Department of Near Eastern

Studies at Johns Hopkins University, Baltimore. He concluded that a tidal wave created by the eruption was responsible for the parting of the 'Sea of Reeds', and that it had happened somewhere in the Nile Delta. If so, where might this have been? According to Exodus 13:17–21:

> And it came to pass that when Pharaoh had let the people go, that God led them not through the way of the land of the Philistines, although that was near; for God said, Lest peradventure the people repent when they see war, and they return to Egypt; But God led the people about, through the way of the wilderness of the Red Sea [Sea of Reeds]: and the children of Israel went up harnessed out of the land of Egypt ... And they took their journey from Succoth, and encamped in Etham, in the edge of the wilderness. And the Lord went before them by day in a pillar of a cloud, to lead them the way; and by night in a pillar of fire, to give them light; to go by day and night.

Unfortunately none of these locations have been identified. The 'way of the land of the Philistines' is almost certainly a later name for the area: as we have seen, the Philistines are not recorded anywhere near Egypt until around 1180 BC, almost a century later (see Chapter Eight). Like the name Pi-Ramesses for Avaris, it was no doubt a later name used for the route. Most Egyptologists, however, think that it refers to a trade route into Egypt, about twelve kilometres wide, between Lakes Ballah and Timsah, about 40 kilometres south-east of Avaris. When the Philistines eventually overran much of Canaan and the area to the east of Egypt, the failing Egyptian empire had much difficulty controlling their borders at this point. This would certainly fit the narrative context. Exodus tells us that the

Israelites had been in Avaris (Pi-Ramesses), and the most direct route out of Egypt towards Canaan would be here. However, it would have been patrolled, and so it would certainly have been prudent to have taken a different route, as Exodus relates.

If the Israelites did head in the direction of the Thera plume from Avaris, then they would have reached the Mediterranean coast some eighty kilometres north-west of Avaris, near the shores of Lake Manzala.

Two verses after the above passage, in Exodus 14:1–2, we are told that God ordered the Israelites to turn and make camp: 'And the Lord spake unto Moses saying, Speak unto the children of Israel, that they turn and encamp before Pi-hahiroth, between Migdol and the sea, over against Baal-zephon: before it shall ye encamp by the sea. For Pharaoh will say of the children of Israel, They are entangled in the land, the wilderness hath shut them in.'

Again these locations are now unknown, although it is quite clear that the 'wilderness' referenced here and in the preceding passage is actually the 'Sea of Reeds' itself. In the former we are told of 'the wilderness of the Sea of Reeds', and here, when they have their backs to the sea, 'the wilderness has shut them in'. In other words, the pharaoh will assume that they are trapped as the 'Sea of Reeds' is barring their escape. Indeed, a great swampy, reed-strewn expanse of water that no ship or person could cross would be aptly described as a wilderness.

At this point in the narrative, the pharaoh decides to bring the Israelites back. Perhaps, by this time, the Egyptians have recovered their wits enough to go after their runaway slaves. Although in Exodus 13:17 we are told that the pharaoh has chosen to let the Israelites go, in Exodus 14:5 he appears to have had no idea they had left, as he has to be informed: 'And it was told the king of Egypt that the people had fled.' When the pharaoh's army reaches the Israelites, the waters of the sea part allowing them to escape. If the Israelites had been following the Thera plume before they turned and made camp beside the 'Sea of Reeds', then Exodus 14:19 makes it quite clear what the 'Sea of Reeds' actually is, and it also reveals the crossing point. We are told that before they crossed, 'the pillar of the cloud went from before their face, and stood behind them'. For this to have happened – if it was the Thera plume – then the Israelites must have made an abrupt turn to face Lake Manzala in a south-easterly direction. Lake Manzala, therefore, would seem to be the 'Sea of Reeds'.

Lake Manzala is now a misleading name, as it is actually open to the sea. However, this was not always the case: in Roman times, and presumably earlier, it was divided from the Mediterranean by a narrow ridge of dry land some fifty kilometres long, broken here and there by a few hundred metres of water at high tide. If the Israelites managed to cross this causeway, then it would have afford them escape from Egypt in the direction of Canaan.

It would have been a sensible policy for the Israelites to attempt to cross the Manzala causeway in any event, as the sections of the land bridge submerged at high tide would be wet and muddy, impeding the passage of chariots and heavily armed soldiers. Exodus 14:25 actually tells us that when the Egyptians tried to pursue the Israelites across the 'Sea of Reeds' they were hampered by the ground 'clogging their chariot wheels so they drove heavily'. Remarkably, it is here that a tidal wave could also have been used to the Israelites' advantage.

During the Krakatau eruption, a series of *tsunami* occurred over a period of two days. The same would certainly be true for Thera. In fact, a succession of *tsunami* may have hit the Egyptian coast for much longer, swilling up and down the Mediterranean

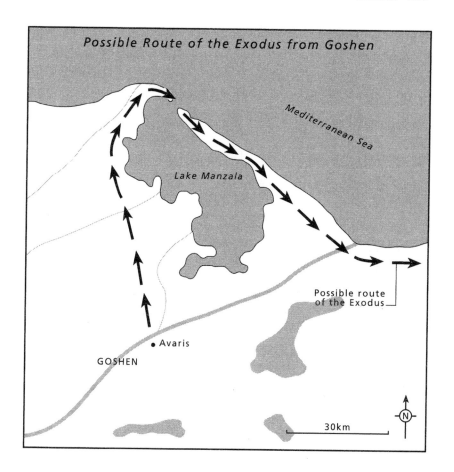

Possible Route of the Exodus from Goshen

like water in a bath. Preceding the arrival of a *tsunami*, the sea withdraws, sometimes for hours. After the Krakatau eruption, a huge coral reef on the coast of Java, usually six feet under sea level, even at low tide, was completely exposed for more than an hour before the wave hit. (It is basically the same phenomenon that causes the sea to withdraw before the breaking of a normal wave, only over a longer duration.)

From Avaris, the Israelites could easily have reached the Manzala causeway within a couple of days of the initial eruption. If a section of the causeway, usually under water, had been exposed by the pre-*tsunami* conditions, then the phenomenon might indeed have saved the Israelites if the Egyptians were in close pursuit. The sea would have been made dry land, as the Bible relates: 'And the Lord caused the sea to go back by a strong east wind all that night and made the sea into dry land, and the waters were divided'. (Exodus 14:21.)

This is an excellent description of what would have happened at the Manzala causeway, with the waters of the Mediterranean having divided from the waters of the Lake Manzala. The pressure drop over the lowering coastal waters of the Mediterranean would even have caused a strong wind to blow from the east over Lake Manzala. The Israelites could have made it safely across and, if the timing was fortuitous, the pursuing soldiers may have been attempting to follow when the *tsunami* hit, washing them all away. 'And the waters returned and covered the chariots, and the horsemen and all the host of Pharaoh that came into the sea after them; there remained not so much as one of them.' (Exodus 14:29.)

In every aspect but one – there would not be a wall of water to the left and right as the Bible says – the scenario precisely matches the biblical account of the crossing of the 'Sea of Reeds'.

The plagues alone, being so similar to the effects of Thera, would be evidence enough that the volcanic eruption was responsible for the Exodus events. That the pillar of cloud and fire, and the parting of the sea also match the Thera effects is all the more compelling. From the scientist's perspective, the Exodus could indeed have happened pretty much as the Bible describes. From the historian's perspective, the unique set of circumstances favoured the Israelites to such a degree that faith in their God endured for generations to come. From the theologian's perspective, such a incredible series of events favouring one group of people is surely beyond coincidence. Whatever way you look at it, if Thera was the cause of the Exodus, then it certainly ranks as one of the most remarkable events ever to have shaped the course of human history. Without it, Judaism might never have developed, nor indeed Christianity – in which case the Western world would be a very different place.

Let us return to the Egyptians at the time of Thera. From the sheer magnitude of the events and the fear that must have been aroused, it is quite understandable that Amonhotep III should frenziedly erect so many statues to Sekhmet. In the north-east, however, spared the worst horrors of the fallout, the priesthood would almost certainly have considered their god Re responsible for the event: he had punished Thebes for the worship of the god Amun. For some reason Akhenaten allied himself with the cult of Re, which may have been because he too was in north-east Egypt when the eruption occurred. Traditionally, the eldest son of the New Kingdom pharaohs – the heir to the throne – would serve as the governor of Memphis, less than fifty kilometres south of Heliopolis. As governor of Memphis, he would have been responsible for Lower Egypt. It is in this role that he may have actually come to associate the Thera eruption with the Hebrew God.

If the Israelites were escaping from Avaris, it would certainly have been Akhenaten's responsibility to bring them back. Akhenaten, therefore, may have been the very pharaoh who pursued the Israelites. Although he would not have been pharaoh at the time, we have seen how the Exodus account often refers to things by their later names. It is quite possible that they might refer to Akhenaten as pharaoh, even though he did not become king until some time later. (Although the popular movie interpretation of events often has the pharaoh being washed away with his army, the Bible does not make it clear whether he was with them or not. We are merely told that all those who followed the Israelites across the sea perished.)

Akhenaten's adoption of the Hebrews' religious beliefs would therefore be quite understandable. The apparently miraculous circumstances surrounding the Israelite escape may have convinced him that the Hebrew God was responsible. That he initially associated his new god with Re does not contradict this hypothesis. Ancient cultures were forever identifying other people's gods with their own. The Romans, for instance, considered the Greek Zeus to be their Jove, and sky god of the Gauls to be their Mercury. There is no reason for Akhenaten to think differently. It would make sense for him to associate the Hebrew God with the Egyptian Re. He was, after all, the god of the sun, and it was the sun's appearance that had been strangely altered. Re had also spared much of the north where the cult of Re flourished. Akhenaten may, therefore, have converted to the Hebrew God, firstly linking Him with Re, then later, aware that Re did not fit the profile of an invisible and omnipresent deity, represented Him as the Aten.

The Thera eruption is just about the only episode that makes any sense of the otherwise bewildering Amarna period: an event which must surely be linked with the biblical plagues and the miraculous flight from Egypt. How, therefore, does the dating of the Exodus to around 1360 BC compare with the traditional dating of the Exodus to the reign of Ramesses II, almost a century later?

SUMMARY

- The effects of the Thera eruption on Egypt bear a striking similarity to the plague of darkness and other ills which the Bible tells us God inflicted upon Egypt when the pharaoh refused to let the Israelites leave. God punishes the Egyptians by a series of plagues including darkness, fiery hailstorms, boils and the Nile turning to blood.

- Within a day of the Thera eruption the fallout cloud would have drifted high over Egypt and the skies would have darkened. After the Mount St Helens eruption the sun was obscured for hours 500 kilometres from the volcano, and after Krakatau the skies were darkened to a much greater distance – it was actually as dark as night for days on end up to 800 kilometres away. Because of the greater magnitude of the Thera eruption, we can assume that the same must have been true for much of Egypt. According to Exodus 10: 22: 'There was thick darkness in all the land of Egypt three days.'

- In Exodus 9:24–25 we are told that Egypt is afflicted by a terrible storm in which, 'there was hail and fire mingled with the hail ... and the hail smote all throughout the land of Egypt, all that was in the field, both man and beast, and brake every tree in the field'. This would be an accurate description of the terrible ordeal suffered by the people on the Sumatran coast after the eruption of Krakatau: pellet-sized volcanic debris falling like hail; fiery pumice setting fires on the ground and destroying trees and houses; lightning flashing around, generated by the tremendous turbulence inside the volcanic cloud.

- 'And it shall become small dust in all the land of Egypt, and shall be a boil breaking forth with blains upon man, and upon beast.' (Exodus 9:9.) Throughout three states after the Mount St Helens eruption, hundreds of people were taken to hospital with skin rashes and sores caused by the acidic fallout ash, while cattle, horses and other livestock perished due to prolonged inhalation of the volcanic dust.

- As well as the grey pumice ash the volcano blasted skywards, Thera had another, more corrosive toxin in its bedrock – iron oxide. In the submarine eruptions that still occur at Thera, tons of iron oxide are discharged which kill fish for miles around. According to Exodus 7:21: 'And the fish that were in the river died.' As iron oxide oxidizes in contact with air, the consequent red-coloured rust stains also turns the sea blood red. According the Exodus 7:20: 'And all the waters that were in the river turned to blood.'

- The 'parting of the Red Sea' may also be accounted for by the eruption of Thera. The name 'Red Sea', used in Exodus for the place where the waters miraculously part to allow the Israelites to escape Egypt, comes from a mistranslation of the Hebrew words *Yam Suph*, which actually means 'Sea of Reeds'. The term 'Sea of Reeds' probably applied to an expanse of water which looked exactly like it sounds: a large shallow lake or inlet covered by reeds. The most likely location of the 'Sea of Reeds' is a broad inlet on the Delta coast now called Lake Manzala. In biblical times it was divided from the Mediterranean by a narrow ridge of dry land some fifty kilometres long, broken here and there by a few hundred metres of water at high tide. If the Israelites tried to cross here, a tidal wave created by the Thera eruption might have worked to their advantage.

- During the Krakatau eruption, a series of tidal waves occurred over a period of two days. The same would certainly be true for Thera. In fact, a succession of such waves may have hit the Egyptian coast for much longer, swilling up and down the Mediterranean like water in a bath. Preceding the arrival of such tidal waves, the sea withdraws, sometimes for hours. If a section of the causeway, usually under water, had been exposed to such conditions, then the phenomenon might indeed have saved the Israelites if the Egyptians were in close pursuit. The sea would have been made dry land, as the Bible relates, and the Israelites could have made it safely across and, if the timing was fortuitous, the pursuing soldiers may have been attempting to follow when the tidal wave hit, washing them all away, just as the Bible relates. Akhenaten's adoption of the Hebrew's religious beliefs would therefore be quite under-standable. The apparently miraculous circumstances surrounding the Israelite escape may have convinced him that the Hebrew God was responsible.

CHAPTER ELEVEN

Strangers in a Strange Land

For many years biblical scholars have tended to place the Exodus during the early thirteenth century BC, some hundred years later than the time that Thera seems to have erupted. This dating is primarily because of the reference in Exodus 1:11, naming the cities where the Israelites were enslaved: 'And they did build for Pharaoh treasure cities, Pithom and Raamses.' The city of Raamses is generally accepted to have been a reference to the city of Pi-Ramesses – meaning 'The Domain of Ramesses' – which was built during the reigns of the first three kings of the nineteenth dynasty. Like Amarna, it was basically two cities in one – an administrative centre and a palace and suburban district. Pithom, therefore, may also be referring to a part of the same city. Work on Pi-Ramesses actually seems to have started in the reign of Ramesses I , the first pharaoh of the nineteenth dynasty, around 1307 BC. Horemheb had been the last eighteenth-dynasty king who, during his thirty-year reign, had purged the country of undesirable elements, such as the Atenists, and restabilized the nation under a virtual military dictatorship. Like his four predecessors, he had no male heir to succeed him, and so his general, the 'Vizier and Troop Commander' Ramesses, became the new king – Ramesses I. This time there were no royal princesses to marry

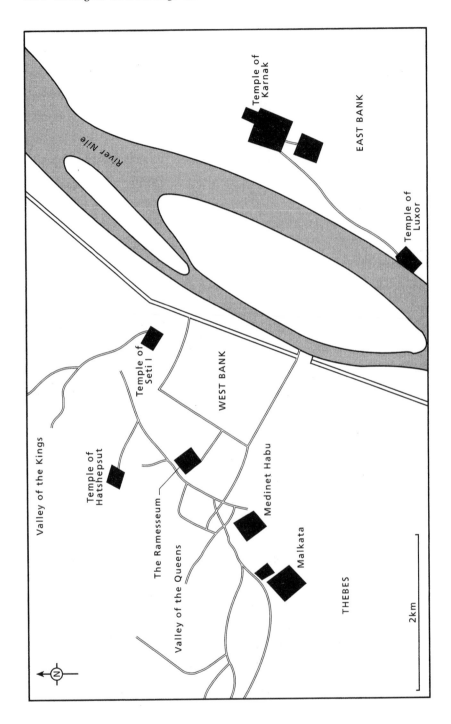

and so a completely new dynasty emerged. To signal a break with the past, the new king decided to move his capital from Thebes to the old Hyksos capital at Avaris, in the north-east Delta of Lower Egypt, and there construction on the new city of Pi-Ramesses began.

Ramesses I only lived for some two years as king and also died without an heir. Ramesses' chief general, Seti, therefore succeeded him as pharaoh. Seti broke completely with tradition and married a commoner named Tuya, the daughter of a humble junior officer. This seems to have been a wise move, for it broke an hereditary bane that had afflicted six pharaohs, not one of them having produced a male heir for over half a century. Although Tuya's first boy died in infancy, the second, also called Ramesses, lived to become Ramesses II.

Ramesses II came to the throne around the age of twenty-five and soon earned his title, 'Ramesses the Great'. He reigned for a remarkable sixty-seven years, making him one of the oldest men recorded in Egyptian history. During his reign he did everything on a gigantic scale, and even exceeded the building projects of Amonhotep III. He added to the great temples of Karnak and Luxor and built one of his own at nearby Abydos. All over the empire he erected monuments that in some ways rival the architectural achievements of the Old Kingdom. In Nubia, for instance, at Abu Simbel, he built the so-called Great Temple. Well deserving its name, it is a remarkable piece of engineering, even by today's standards: a huge artificial cave cut into a mountain, some 60 metres deep and 40 metres high. Inside the vast excavated dome are a series of temples, and outside the imposing entrance is flanked by four 18-metre-high statues of the king, hewn from solid rock.

These remarkable building projects required a vast labour force. On the west bank of the Nile, at Thebes, Ramesses constructed a massive mortuary temple called the Ramesseum, and inscriptions from a nearby quarry reveal that 3,000 workers were employed in the cutting of its stone alone. This must have been a tiny portion of the complete work force necessary to erect the temple which, by Ramesses' standards, was a modest undertaking. When we consider that the entire army, as described on the south wall of the Hypostyle Hall at the Ramesseum, only numbered some 20,000 men, we can gather that large numbers of conscript workers were needed – and many of them would have been foreign captives. The majority of these would have been used in the construction of the new city of Pi-Ramesses which, when completed, became the wonder of its age. It was here, it is argued, that the Hebrews were used as slaves.

Apart from the name of the city being mentioned in the Exodus account (which we shall examine shortly), the advocates of a Ramesses II Exodus also draw attention to references to the *Apiru* at this time. As we have seen in Chapter Eight, the *Apiru* were used in construction gangs, and are recorded making bricks in Fayum and erecting a pylon at Memphis during the reign of Ramesses II. In Exodus 1:14, this is exactly what the Hebrews are made to do: 'And they made their lives bitter with hard bondage, in mortar, and in brick.'

If these *Apiru* are the Hebrews, which they certainly seem to be, then their presence in Egypt at this time does not necessarily imply that the Exodus had not yet occurred. They may have been recaptured during Ramesses' fierce campaigning in the early part of his reign. In his fifth regnal year, around 1287 BC, Ramesses assembled one of the greatest war machines the country had ever seen – around 20,000 soldiers – for an all-out offensive against the hated Hittites. Following in the footsteps of Tuthmosis III, some 200 years earlier, Ramesses moved north through Canaan and up the Gaza Strip, so as to attack the Hittites in their Syrian strongholds. However, he had not banked on the Hittites' similar resolve to crush the Egyptians: they had assembled an even bigger army, a staggering 40,000 strong. Remarkably, Ramesses managed to survive the conflict with his army intact, neither side gaining the advantage. For the next fifteen years there were repeated battles between the Hittites and the Egyptians with no one getting the upper hand. Eventually, both sides agreed on a ceasefire. The consequence of all this fighting was that Ramesses was continually storming through Canaan, often returning with Hyksos captives to be used to support the war effort. A number of Israelites could easily have been among them.

There are, in fact, *Apiru* captives in Egypt a century later, working for the twentieth-dynasty pharaoh Ramesses III, both as attendants at the Atum temple at Heliopolis and elsewhere as quarry workers (see Chapter Eight). This is around 1180 BC, well after the Exodus must have occurred. We know from the Israel Stela that the Israelites had established some kind of kingdom in Canaan by the reign of Merenptah, some thirty years earlier. If these *Apiru* had been recaptured, then so equally could those referred to in the reign of Ramesses II. In fact, one the *Apiru* references actually shows that they were already in Canaan a few years before Ramesses' time. In the reign of Seti I, around 1300 BC, they are recorded as having been involved in a revolt at Beisham in Palestine (see Chapter Eight). Seti I had initiated the conflict with the Hittites which, although not on the scale as his son's campaigns, did necessitate repeated excursions along the Canaan coast. During such forays, he may well have become embroiled in skirmishes with the Israelites.

The Exodus narrative can be somewhat misleading from an

historical perspective, as it gives the impression that the Israelites experienced no immediate trouble from the Egyptians after they had settled in Canaan. Historically, although their main foes would have been the native Canaanites and the marauding Philistines, as the Bible relates, they would also have been stuck in the middle of an ongoing war between the two biggest empires of the day – Egypt and the Hittites. Although usually out of harm's way in their hilltop fortifications, they would have been no match for either side should they decide it was to their advantage to occupy their encampments.

The references to the *Apiru* in Egypt during the reign of Ramesses II, therefore, cannot be taken as evidence that the Exodus had not yet occurred. On the contrary, the Seti reference appears to show that it had already taken place some years before Ramesses II's reign.

We move, therefore, to the principle arguments for placing the Exodus in the early nineteenth dynasty. Firstly, that Ramesses II was the chief architect of the city that the Hebrews were forced to build. Secondly, that Eastern Delta was named the Land of Ramesses at this time, and Exodus 12:37 refers to it by this name as the starting point of the Exodus: 'And the children of Israel journeyed from Ramesses to Succoth...'

It would therefore *seem* fairly straightforward that the Exodus occurred during the reign of Ramesses II. However, we must remember how the Pentateuch often use later names for locations, and not always those contemporary with the events being described. In this particular instance, there can be no doubt whatsoever that the Bible is using a later name for the area. The Old Testament actually refers to the area around Avaris as Ramesses when it speaks of a period hundreds of years before Ramesses II was born. In Genesis 47:11, Ramesses is the name given for the land where the Israelites are allowed to settle on their arrival in Egypt. 'And Joseph placed his father and his brethren, and gave them a possession in the land of Egypt, in the best of the land, in the land of Ramesses . . .'

As we have seen, this is hundreds of years before the time of Ramesses II, during the Hyksos era (see Chapter Eight) – even

Approximate Date BC	Pharaoh	Throne Name
1570–1545	Amosis	Nebpehtyre
1545–1524	Amonhotep I	Djeserkare
1524–1518	Tuthmosis I	Akheperkare
1518–1504	Tuthmosis II	Akheperenre
1504–1483	Queen Hatshepsut	Maakare
1483–1450	Tuthmosis III	Menkheperre
1450–1416	Amonhotep II	Akheperure
1416–1389	Tuthmosis IV	Menkheperure
1389–1364	Amonhotep III	Nubmaatre
1364–1349	Akhenaten	Neferkheperure
1349–1347	Smenkhkare	Ankhkheperure
1347–1338	Tutankhamun	Nebkheperure
1338–1334	Ay	Kheperkheperure
1334–1307	Horemheb	Djeserkheperure Setepenre
1307–1305	Ramesses I	Menpehtyre
1305–1292	Seti I	Menmaatre
1292–1225	Ramesses II	Usermaatre
1225–1215	Merenptah	Baenre-merynetjeru

Independent reigns of the 18th- and early 19th-dynasty pharaohs

the Bible tells us that this was over four centuries before the Exodus (Exodus 12:40). As Genesis calls the Eastern Delta the land of Ramesses when referring to a time well before it was actually called by that name, the same could equally be true of the Ramesses references in connection with Goshen and the city of Avaris in the Exodus account.

Neither the references to the *Apiru* in Egypt nor the biblical allusions to Ramesses can therefore be taken as a case for placing the Exodus in the reign of Ramesses II, or during the reigns of his immediate nineteenth-dynasty predecessors. So is there *any* historical evidence to tell us when the Exodus took place?

Dr Manfred Bietak's excavations of ancient Avaris (see Chapter Eight) revealed four distinct levels of occupation: a Middle Kingdom layer; a Hyksos layer, dating from around 1650–1550 BC; a period of abandonment and relative inactivity; and a level of extensive rebuilding from around 1300 BC – the period of Ramesses I, Seti I and Ramesses II. It has been suggested that between the expulsion of the Hyksos and the rebuilding by these first nineteenth-dynasty kings, the city was completely abandoned. However, although it may not have been a major centre, this clearly was not the case. The reason why these kings – principally Ramesses II – decided to build their new city at Avaris, rather than anywhere else, is that it seems to have been their family home. Horemheb's regime had succeeded in dislodging the old ruling elite, and replaced them with army officers. For three decades, the country had been run by something approaching a military junta. Like most of Horemheb's senior officials, Ramesses I had been a professional soldier. Ramesses I's tomb was found by Belzoni in the Valley of the Kings in 1817, and hieroglyphic inscriptions from its modest decorations reveal that the pharaoh had been the son of a troop commander, Seti, who had been stationed at Avaris. Accordingly, Avaris *must* have been occupied to some extent.

It would seem as though Ramesses I was somehow related to his successor, Seti I, as his father bears the same name. Besides which, the military elite were trying to establish a new dynasty, and for Seti to have been accepted as pharaoh, he must have had some family connection to his predecessor. Accordingly, all three pharaohs probably had family links with Avaris. The most likely conclusion is that Avaris had been a garrison town. As it was the nearest large settlement to the major trade route – or potential invasion route – into Egypt at the time (the Ballah–Timsah crossing), it would make sense for it to have housed a military barracks. In any age, whenever you have a important military base, a town grows up around it. Exactly such a thing happened in Roman times, with many of Europe's largest cities having begun life as a fort of the Roman army. It is, at present, impossible to tell from the excavations at Avaris when such an occupation may have begun, as so little of the site remains. However, one particular Egyptian reference to the town does survive which suggests that it was reoccupied during the time of Amonhotep III.

The account appears in Manetho's *Aegyptiaca*, in the third century BC, which was reproduced in the work of the Jewish historian Flavius Josephus around AD 70. According to Manetho, a king named Amonhotep was advised by one of his officials, a man also called Amonhotep, to purge the country of 'undesirables' and set them to work in the stone quarries. After many miserable years in bondage, the king grew sorry for the wretched slaves and allowed them to live in their 'ancestral home' at Avaris. However, although they lived in better conditions, they still remained as slaves. In Avaris, the slaves were joined by a priest from Heliopolis, who had himself abandoned the Egyptian ways, and preached to them not worship the gods of Egypt. Ultimately, the priest decided to free them from captivity by training them to fight the Egyptians. He sent an emissary to the 'shepherds who had been expelled by Tuthmosis' asking for their help. 200,000 men apparently responded, and eventually they all manage to leave Egypt.

This was obviously a legendary account that the Grecian Manetho had heard from some native Egyptians. However, it seems to contain certain elements of truth. The only king called Amonhotep who also had a chief minister of the same name is Amonhotep III. In Amonhotep III's reign, a certain Amonhotep, son of Hapu, was the master of works responsible for the country's labour force. He oversaw the conscription of site workers and the allocation of foreign captives for quarrying, transportation and building. He also filled the post of 'Scribe of the Elite Troops', making him responsible for army recruitment. In short, Amonhotep, son of Hapu, was responsible for the country's entire work force. Such a man would be responsible for conscripting quarry workers, just as the story relates.

In essence, therefore, there is no reason to doubt the account. If it is true, then it not only demonstrates that Avaris was occupied during the reign of Amonhotep III, but it shows that slaves were employed there. Might they have been the Israelites?

The 'shepherds who had been expelled by Tuthmosis' are quite clearly the Hyksos, as elsewhere in his works Manetho describes them as the 'Shepherd Princes'. The 'undesirables' must have been related to them in some way: not only do the Hyksos come to their aid, but Avaris – once the Hyksos capital

– is said to be their 'ancestral home'. As the Israelites do appear to have been an important Hyksos faction (see Chapter Eight), Manetho's account is the nearest thing we have to an historical report of the Hebrew bondage in Egypt outside the Bible. Moreover, as the 'undesirables' rebel and ultimately leave the country, it may also be an allusion to the Exodus itself. It is possible that the story arose to cover the humiliating truth. The Israelites had escaped in large numbers, and later made it an issue of propaganda: the Egyptians countered by claiming that 200,000 Hyksos had actually helped them. This is blatantly an unrealistic figure, as the greatest army that Egypt ever assembled numbered only 20,000 men.

We turn finally to the archaeological evidence. Can this tell us when the Exodus occurred? The first archaeological signs of an identifiable Israelite presence in Palestine appear around the early-to-mid thirteenth century BC, and from the distinctive style of Mycenaean pottery found on the site, we know that Hazor had fallen to the Israelites around 1250 BC, give or take thirty years (see Chapter Eight). According to the Bible, the Israelites were in the wilderness for forty years before they arrived in Canaan, which, if based on any historical truth, would place the Exodus somewhere between 1340 and 1290 BC. However, the latest radiocarbon tests to date the fall of Jericho may provide a somewhat earlier date.

In 1952, when Kathleen Kenyon excavated the site of ancient Jericho, she concluded that the city was destroyed by fire around 1500 BC – much too early to have been the work of the Israelites. However, the recent radiocarbon tests, at the Centre for Isotope Research at Groningen University in Holland, have determined a much later date for the destruction. In July 1996, Hendrik J Bruins and Johannes van der Plicht published their findings in the journal *Nature* (see Chapter Nine), after they had dated ancient cereal grains found in the burned layer of the citadel excavation. (The samples had actually been excavated by Kathleen Kenyon herself in the 1950s.) Caution is called for with regards radiocarbon dating, due to the margins of error involved (see Chapter Nine). In this case, however, six separate sets of samples were tested, providing dates spanning a period of 150 years. The dates arrived at were: 1316, 1292, 1335, 1316, 1244 and 1397, giving a central date of 1315 BC. This would actually fit with the Biblical account.

According to the Bible, the Israelite conquest of Canaan began with the fall of Jericho and was followed by a lengthy campaign, as a number of city states were taken in succession, culminating in the fall of Hazor. In the fifteenth century BC, Tuthmosis III also conquered Canaan, and we can use his campaign as a comparison to arrive at a plausible chronology. We know from inscriptions on the Seventh Pylon at Karnak, that in the Year 42 of his reign Tuthmosis completed the conquest by capturing Kadesh. He did not come to the throne in his own right until his mother, Hatshepsut, died in his ninth regnal year, and the campaign did not start until this time. His conquest of Canaan therefore took around thirty-three years. Taking into account that the city states were far less formidable by the period Joshua was campaigning, with a lesser, but growing army of Hyksos recruits, it may have been possible for him to have completed the conquest in about the same time. Consequently, if the Israelite campaign started with the fall of Jericho around 1315 BC, the conquest may have been completed around 1280 BC, a date which falls within the parameters of the dating of Hazor's fall.

As the biblical account of the conquest of Canaan fits so well into the archaeological chronology, then perhaps the forty years in the wilderness also reflects an historical framework. Based on these findings, forty years earlier than Jericho's fall places the Exodus around 1355 BC. When we allow for a certain margin of error, this makes an Exodus in the 1360s BC, in the reign of Amonhotep III, a very real possibility.

Let us, therefore, summarize the historical and archaeological evidence available. Give or take ten or twenty years, these are the historical events as best we know them:

- *Circa* 1315 BC: The burning of Jericho.

- *Circa* 1300–1250 BC: Earliest archaeological evidence for Israelites in Palestine.

- *Circa* 1300 BC: *Apiru* involved in a revolt in Palestine.

- *Circa* 1250 BC: The burning of Hazor.

- *Circa* 1220 BC: Israel Stela reveals that the Israelites had established some kind of state in Canaan.

This completely tallies with the biblical account: the Israelite conquest of Canaan, starting with Jericho, which was razed to the ground, and finishing, after a lengthy campaign, with the burning of Hazor. The Bible also tells us that the Israelites spent forty years in the wilderness before they took Jericho. Because of the remarkable accuracy so far, we might assume that the Bible is also right on this point. If so, then the Exodus would have taken place around 1355 BC, give or take ten or twenty years either way.

Let us now look at what the historical and archaeological evidence tells us concerning events in the 1360s BC – a time which, based on the above chronology, falls well within the margin of error for the date of the Exodus:

- *Circa* 1360 BC: Egypt is at the height of her power. The pharaoh Amonhotep III is firmly entrenched as absolute ruler. The God Amun-Re is unquestioned as supreme deity.

- Amonhotep suddenly behaves strangely, makes Sekhmet – the goddess of devastation – chief goddess and erects more statues to her than any other god in Egypt's history. Soon after, he hands over complete authority to his son Akhenaten.

- Akhenaten abandons two thousand years of tradition, denies the existence of all the old gods, and establishes the previously obscure Aten – which is not actually a god at all – as a universal and omnipresent deity. There is no evidence of dissention.

- Akhenaten's new religion is almost identical to the Hebrew religion.

According to the Bible, the Exodus occurred after God had afflicted Egypt with a series of dreadful plagues. The terrifying events left the country devastated and demonstrated to the Egyptians the power of their God. From what we see above, it is quite clear that around 1365 BC something frightening and devastating had challenged the nation's beliefs. Moreover, it seems to have had something to do with the Hebrews. Remarkably, even without the inclusion of the Thera eruption, everything fits with the Exodus having happened at this time.

The latest scientific evidence, from both the ice core samples and the independent radiocarbon tests, does show that Thera erupted in the early fourteenth century BC. Not everyone, however, would agree with this date. Even at the present time of writing, scientists are disagreeing by hundreds of years: some placing the eruption as early as the seventeenth century BC, others as late as the twelfth century BC (see Chapter Nine). It is the same with archaeologists: some, having found traces of pumice in Egyptian ruins dating from the period of Tuthmosis III, have suggested that Thera erupted in the fifteenth century BC; while others, having found similar pumice in the Avaris region dating from the Hyksos period, have suggested that the eruption occurred in the eighteenth century BC.

The confusion may well be due to a number of lesser eruptions of what was an extremely active volcano. A decade before the *Vema* survey of 1956, a Swedish survey ship called the *Albatross* conducted an analysis of the eastern Mediterranean, taking core samples from the seabed. These marine geologists discovered evidence of an earlier Thera eruption than the one uncovered by Ninkovich and Heezen, the fallout from which had drifted further to the north. The *Vema* itself found evidence of a third, and possibly a fourth, dating back some 25,000 years. The *Albatross* eruption has not been dated, but all these findings clearly demonstrate that Thera had erupted on a number of occasions with enough force to cover vast areas of the Mediterranean seabed with ash. Indeed, Thera is still active today, and last erupted on 26 June 1926. Although a minor event compared to the ancient eruptions, it was of sufficient magnitude for its accompanying tremors to destroy over 2,000 houses on the island itself and a further 50 on neighbouring Crete, with considerable damage to a further 300. There was only ever one massive *explosion*, however: the one with sufficient magnitude to have been responsible for the plagues described in Exodus.

Datable archaeological evidence from outside Egypt which does suggest that the big one happened around 1365 BC comes from the Mitannian city of Ugarit, an ancient port on the coast of Syria, some twelve kilometres north of modern Latakia. Excavations conducted on the site since the 1930s have shown that a massive tidal wave washed away half the city sometime between the fifteenth and thirteenth centuries BC. By a remarkable stroke of luck, this event can be dated to within a few years of the Amarna period in Egypt. One of the Amarna letters sent to Akhenaten by King Abimilki of Tyre, talks of the king's horror on visiting Ugarit to find the population gone and half the city washed away into the sea. Some massive seismic activity must therefore have been responsible for the destruction either during – or shortly before – Akhenaten's reign.

The debate will no doubt continue. It is a virtual certainty, however, that Egypt *was* subjected to the devastating effects of the massive Thera eruption: the only question is when? From the widest scientific perspective, the independent ice core studies and separate radiocarbon tests show that Thera erupted in the early fourteenth century BC. From the historical perspective, the eruption of Thera around 1365 BC is just about the only event that makes any sense of the otherwise bewildering Amarna period. From the archaeological perspective, if the Exodus did occur, then it had to have happened around 1365 BC, and the Thera eruption is about the only natural phenomenon that could have caused the events the Bible describes. We can say with a high degree of confidence, therefore, that the eruption was responsible for both the sudden rise of Atenism and the Exodus plagues; and, as such, explains why Akhenaten seems to have been influenced by the Hebrew religion.

The next question concerns a Hebrew presence in Egypt during Akhenaten's reign. Realistically, it seems unlikely that all the Israelite slaves in Goshen at the time would have left when their fellow countrymen escaped. As Akhenaten had essentially

Tutankhamun's solid gold death mask which covered the face of the mummy. (*Cairo Museum.*)

The face depicted on the middle coffin is completely unlike Tutankhamun as he is depicted elsewhere – for instance, on the death mask. The cheekbones are more pronounced, the jaw is firmer and broader, the lips are less full and the nose is not so long. (*Cairo Museum.*)

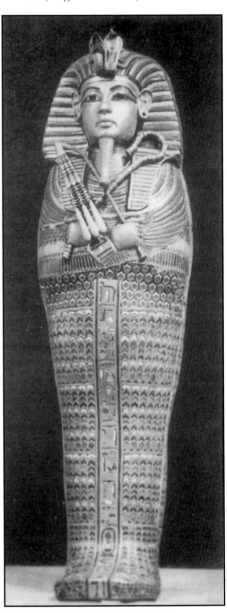

Left: The Treasury of Tutankhamun's tomb, where the figure of the jackal god Anubis guarded the splendid Canopic shrine. (*Griffith Museum.*)

Close up of one of Tutankhamun's Canopic coffinettes which were of identical design to the middle coffin. (*Cairo Museum.*)

One of the four Canopic coffinettes which contained Tutankhamun's removed internal organs. They were clearly part of the same burial equipment that had been made for another king. (*Griffith Institute.*)

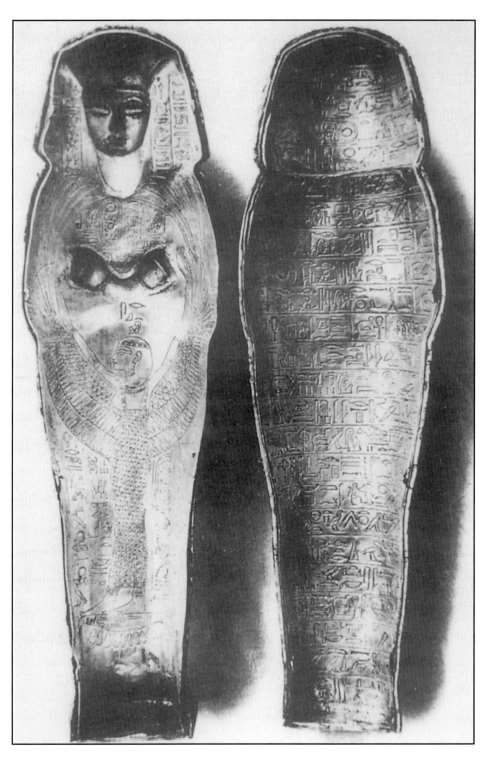

The interior of one of Tutankhamun's Canopic coffinettes, showing the inscriptions revealing that they were originally made for Tutankhamun's brother and predecessor, Smenkhkare. (*Griffith Institute.*)

Left: The only known statue of Smenkhkare as pharaoh, showing the same facial features as depicted on Tutankhamun's middle coffin and his Canopic coffinettes. Like Akhenaten, he is depicted with female breasts. (*The Lovvre, Paris.*)

Below: Two statuettes of Tutankhamun, showing his distinctive, soft features, so different from the figure depicted on the middle coffin and Canopic coffinettes. (*Cairo Museum.*)

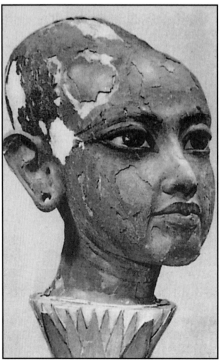

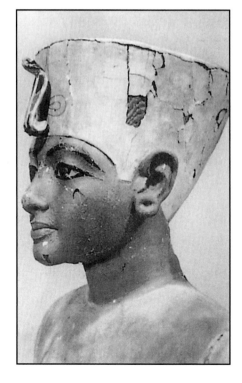

The carved limestone tablet found during excavations of the Great Temple of Amarna in 1933. It appears to show Akhenaten and Smenkhkare as co-regents. (*Cairo Museum.*)

The painted slab found at Amarna in the early 1900s which shows Smenkhkare and Meritaten reigning alone as king and queen. (*Berlin Museum.*)

One of the many Great Temple reliefs in which the eyes have been gouged from Kiya's image by her arch-rival Meritaten. (*Ny Carlsberg Glyptotek, Copenhagen.*)

Scene from Tutankhamun's golden throne, showing the king and his queen, Ankhesenpaaten, beneath the rayed symbol of the Aten. (*Cairo Museum.*)

Above: A typical domestic scene of Akhenaten, Nefertiti and their infant daughters embracing one another. No other Egyptian pharaoh ever allowed himself to be depicted in such an intimate manner. (*Berlin Museum.*)

Right: Limestone relief of Akhenaten, Nefertiti and Meritaten found in the royal tomb at Amarna. Although the names and faces of the king and queen remain intact, Meritaten's image has had the face chiseled away, probably after Tutankhamun came to the throne.

The lion-headed Sekhmet, goddess of devastation. Was it her demonic influence that Tutankhamun and his chief minister Ay believed they had imprisoned in Tomb 55? (*British Museum.*)

embraced the Israelites' religious ideas, would not some of them have freely remained behind in the new Egypt?

Akhenaten certainly seems to have undergone not only a religious, but a moral conversion. Scenes from the earliest years of his reign show him executing foreign captives with as much gusto as his predecessors. In the porch of the Third Pylon at Karnak, for instance, he is depicted smiting his foes with a huge club. The Karnak Talatat, as well as depicting similar acts of violence, include a remarkable picture of a bitter-faced Akhenaten ringing the neck of a sacrificial duck. This is hardly the Akhenaten we know from Amarna: the king who so enthusiastically praises all his god's creations, the 'good ruler that loves mankind', the man who was never depicted hunting animals for sport.

It would seem that, although Akhenaten established the Aten as supreme deity right from the beginning of his reign, his conversion to a religion which is almost identical to the Hebrew faith was more of a gradual process. In the fifth year he breaks with his former identity, adopts his new name and builds his new city. By this time he had also adopted his humanitarian doctrines. Four years later he proscribes the use of graven images and totally separates his omnipresent god from the old notions of Re-Herakhte. This would all suggest that, although the Thera experience may have persuaded him to accept the supremacy of the Hebrew God (at least his own perception of it), something was continuing to move him ever closer to an Israelite view of religion. This not only implies that there were still Israelites in Egypt, but also that they were somehow close to the pharaoh.

If any Hebrew slaves remained in Egypt, we can assume that Akhenaten would have set them free. There is no evidence that any Hyksos slaves were being used during his reign. On the contrary, he seems to have employed them in his praetorian guard. The Karnak Talatat, coming from the *Gempaaten*, show what can only be described as a foreign legion in attendance on the king. There are almost no soldiers in native Egyptian dress depicted anywhere near Akhenaten. Among foreigners, quite obviously of African origin, are a large number of figures who appear to be officers in Asiatic dress, identical to that worn by the Hyksos in scenes discovered at Avaris (see Chapter Eight). Identifiably Hyksos guards are also shown in great numbers in the Jubilee event of the Year 12, shown in the tombs of Huya and Meryre (see Chapter Six). Whether these soldiers included the Israelites, there is no way of knowing. All the same, it does demonstrate Akhenaten's complete change of policy towards the peoples who included the Israelites, and that the Israelites could have been in close attendance of the pharaoh. However, one remarkable piece of evidence, which has only recently come to light, suggests that some Israelites were actually appointed senior ministers.

In 1989 the French archaeologist Alain Zivie discovered a rock-cut tomb in the Bubasteion cliff at Saqqara, right beneath a guest house belonging to the Egyptian Antiquities Organis-ation. The tomb was still sealed, but it had been plundered in antiquity and patched up by the necropolis attendants at the time. Inside were the decomposed mummies of one Aper-el, his wife Tauret and their son Huy. A number of items did remain, including the coffins, wine jars, a number of *ushabti* figures, statuettes, jewellery, and a complete set of Canopic jars. Most important of all, however, were the inscriptions that still remained intact, identifying the occupants and their place in Egyptian history.

Aper-el was practically unknown before the discovery, which made the find all the more astonishing. It turned out that he

was one of the most important figures in Akhenaten's government. He was both the vizier of Memphis – the governor of
northern Egypt – and an important religious figure, as he bore
the title 'Father of the God'. This made him of equal status to
Akhenaten's chief minister Ay. Aper-El's son had been an
important figure: the general in charge of all the chariotry of
Lower Egypt, and the 'Scribe of Recruits', making him responsible for all army recruitment in the area.

Wine jars in the tomb are dated as the Year 10 of Akhenaten's reign, but more significantly cartouches of both Akhenaten
and Amonhotep III were found. As Alain Zivie observed in an
article in the summer 1991 issue of *Egyptian Archaeology* magazine: 'taken together [these] could be used as evidence in the
old "Loch Ness monster" question of Egyptology – that of a
possible co-regency of the two kings...'. This was nothing,
however, compared to apparent identity of Aper-El himself. The
remarkable thing was that Aper-El was not a native Egyptian
but an Asiatic – which in itself would be unusual enough, as no
other pharaoh of the eighteenth dynasty is known to have
appointed an Asiatic to such high office. More specifically,
however, he seems to have been an Israelite. His name, Aper-El,
Alain Zivie, realized with surprise, appeared to have been a title,
an Egyptian form of *Abed* or *Oved-El*, meaning 'The Servitor of
[the god] El'. *El* is an abbreviated form of the Hebrew word
Elohim, meaning Lord, which is the form in which God is
usually addressed in the original Hebrew of the Old Testament.
(In the original Hebrew version of the Old Testament the name
for God appears simply as the word *El* many times. For example,
in Genesis alone we find it used frequently in place of the word
God: Genesis 14:18, 16:13, 21:33, 33:20, 35:7.)

It may seem strange that someone of Hebrew origin would
allow himself to be mummified in an Egyptian manner. How-

ever, the Bible makes it quite clear that the Israelites saw nothing wrong in this. The Patriarch Joseph, for example, is buried according to Egyptian custom: 'So Joseph died, being an hundred and ten years old, and they embalmed him, and he was put in a coffin in Egypt.' (Genesis 50:26.)

However, this is nothing compared to the most astonishing discovery of all. The depictions of the Aten in the tomb, together with other Amarna-style illustrations, make it blatantly apparent that Aper-El was also an Atenist. Alain Zivie even suggests that Aper-El was a prophet of the Aten in Memphis. The title 'Father of the God' would certainly imply this.

Here we not only have evidence of a shared link between the Hebrew religion and Atenism, but a corporeal example of someone who seems to have been a prophet of both religions and saw nothing contradictory about it. Unfortunately, the tomb was badly damaged and robbed of most of its treasures – if it had been intact, it may have shed an incredible new light on the entire mystery of the Israelites in Egypt.

It may actually have been people such as Aper-El who made up the 'bull-worshipping' faction among the early Israelites, as evidenced by Dr Amihay Mazor's discovery at biblical Shechem, and the Exodus story of the 'golden calf' (see Chapter Seven). Perhaps when the Atenists were eventually suppressed by Horemheb, many of them had fled from Egypt and joined up with the Israelites, somewhere in the Sinai desert.

In Manetho's account we have evidence of interaction between the Heliopolis cult and the Israelites. He tells us that, while in Avaris, the slaves (who seem to have been the Israelites) were joined by a priest from Heliopolis, who preached to them not to worship the Egyptian gods. It may be that the Egyptians had tried to force the Israelites to accept their gods and some of them may have been tempted. The fact that a priest from

Heliopolis – the centre for the Re cult – should join them and persuade them otherwise, suggest that he had already be converted to *their* God. This is, once again, a possible link between the Hebrews and the Atenists, for it was in Heliopolis that Atenism seems to have begun. Perhaps the cult of Re was already being influenced by the religion of Egypt's reluctant guests, even before the time of the Exodus.

Before moving on, there is one final person we must consider: Moses. As everything else in the Exodus account would seem to be based to a remarkable degree on historical events, Moses himself may also reflect an historical figure. The Bible tells us that Moses was the son of a Hebrew of the house of Levi: we are told he has a brother called Aaron, but the identity of his father remains vague, as he is named both as Reu'el and later as Jethro. After he is saved in the little boat of bulrushes, Moses is actually brought up by the pharaoh's daughter: 'And the child grew, and she [Moses' sister] brought him unto Pharaoh's daughter, and he became her son.' (Exodus 2:10.) He even becomes an Egyptian prince. According to Exodus 2:14, the Hebrew whose life Moses has saved questions Moses about himself: 'Who made thee and prince and judge over us?'

Surely, such a person should be found somewhere in Egyptian records? Unfortunately not – not during the reign of Amonhotep III, or of any other Egyptian pharaoh. However, his name may be misleading. In its original Hebrew, the name Moses is *Moshe*. Exodus 2:10 tells us that the pharaoh's daughter decides to call him this: 'Because I drew him out of the water'. The Hebrew word *Msha* means 'to draw', and *Moshui* is 'one who has been drawn out'. Some biblical scholars have concluded that the later copyists of Exodus, in the seventh century BC, tried to offer a Hebrew origin of the name that was not originally intended. They point out that it is unlikely that an Egyptian princess would call an adopted son by a Hebrew name if she wished to keep his Semitic background a secret from the rest of the court. Even if she had no fear of being discovered, then why not use the name his true mother had given him, which, incidentally, we are never told. In its original Hebrew, the name Moses is pronounced *Moshe*. As the Egyptian equivalent of *sh* is the simple s sound, *Moshe* would be pronounced *Mose* in Egyptian, a word which simply means 'son'. If we look at Exodus 2:10 we can see what might have happened: 'And the child grew, and she brought him unto Pharaoh's daughter, and he became her son. And she called his name Moses.'

If we exchange the word Moses for 'son', then the pharaoh's daughter is simply repeating what she has promised – that she will raise him as her own son. The first Greek translators of the Old Testament certainly interpreted it this way. When the Greeks later occupied Egypt in the fourth century BC, the Egyptian word *Mose* became *Mosis* – hence names such as Tuthmosis – 'Born of [the god] Thoth', or 'Thoth – son'. (When he lived, Tuthmosis' name would have been pronounced 'Tut-mose'.) In the Greek version of the Bible, Moses' name was actually written *Mosis*, from which we now get the name 'Moses'.

Consequently, whoever it was who led the Israelites out of Egypt during the Exodus was probably not known as Moshe or Moses when he was alive. This may account for why his name does not appear in Egyptian records.

The story of Moses being hidden in the river may also have been a later addition to the account, taken from an old Mesopotamian myth. Magnus Magnusson, the British broadcaster and author, draws attention to a remarkable similarity between the Moses story and an ancient myth, in his book, *BC: The Archaeology of the Bible Lands*. In Exodus 2:3 we are told how Moses' mother hides him: 'And when she could no longer hide him, she took for him an ark of bulrushes, and daubed it with slime and with pitch, and put the child therein; and she laid it in the flags of the river brink.'

In a Mesopotamian myth, concerning King Sargon I of Akkad, dating from around 2350 BC, Sargon says of himself: 'My changeling mother conceived me, in secret she bore me. She set me in a basket of rushes, with bitumen she sealed my lid. She cast me in the river which rose not over me . . . Akki, the drawer of water, took me as his son and reared me.'

Whether or not Moses really was placed into the river or not, the fact remains that he was said to have been brought up as a prince. Is there anyone who appears as a prince in the royal court during the reign of Amonhotep who fits the profile of Moses? Apart from Akhenaten, the only other royal prince to be found in Egyptian records from the reign of Amonhotep III is Akhenaten's elder brother – a shadowy figure named Tuthmosis (not to be confused with the pharaohs of the same name). He was actually the true heir to the throne before he mysteriously disappears.

The Bible tells us that Moses is eighty years of age when he confronts the pharaoh, which would make him far too old to have been Prince Tuthmosis. However, as we have seen, one has to treat biblical ages with caution. We often read of people living to more than a century when forty or fifty was considered a good life span. Moses himself, we are told, lives to be 120. Some figures in the Old Testament reach impossible ages: Abraham's father Terah reaches 205 and Noah lived until he was 950. In all probability, the ages of the characters were not included in the oral accounts that were handed down from generation to generation, and the later copyists attributed them with great old age to intimate extreme wisdom.

Prince Tuthmosis was recognized as heir of Amenhotep III and, as such, filled the office of governor of Memphis. (An office that Aper-El filled in Akhenaten's reign as the pharaoh had no sons.) He was also installed as high priest of its temple, dedicated to the creator god Ptah. The Priest was responsible for burying the sacred Apis bull (not to be confused with the Mnevis Bull [see Chapter Seven]), in which Ptah was thought to incarnate, and which died during Amonhotep's reign. Tuthmosis is recorded officiating with his father at the bull's funeral. Apart from an ivory whip, found in Tutankhamun's tomb, which he apparently used as commander of the king's chariot forces, nothing more is heard of Tuthmosis.

It is difficult to tell how much earlier than Akhenaten's reign Tuthmosis disappears, as only one reference to Akhenaten survives from the period before he became pharaoh. This is the wine-jar seal from Malkata (see Chapter Seven), referring to 'the estate of the true king's son Amonhotep'. Intriguingly, Akhenaten (under his original name, Amonhotep) is described as the *true* king's son, implying that someone else was not. It is tempting to speculate that this might have been intended as a slight on Tuthmosis. There is certainly one piece of evidence which shows almost conclusively that Tuthmosis had fallen from favour and had been executed or exiled. A tomb was being prepared for him in the Valley of the Kings when – for some unknown reason – it was suddenly abandoned. It was found by Giovanni Belzoni in 1816 at the far end of the western Valley of the Kings, and was the one later used for the pharaoh Ay. If Prince Tuthmosis died while still in favour, why was he not buried in it? Many of the pharaohs were buried in unfinished tombs.

If Moses really was brought up as a royal prince during the reign of Amonhotep III, then Tuthmosis is the only known historical figure who fits the profile. According to the Bible, Moses has to flee into exile, and something very similar may well have happened to Tuthmosis. Moreover, like Moses, Tuthmosis might not actually have been the king's true son. Perhaps this was discovered and he was enslaved with the Israelites. He might even have been the priest from Heliopolis that Manetho tells us helped the 'undesirables' to escape. Manetho calls him Osarseph, which certainly sounds like a Hebrew name. Might this have been Moses' birth name? Unfortunately, at present, there is no way of knowing. It is an intriguing thought, however, that if Tuthmosis had abandoned the old gods and decided to drop the god-element *Tuth* from his name, he would actually have been called *Mosis*.

Before finally returning to the mystery of Tomb 55, there is one additional aspect of the Exodus story we have not yet examined: the last plague which the Bible tells us God inflicted upon the Egyptians: the deaths of the firstborn. It is this that may provide the final clue to the mystery of Tomb 55 – indeed, the entire Exodus enigma.

SUMMARY

- According to the Bible, the Israelite entry into the Promised Land of Canaan began with the conquest and burning of the city of Jericho, forty years after the Exodus from Egypt. In

1996 radiocarbon tests on the charred remains were able to date the destruction to around 1315 BC. Based on these findings, forty years earlier than Jericho's fall places the Exodus around 1355 BC. When we allow for a certain margin of error expected in radiocarbon dating, this makes an Exodus in the 1360s BC, in the reign of Amonhotep III, a very real possibility.

- In 1989 the French archaeologist Alain Zivie discovered the tomb of Akhenaten's chief minister, Aper-El. The remarkable thing about Aper-El was that he seems to have been an Israelite.

- In the tomb of Aper-El we not only have evidence of a shared link between the Hebrew religion and Atenism, but an example of someone who seems to have been a prophet of both religions and saw no contradiction in it. It may actually have been people such as Aper-El who made up the 'bull-worshipping' faction among the early Israelites, as evidenced by the archaeological discoveries and the Exodus story of the 'golden calf'. Perhaps when the Atenists were eventually suppressed by Horemheb, many of them fled from Egypt and joined up with the Israelites somewhere in the Sinai desert.

- According to the Bible Moses, although born an Israelite, is brought up by the pharaoh's daughter as a prince at the royal court. However, no record has yet been discovered of any Egyptian prince of this name. The name, though, may be misleading. In its original Hebrew, the name Moses is *Moshe*. As the Egyptian equivalent of the letters *sh* is the simple *s* sound, *Moshe* would be pronounced *Mose* in Egyptian, a word which simply means 'son'. The first Greek translators of the Old Testament certainly interpreted it this way. When the Greeks later occupied Egypt in the fourth century BC, the Egyptian word *Mose* became *Mosis*. In the Greek version of the Bible, Moses' name was actually written *Mosis*, from which we now get the name 'Moses'.

- Whoever it was who led the Israelites out of Egypt during the Exodus he was probably not known as Moshe or Moses when he was alive. This may account for why his name does not appear in Egyptian records. Apart from Akhenaten, the only other royal prince to be found in Egyptian records from the reign of Amonhotep III is Akhenaten's elder brother — a shadowy figure named Tuthmosis. He was actually the true heir to the throne before he mysteriously disappears from the record a few years before Akhenaten's reign.

- There are very few surviving records of Akhenaten before his accession to the throne, but one, on a wine-jar seal, refers to him as 'the true king's son'. Intriguingly, Akhenaten is described as the *true* king's son, implying that someone else was not. It is tempting to speculate that this might have been intended as a slight on Tuthmosis. There is certainly one piece of evidence which shows almost conclusively that Tuthmosis had fallen from favour and had been executed or exiled. A tomb was being prepared for him in the Valley of the Kings when, for some unknown reason, it was suddenly abandoned. If Prince Tuthmosis died while still in favour, why was he not buried in it? Many of the pharaohs were buried in unfinished tombs.

- If Moses really was brought up as a royal prince during the reign of Amonhotep III, then Tuthmosis is the only known historical figure who fits the profile. According to the Bible, Moses has to flee into exile, and something very similar may well have happened to Tuthmosis. Moreover, like Moses, Tuthmosis may not actually have been the king's true son. It is an intriguing thought, however, that if Tuthmosis had abandoned the old gods and decided to drop the god-element *Tuth* from his name, he would actually have been called *Mosis*.

CHAPTER TWELVE

The Angel of Death

Let us try to imagine the ancient city of Thebes immediately after the fallout cloud has dispersed. The lush strip of land to either side of the Nile now appears as barren as the surrounding desert, with ruddy-streaked, grey ash blanketing everything like the surface of the moon. Charred trees, having been set ablaze by falling cinders, now stand smouldering in stark silhouette, like black skeletal fingers clawing at the sky. On the river banks, boats lie abandoned, some broken apart, others beached high on the embankment by the great waves that have surged upstream. The carcasses of animals – goats, donkeys, cattle – lie stiff and cold, their open mouths a frozen testament to their last lungfuls of choking ash. The Nile is now a parody of its life-giving self, with dead fish floating along on a stinking foam of red mud. A bizarre cacophony fills the air: muffled moans drifting from buildings, the howling of dogs out in the desert, the hiss of volcanic dust as it streams from the rooftops of temples, palaces and shrines.

Through the smoke which hugs the ground like a morning mist, the survivors emerge one by one. Some are unscathed, but their eyes are wide with horror; some are covered with sores, their eyes bloodshot and swollen. Filing into the streets, they huddle together in shocked silence. Someone points to

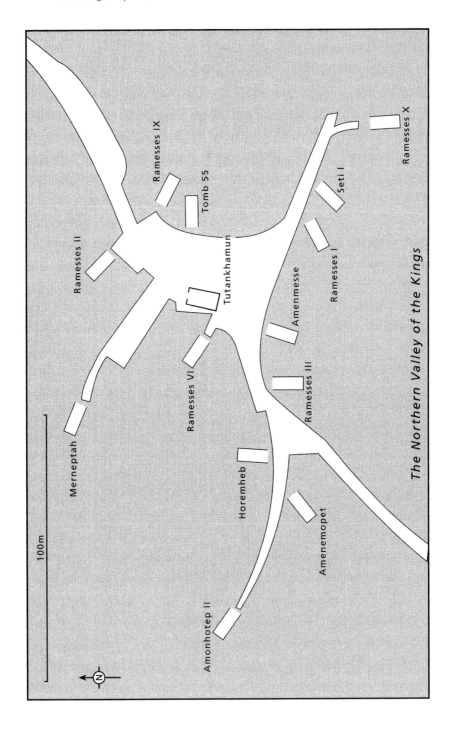

Amonhotep II

Merneptah

Ramesses II

Horemheb

Amenemopet

Ramesses VI

Ramesses IX

Tomb 55

Tutankhamun

Amenmesse

Ramesses III

Seti I

Ramesses I

Ramesses X

100m

The Northern Valley of the Kings

the sky. The others look up – the sun shines sickly green overhead!

In the great temple of Karnak, the priesthood gathers in secret conclave, away from the staring image of Amun-Re. Surely they have carried out all the prescribed rites, observed all the necessary festivals, attended to all the god's needs. What more should they do to serve? In the palace, the pharaoh consults frantically with his ministers. He is the son of the god. How can he restrain the wrath of his divine father?

An answer is found in the ancient texts. Once before, at the dawn of time, the goddess Sekhmet had tried to destroy mankind. She is the goddess of devastation, of carnage and destruction. It is she who must be appeased. She must be made supreme goddess and worshipped by all Egypt.

Far to the north, in the north-east Delta, followers of the cult of Re have been spared. They hear of the devastation inflicted on the south and all agree – it is their god who has been enraged. The cult of Amun has gone too far. The statues, the temples, the shrines, that cover the land are erected in the name of Amun-Re. Re must be revered in his own right – no longer as an aspect of a lesser god. The once supreme deity of all Egypt must be supreme again. If not, then he will no longer curb his rage.

The governor of Lower Egypt and heir to the throne, the young Amonhotep, does not agree. This, he says, has been the work of the Hebrews' God. They too have been spared. It is their God who must be worshipped if the world is to live. Overhead, the sun still shines forth its vile green rays, casting an eerie glow over the land of the Nile. There can be no doubt that this is a sun-god's deed. Perhaps the God of the Hebrews and the sun-god Re are one and the same! Yet the Hebrew God is the *only* god and he has no name! It must be Re in his aspect as the Aten – the sunlight that shines over all – that is the true god of mankind.

The weeks pass. Back in Thebes, the priests have made Sekhmet the divine consort of Amun-Re, hundreds of her statues line the temple precincts, and the pharaoh issues up daily prayers to the new goddess. Yet still the sun shines green. Worse! Plagues of locusts have ravished the crops, descending in their thousands to devour the city's food. Swarms of flies and stinging insects fill the air. Why has the goddess not been appeased?

When Prince Amonhotep returns to Thebes and proclaims his new god, many flock to his side. He tells them how the north has been spared, and how, if they adore the Aten, and make him king, they too shall live in a pure land. As more and more follow the new prophet, the skies are cleansed and the pestilence retreats. Egypt has been saved! The young Amonhotep is accepted by all alike – the priesthood, the soldiery, the people – as the sole voice and true son of the one and only god. Even the king concedes to his son's demands. He is made co-regent and appointed with full pharaonic power. He is the pharaoh Amonhotep IV. He is Akhenaten – 'The living spirit of the Aten'.

This may not be exactly how it happened, but Atenism would appear to have come about under circumstances some-where along these lines. The important point is that when Akhenaten came to the throne he appears to have enjoyed wide support. Within five years he was building a completely new capital, two years later the entire administration had moved there, and two years after that Atenism had fully developed into what we would now consider a modern religion. The Aten was the omnipresent and only god, it could not be represented by an idol or its power called upon by amulets, and it communed solely with its infallible prophet, Akhenaten. It was a religion of love, peace, and goodwill to all creation. On paper, there is almost no difference between Atenism and early Christianity. It worshipped one omnipresent God – a God forbidden to be shown as a graven image or His power summoned by talismans – and His sole emissary on earth was the pontiff. Like, Atenism, Christianity preached universal love. Christianity, sprung from the Hebrew faith, was adopted by the greatest empire in the world – the Romans – and has survived for centuries, spreading its teachings around the globe. Atenism seems to have emerged from the Hebrew faith, it was the religion of the greatest empire in the world – the Egyptians – but it survived for less than two decades. What went wrong?

Theological considerations or matters of faith aside, from the purely psychological standpoint Atenism failed because it was too much too soon, but most of all because it was inflexible. To begin with, there was the entire concept of monotheism. We can see from all the tomb and temple decorations that during the later Amarna period the Aten was the only god allowed to be venerated under Atenism. Although previously the Egyptians could pray to a pantheon of gods for an infinite variety of matters, the shrines in the private dwellings reveal that only by beseeching Akhenaten to intercede on their behalf could the citizens of Amarna pray for help, protection or guidance.

We live in a world of uncertainty, where much in life is beyond our control. In ancient times, life was all the more uncertain, and there were no scientists to explain why things happened the way they did. Each force of nature, each daily routine, every aspect of life, was the domain of a specific divinity. There were gods for love, gods for war, gods for protection, and gods to grant wisdom. There were gods for everything. Although Amun-Re was the chief god of Egypt and responsible for the nation's prosperity, individual fate and fortune were governed by a myriad gods. If you hoped for a favourable ruling in a court of law, you might pray to Mafdet, the goddess of the judiciary; if you wished to be successful in hunting, you might pray to Neith, the goddess of the wild chase; and if you wanted your land to be fertile, you might prey to Geb, the god of the earth. Egyptians had been doing this for centuries, and suddenly those that accepted Akhenaten's teachings could never do so again. An entire nation cannot change overnight, and old habits die hard.

The Roman Catholic Church survived its early years because it was flexible; an institution developed that allowed the polytheistic citizens of the Roman Empire, and the pagan peoples of its domains, to pray to a variety of higher beings without breaking the taboos of a single God – the saints. Christian martyrs, early missionaries and performers of miracles were made saints, and there were soon as many saints as there had been gods. Although the canonization of saints is now the prerogative of the Vatican, in early Christian times local communities appointed saints as they saw fit. This continued well after the fall of the Roman empire, right through the Dark Ages and even into medieval times. A successful warrior could be made a saint, like the Saxon king Edgar; so could a popular benefactor, like the Danish princess Fraith: in some cases even one of the old gods managed to sneak in unnoticed, like the controversial English patron saint St George – once a pagan sun-god.

Generally speaking, however, the saints were Christian holy men and women, and each of them had a specific role to play. St Francis, for instance, became the patron saint of animals, St Christopher became the patron saint of travellers, and St Jude became the patron saint of lost causes. Just as in the old religions, the people of Christendom could pray to different immortals for different reasons. Atenism, however, allowed for none of this. You prayed to the Aten or to Akhenaten or to no one at all – the god and his prophet saw to everything personally.

The second drawback for Atenism was that it did not allow the making of idols. The Aten had no earthly shape, so it could not be represented in corporeal form – only by the image of the sun disc. Once again, the Egyptians had spent two thousand years praying to tangible figures in which their gods could reside. Like the jackal-headed Anubis, the ibis-headed Thoth, or the crocodile-headed Suchos, all the gods had physical forms, and when their images were made and consecrated, something of the god's power would inhabit them. Once more, it was impossible for all but the most pious to abandon such ingrained traditions overnight. The Catholic Church also proscribed the making of images of God: yet they still had the saints, and their images could be made and prayed to without offending the Lord.

Another disadvantage facing Atenism was its proscribing the use of talismans. Talismans or amulets, such as jewellery or tokens consecrated to a specific god and thought to secure their aid or protection, were forbidden. Again, after centuries of habitual reliance on talismans, such a decree would have left the Egyptians feeling naked and vulnerable. Like the Christians being permitted to wear the cross, the Atenists were allowed to wear the *ankh*, the symbol of the Aten's life-giving power. However, this in no way made up for the hexes, spells and conjurations that talismans were believed to perform. For someone in Akhenaten's Egypt to be prevented from employing such icons would be like expecting someone from the modern world to work in a hazardous environment without protective clothing, or to go into battle without a weapon. The Catholic Church avoided this problem through the sanctioning of relics.

Atenism had no Grail, it had no Turin Shroud, no bones of saints or anything to channel the power of its gods – only the sun itself and its prophet, the king.

The greatest problem of all for Atenism, however, was that it was too naive – it made no allowance for evil. The idea of a single, all-encompassing god is a fine philosophy until you run into trouble. If there is only one divinity responsible for everything, then whom do you blame when things go wrong? Akhenaten gained power, and his religion achieved prominence, seemingly because his god had smitten Egypt for worshipping other gods. The Aten was responsible for everything! This concept had thrust Atenism to supremacy, but it also seems to have initiated its rapid demise. The Christian Church survived the fall of the Roman empire, the Dark Ages, even the Black Death, because it had someone else to blame – the Devil. Atenism seems to have had no such concept. If disaster struck, then it was totally down to the Aten. True, it could be argued that the god had not been properly venerated or its people had abandoned it. But what if they had done everything their prophet demanded – and still disaster struck? It is just such a scenario that seems to have led to the sudden eclipse of Atenism.

After only ten halcyon years in Amarna, the people who had embraced the new religion with fervour, and had joyfully revered their prophet king, totally abandoned the city and reinstated the old gods. In fact, the downfall of Atenism seems to have started after a mere seven years in Amarna, when Akhenaten retired almost completely from public life, and his daughter and co-regent began a three-year reign of religious oppression.

Somewhere around year 14 of Akhenaten's reign, something begins to go terribly wrong. In fact, it is so sudden that it cannot be accounted for by the populace simply growing hungry for the old ways – this would surely have been a more gradual process. Moreover, for the Egyptians to have abandoned a god that evidently had the power to inflict wholesale catastrophe – the likes of which had never been seen before – must imply that something equally horrific was happening again. Something which persuaded them that Akhenaten's doctrines were not the answer after all.

Amonhotep III seems to have handed power over to his co-regent, Akhenaten, because he had failed to appease whatever forces were responsible for the Thera holocaust. Around his fifteenth regnal year Akhenaten also withdrew from public life and handed over power to *his* co-regent Smenkhkare. We can only infer that some calamity of a similar magnitude had again occurred. The very fact that Smenkhkare and the new queen, Meritaten, immediately initiated a savage desecration of the Amun temples at Thebes, only adds weight to this hypothesis. As we have seen, there was now nothing but the Aten to blame. If Egypt was plagued by some misfortune, and the Aten was responsible, then, from the Atenist perspective, it could only mean that the Aten was displeased. Only by doing something from which Akhenaten had refrained, could matters be put to right: by destroying the temple at Karnak and persecuting any who may still adhere to the old ways.

Presumably this must have been deemed to have failed, as Akhenaten himself is then apparently held to account. We have seen in Chapter Five how the macabre burial, ultimately destined for Smenkhkare, was originally planned – and probably implemented – for Akhenaten. Add to this the fact that Smenkhkare then returned to Thebes to realign himself with the cult of Amun, and that his successors almost immediately abandoned Amarna, and we have all the signs of a nation in the throes of desperation. Everything they try is to no avail! When we look again at Amarna's last years, we see all the signs of a further natural disaster – an epidemic.

If the royal family is anything to go by, then the population was dropping like flies. Some three years before the end of Akhenaten's reign, there are many members of the king's household recorded and pictured in the Amarna tomb, palace and temple scenes. We have the queen, Nefertiti, the second wife, Kiya, the queen mother, Tiye, and her daughter Beketaten; together with the princesses: Meritaten, Meketaten, Ankhesen-paaten, Neferneferuaten-ta-sherit, Neferneferure and Sotepenre. In the year 12 they are all joyfully present at the Jubilee event, and in the year 14 they are still alive and well. But after the year 17, only one of them – Ankhesenpaaten – is ever heard of again (see Chapter Five). Even the two latest additions to the family, Ankhesenpaaten-ta-sherit and Meritaten-ta-sherit, vanish from the record after Amarna is abandoned. Apart from Akhenaten himself and Smenkhkare, both of whom appear to have died within a year of each other, many of the chief ministers – such as the chamberlain Tutu, the cupbearer Perennefer and the high priest Meryre – simply disappear at the end of Akhenaten's reign.

There does not seem to have been a palace coup or a purge by Smenkhkare, as we can be fairly sure that the most important official, Ay, would have been first on the list. Besides which, if someone wanted to be rid of the whole royal family, why leave Ankesenpaaten alive, and why should the next four kings all have married Akhenaten's relatives to legitimate their rule? We certainly know that Akhenaten, Nefertiti, Meketaten, and another princess (probably Neferneferure) were not purged in a coup as they were all interred in the royal tomb (see Chapter Five).

Of the common citizens of Amarna there survives no record, but if we take the royal family and the ruling elite as a statistical cross-section, then it would appear that something was killing off the population in droves. This is surely evidence of some type of epidemic. In fact, we have proof positive that a virulent plague was sweeping through the Egyptian vassal states. The king of Alashia writes to Akhenaten in one of the Amarna letters that Nergal – the god of disease and pestilence – was abroad in his land, reducing the production of copper ingots for the pharaoh. Completely independent accounts from Byblos and Sumura also record vast numbers dying of plague. Even the Hittites, who seemed to have been keeping their distance from Egypt, eventually succumbed.

From excavations at Hattusas (modern Boghazkoy) in Turkey, the Hittite capital, the archives of King Suppiluliumas I were discovered. Among the clay tablets inscribed with records of his reign was found a fascinating reference to the letter that Ankesenpaaten had sent to Suppiluliumas when Tutankhamun died (see Chapter Six). As we have seen, she asked the king to send her one of his sons so that she could marry him and make him pharaoh. When the prince was attacked and killed, it led to a revenge raid by the Hittites on Egyptian-occupied Amqa (in Lebanon). The archives record that after the attack, the Egyptian prisoners they brought back to the capital carried with them a plague that not only killed the king but afflicted the Hittites for years to come.

Such a plague may actually account for the abandonment of Amarna. Even though the ancients may not have known the true cause of disease, they knew well enough that contagious illnesses were passed from person to person. What type of epidemic this might have been is hard to tell, although it seems to have had a lengthy duration. In fact, it may have been a series of different viruses, perhaps started by the after-effects of the Thera eruption. With the number of dead carcasses littering the countryside, the abundance of rodents, and the mass of disease-carrying insects, who knows how many outbreaks of disease could have resulted. An ongoing series of epidemics in Thebes, and elsewhere, may even have accounted for Akhenaten's move to Amarna in the first place.

It is with disease in Egypt that we again find a familiar echo in the Exodus account. According to Exodus 7:29–30, the last plague that God brought down upon the Egyptians was the most terrifying of all:

> And it came to pass, that at midnight the Lord smote all the firstborn in the land of Egypt, from the firstborn of the Pharaoh that sat on his throne unto the firstborn of the captive that was in the dungeon; and all the firstborn of cattle. And Pharaoh rose up in the night, he, and all his servants, and all the Egyptians; and there was a great cry in Egypt; for there was not a house where there was not one dead.

Might this be a reference to such an epidemic? Although in the biblical narrative, the deaths of the firstborn occur before the Exodus from Egypt, we have already seen how the order of events may have been rearranged at a later date (see Chapter Ten). The specific reference to the firstborn could also be a confusion of two separate calamities to have affected Egypt.

From the moment Akhenaten comes to the throne – seemingly right after the 'plagues' caused by Thera – no pharaoh sires a male heir for well over half a century. Akhenaten, despite having at least six daughters, has no son that we know of. Smenkhkare also appears to have sired only a daughter, Merita-ten-ta-sherit: he certainly left no male heir. Tutankhamun's queen, Ankhesenpaaten, only seems to have conceived daughters, one (perhaps) by her father – Ankhesenpaaten-ta-shertit – and two stillborn foetuses of baby girls. Aborted after five and eight months, they were found mummified in the Treasury of Tutankhamun's tomb. Ay never sired a male heir, and neither did Horemheb, despite the fact that they both lived to a ripe old age. Even the first nineteenth-dynasty king, Ramesses I, had no male issue. It is not until Seti I, around 1300 BC, that the chain is finally broken. This is a period of some sixty-odd years. For a people whose pharaoh was considered the personification of the chief god on earth, around whom the whole of society revolved, it must have seemed as if they were indeed a cursed nation. It certainly led to instability and ultimately what seems to have been a military dictatorship.

It is possible that a combination of these two afflictions inspired the story of the final plague in the Exodus account. As we have seen in the previous chapter, some Israelites would appear to have stayed in Egypt after the Thera event. Some, like Aper-El and his son, even achieved exalted office during Akhenaten's reign. Surely, if one of them rose to be the equivalent of a prime minister, there must have been many more. Staying in a foreign country, in which they were now respected, possibly feared, must have been infinitely preferable to wandering in the desert, or holding their own against hostile marauders in Canaan.

Once the anti-Atenist persecutions began under Horemheb, however, any Hebrews that had allied themselves with Akhenaten would almost certainly have suffered too. We know that by the beginning of Seti's reign there are *Apiru* slaves again being used in Egypt, having been absent from the surviving records for many decades (see Chapter Seven). Perhaps, during such oppression, many of the remaining Israelites managed to flee from Egypt and join up with their countrymen – possibly the golden-calf worshippers of Exodus 32. Although the Hebrews who remained in Egypt seem to have influenced the course of Atenism, Atenism may also have influenced them. To an extent, they may have gone native, and the Exodus story of the golden calf may reflect this. Even though Exodus tells us that calf-worshippers were put to the sword, we know from the archaeological evidence that in its early days in Canaan, the Hebrew religion was tainted with bull worship more than the Old Testament writers actually cared to admit.

Interestingly, if the calf-worshippers were recent arrivals among the wandering Israelites, it might explain the reference in Exodus 32: 35: 'And God plagued the people, because they made the calf.' Perhaps they had brought the epidemic with them. It would certainly be taken as additional evidence – if any was really required – that the Lord wanted no part of Egyptian religion, even if it was a monotheistic one. As God says when telling Moses of His plans to kill the firstborn in Exodus 12:12: 'Against all the gods of Egypt I will execute judgement.'

It is with the wandering of the Israelites in the wilderness that we might again interpret evidence of plague. In the previous chapter we saw how the forty-year wandering before the conquest of Jericho would seem to have been based on historical events. The period between the Thera eruption – the Exodus – and the burning of Jericho – the arrival in Canaan – was indeed around forty years. In which case we must ask ourselves why? Why should the Hebrews spend four decades waiting to return to their ancient homeland? Might it have been because a plague was pandemic throughout the entire region. We know that Egypt was affected, so also were the Egyptian territories along the Canaan coast as far north as Turkey. In fact the safest place to be was right in the middle of the Sinai Desert – precisely where we find the Israelites. Moreover, they would appear to have been there for approximately the duration of the epidemic – or series of epidemics. By the time Jericho is taken around 1315 BC, there is no further evidence of plagues in any of the countries mentioned. Once again, what was a catastrophe for everyone else, just so happens to have benefited the Israelites. By the time they arrived in Canaan, the population of the city states would have been greatly reduced and hard pressed to defend themselves.

With the Amarna years now no longer so mysterious – yet all the more astonishing – and many aspects of the Exodus story fitting, for perhaps the first time, into a genuine historical framework, we finally return to the mystery that began this unusual investigation: the strange case of Tomb 55.

We have already concluded, from the evidence examined in earlier chapters, that Smenkhkare was entombed in such a way that his burial was believed to have imprisoned some kind of malevolence – something that had inhabited his corporeal form. If Smenkhkare himself had been considered the source of that evil, it seems unlikely that Tutankhamun would have been interred in a coffin that bore his brother's image. We know that this presumed entity – for want of a better word – is either an androgynous or feminine being, because of both the specially adapted female effects and way in which the body was mummified in the attitude of a woman. We have speculated that such an entity might have been the Aten, for the new god was considered to be of both genders. However, we have also seen how both Ay and Tutankhamun – those responsible for the condition of Tomb 55 – continued to respect, if not actually practise Atenism themselves. There is therefore only one 'immortal being' that fits the bill – the goddess Sekhmet.

If we consider it from Ay's and Tutankhamun's point of view, it is hardly surprising that they took such unprecedented and – as far as we know – unique measures. From being at the height of its power and prosperity, just two decades earlier, Egypt had apparently been subjected to a hellish storm of volcanic ash, had its coast and rivers lashed by violent tidal waves, had its crops and livestock decimated, suffered sickening plagues of vermin and repeated epidemics, and its royal household was failing to produce a legitimate male heir. Amonhotep had attributed it to the wrath of Sekhmet and had tried to appease her. It hadn't worked! Akhenaten had attributed it to the Aten and had proclaimed it as chief and only god. That hadn't worked either! The plagues were continuing, and people were dropping like flies all over the empire. What were they to do?

Even though they may have considered Atenist philosophy sound, Ay and Tutankhamun had reinstated Amun-Re and the old gods, so presumably believed in their power. Tutankhamun's tomb certainly contains images of many gods. It therefore makes sense – indeed the only sense that Egyptian thought could make of it – that Sekhmet was responsible after all. She *was* the goddess of devastation. Just as the king of Alashia had written to Akhenaten about Nergal – *his* god of disease and pestilence – being abroad in his land, Sekhmet – the Egyptian equivalent – was abroad in Egypt. Amonhotep had been right about the cause, but he had been wrong about the remedy. He had tried to appease a goddess who, quite obviously, could not be appeased. As the goddess was immortal, and could not be destroyed, there was only one course of action left open: to contain her – to imprison her for eternity.

Why, though, should they think she had inhabited the body of Smenkhkare? Well, for a start, he was the king. From the very beginning of pharaonic Egypt, the entire nation had revolved around the king. He was the incarnation of the chief god and, as such, the well-being of all Egypt depended on him. All his subjects could only hope to gain divine favour in this life and participation in the afterlife vicariously, by attending to the pharaoh's needs. The king and the land were one. If the land was sick, rather than having been punished by the chief god – as clearly, from the Egyptian standpoint, it was – then at the end of the day there was only the king to blame. By inhabiting the king – just as the principal god would normally have done – Sekhmet had been able to afflict the land and bring about her planned devastation of Egypt.

This was almost certainly the manner in which the new regime, its priests and its ministers, were thinking. However, there may have been an additional, and more specific, reason why they might have considered Sekhmet to have possessed the body of Smenkhkare. He had been born when all the trouble began.

Forensic analysis of the mummy revealed that Smenkhkare had been around twenty years of age when he died. We know he died in the same year as Akhenaten – the seventeenth year of Akhenaten's reign. He must, therefore, have been born around three years before Akhenaten came to the throne. As Amonhotep had enough time to erect over seven hundred statues of Sekhmet before Akhenaten assumed power, the Thera eruption must have occurred a few years before. It seems, therefore, that Smenkhkare had been born very close to the time the volcano exploded. From Ay's and Tutankhamun's perspective, like some Egyptian anti-Christ, the evil goddess would have been hiding among them all the time.

With the mystery of Tomb 55 perhaps solved, we turn to one final piece of speculation: the mystery of Tutankhamun. Why did *his* tomb remain intact? We know that Horemheb tried to obliterate all evidence of Atenism, and all record of the kings who had sanctioned it. Every pharaoh between him and Amonhotep was erased from history – including Tutankhamun! We do not know what happened to the final resting place of Akhenaten, as it has never been found, but we do know that Ay's tomb was smashed to pieces and his mummy was torn to shreds. Despite all this, Horemheb not only left Tutankhamun's tomb alone – he even had it repaired. There it remained, just like Tomb 55, undisturbed for over three thousand years. We have even seen evidence suggesting that both tombs were deliberately hidden deep underground – as if to prevent anyone from ever finding them.

Such behaviour by Horemheb is understandable with regard to Tomb 55 – it was already desecrated – but why protect the tomb of Tutankhamun? Lying in splendour with all his finery, surrounded by family heirlooms and everything he would need in the afterlife – his name, his image, his mummy, fully intact – Tutankhamun has been entombed with every honour that Egypt can bestow. There may be only one reason why a pharaoh who wanted to wipe out all evidence of the Amarna kings would have left Tutankhamun's tomb alone: if it was somehow related to the bizarre interment in Tomb 55.

When Weigall, Ayrton and Davies first entered Tomb 55 on the morning of 19 January 1907, the condition in which they found it was more or less exactly as it had been left over three thousand years before. Although some items had been damaged by water, the entrance was intact and nothing had been removed. From the condition of Tomb 55, we have been able to determine the thinking behind the strange interment. However, the material items in the tombs – the inscriptions, the artefacts, the mummy – are only half the story. The other half we can only guess – namely, the rituals that accompanied the macabre burial, and the magical procedure by which the mummy was being imprisoned. Far more preparation must have been involved than evidenced by the tomb alone. The perpetrators were attempting to imprison a goddess. In Egyptian thinking, the only one who could banish a god – let alone imprison one – was another god: the pharaoh himself. To his subjects Tutankhamun was exactly what his name implies – 'The living image of Amun'. Tutankhamun's seal was on the door of Tomb 55, and it was his influence, as the incarnation of Amun-Re, which would ultimately be the power that would keep the goddess trapped.

Tutankhamun's tomb is only thirteen metres across the valley floor from Tomb 55 – and their entrances directly face each another. Remarkably, it seems that it was deliberately planned this way. The tomb found by Giovanni Belzoni in 1816 at the far end of the western Valley of the Kings, the one originally intended for Prince Tuthmosis and ultimately used by Ay, had been reconstructed for its new intended occupant – Tutankhamun. The traces of decorations on the walls clearly showed that it had been made ready for Tutankhamun some years before he died. Yet despite this, it was not used for his burial. Of all the places in the valley where Tutankhamun could have been buried, his final tomb is positioned right opposite the very tomb that had been desecrated in his name. Knowing what they had done to the occupant of Tomb 55, it is unthinkable that Tutankhamun would want to be interred as his eternal nextdoor neighbour, or that Ay would have allowed it. Unless, of course, it was essential.

As the living incarnation of the god Amun-Re, Tutankhamun was believed to have within him the life-force of the god Re. Re had been the father of Sekhmet and he had restrained her when she had tried to destroy mankind before. In Egyptian thinking, it would be his power that was needed to restrain her once again. Accordingly, it may have been essential for the body of Tutankhamun to be buried close to Tomb 55. So long as the Tutankhamun's tomb remained intact, the king – in his personification as Re – could continue to revisit the earth and so keep watch over the prisoner in Tomb 55. This may even be why he used Smenkhkare's coffin and Canopic coffinettes, even when he would surely have had his own. Perhaps he hoped that his brother's true spirit would reside alongside him, free from Sekhmet; the two of them remaining together as eternal guardians, standing sentinel over Sekhmet – the captive goddess of devastation.

All that now remain of the religion of the ancient Egyptians are its ruined temples, its broken statues and its faded texts; its adherents long since gone. The religion of the Israelites, however, still survives. Not only the Jews, but other great religions now revere their God. Those who worship Him are numbered in the hundreds of millions. If the Thera eruption really was responsible for the Israelite Exodus from Egypt, then its cataclysmic effects were the salvation of a people whose faith was to influence profoundly the entire course of human history. Was this all a remarkable coincidence, or was it really an act of God?

SUMMARY

- The final years of Akhenaten's reign show all the signs of a further natural disaster. If the royal family is anything to go by, then the population was dropping like flies.
- In fact, we have proof positive that a virulent plague was sweeping through the Egyptian vassal states. The king of Alashia writes to Akhenaten in one of the Amarna letters that Nergal – the god of disease and pestilence – was abroad in his land.
- In fact, it may have been a series of different viruses, perhaps started by the aftermath of the Thera eruption. With the number of dead carcasses littering the countryside, the abundance of rodents, and the mass of disease-carrying insects, many outbreaks could have resulted. It is with disease in Egypt that we again find a familiar echo in the Exodus account. According to Exodus 7:29–30, the last plague that God brought down upon the Egyptians was the most terrifying of all: 'And it came to pass, that at midnight the Lord smote all the firstborn in the land of Egypt ... there was not a house where there was not one dead.'
- The specific reference to the firstborn could be a confusion of two separate calamities to have affected Egypt. From the moment Akhenaten comes to the throne – seemingly right after the 'plagues' caused by Thera – no pharaoh sires a male heir for well over half a century. For a people whose pharaoh was considered the personification of the chief god on earth, around whom the whole of society revolved, it must have seemed as if they were indeed a cursed nation.
- The mystery of Tomb 55 may at last be solved. Following such a terrible series of natural disasters, Smenkhkare may

have blamed Akhenaten for abandoning the old gods and had him blasphemously reinterred in the belief that it would break the curse. In the reign of Tutankhamun, however, with the plague still persisting, Smenkhkare himself may have been blamed and was reinterred in the manner he had entombed Akhenaten.

- Although Smenkhkare may have believed that the androgynous Aten was responsible, both Ay and Tutankhamun continued to respect, if not actually practise, Atenism themselves. Smenkhkare, therefore, may have been buried in the desecrated female effects because he was thought to have personified the goddess of devastation, Sekhmet. Apart from being the king – whose destiny was deemed to be linked to the land of Egypt – Smenkhkare appears to have been born at the very time the problems began. By burying him in this way, the goddess herself may have been thought to have been entombed and imprisoned with him.

- This may also explain why Tutankhamun's tomb was also left intact by Horemheb. The perpetrators were attempting to imprison a goddess. In Egyptian thinking, the only one who could banish a god – let alone imprison one – was another god: the pharaoh himself. To his subjects, Tutankhamun was exactly what his name implies – 'The living image of Amun'. Tutankhamun's seal was on the door of Tomb 55, and it was his influence, as the incarnation of Amun-Re, which would have been considered the power that would keep the goddess trapped.

- Tutankhamun's tomb is only thirteen metres across the valley floor from Tomb 55 and their entrances directly face each another. Knowing what they had done to the occupant of Tomb 55, it is unthinkable that Tutankhamun would want to be interred as his eternal nextdoor neighbour, or that Ay would have allowed it. Unless, of course, it was essential.

- As the living incarnation of the god Amun-Re, Tutankhamun was believed to have within him the life-force of the god Re. Re had been the father of Sekhmet and he had restrained her when she had tried to destroy mankind before. In Egyptian thinking, it would be his power that was needed to restrain her once again. Accordingly, it may have been essential for the body of Tutankhamun to be buried close to Tomb 55. So long as Tutankhamun's tomb remained intact, the king – in his personification as Re – could continue to revisit the earth and so keep watch over the prisoner in Tomb 55.

Appendix

LATEST RADIOCARBON DATES FOR
THE ERUPTION OF THERA

In order to date the eruption of Thera by radiocarbon tests, organic matter was obtained from Akrotiri which had perished when the city was covered in volcanic material. Because most of the wood found at the excavation was in a bad state of preservation, having been burned beyond utilization, the best remains were those which had been protected inside storage vessels: foodstuffs such as fruit and grain. However, much of this was contaminated from two main sources. Firstly, volcanic carbon dioxide emanating from fissures in the ground had been assimilated into the plants before the eruption. Secondly, wooden lids that were used on the storage vessels had been charred during the eruption and mixed as organic dust into the contents. Fortunately, some organic material was found to be relatively uncontaminated and acceptable for dating purposes, the best samples being seeds from the *Lathyrus cicera* plant.

Tests on the *Lathyrus* samples were conducted separately in 1990 at the Radiocarbon Dating Laboratory of Copenhagen and the AMS facility at Oxford University. Both sets of results were published in that year by the London-based Thera Foundation

315

in the society's journal *Thera and the Aegean World: Volume III.*
The Copenhagen group, W. L. Friedrich, P. Wagner and H.
Tauber, obtained three sets of results and the Oxford team, R.
A. Housley, R. E. M. Hedges, I. A. Law and C. R. Bronk, gained
seven, providing the following dates as years before the time of
the tests (1990):

*Lathyrus results from the Radiocarbon
Dating Laboratory of Copenhagen*

3310 plus or minus 65 years
3430 plus or minus 90 years
3340 plus or minus 55 years

Central date: 3360 years before time of testing – 1370 BC

*Lathyrus results from the AMS facility
at Oxford University*

3390 plus or minus 65 years
3245 plus or minus 65 years
3335 plus or minus 60 years
3460 plus or minus 80 years
3395 plus or minus 65 years
3340 plus or minus 65 years
3280 plus or minus 65 years

Central date: 3349 before time of testing – 1359 BC

Both these findings taken together place the eruption of Thera
to around 1365 BC, a year or two before the reign of Akhenaten,
as proposed in the current work.

Some researchers (see Chapter Nine), believing that the

dates were too late for the eruption of Thera, have applied a so-called 'calibration curve' to the results. This highly controversial procedure places radiocarbon dates of the period very much earlier than the generally accepted chronology.

Events of the fourteenth century BC, for example, are recalibrated to around 310 years earlier. Accordingly, the Copenhagen group dated the Thera eruption to around 1675 BC. If the procedure is correct, however, it would mean that all radiocarbon dates obtained for this era would also need to be moved some 310 years into the past. Tutankhamun's tomb, for instance – having been radiocarbon dated from cereal grains and the mummy remains – would need to be redated to around 1648 BC, as opposed to around 1338 BC. The reigns of the Amarna kings would therefore be as follows:

> 1737–1676 BC: Reign of Amonhotep III
> 1676–1659 BC: Reign of Akhenaten
> 1659–1659 BC: Reign of Smenkhkare
> 1659–1648 BC: Reign of Tutankhamun
> 1648–1644 BC: Reign of Ay

From these dates we can see that the eruption of Thera still falls within a couple of years of the start of Akhenaten's reign. However, if this recalibration procedure is correct, it would mean that virtually every historian and archaeologist who has ever studied the period in question has been completely wrong concerning ancient chronology by over three centuries. In the opinion of the present author this seems highly unlikely.

THE RE-CALIBRATION CONTROVERSY

All organic matter absorbs the radioactive isotope Carbon 14 which gradually decays once an organism has died. As the rate of decay is constant, the period which has elapsed since the organism's death can be gauged by measuring the amount of Carbon 14 which still exists in its remains. The amount of Carbon 14 to which a living organism is exposed was thought to have been constant over time. However, recent scientific evidence suggests that the level of Carbon 14 in the atmosphere may have decreased permanently around 3,500 years ago due to changes in the earth's magnetic field. If so, the quantity of Carbon 14 present in any organism that died before this time would be greater than had previously been supposed and, accordingly, more time would have elapsed since the organism's death than had been estimated. A radiocarbon date derived from such a sample would therefore need to be placed further back in time than was originally thought. The problem facing archaeologists was when and when not to adjust their dating, as the time when the level of atmospheric Carbon 14 dropped could only be estimated approximately to between 1500 and 1000 BC. At what point during these five centuries should they start recalibrating radiocarbon dates? Some turned to dendro-chronology – tree ring dating – in an attempt to resolve the issue.

Trees have annual growth rings which are wider when the weather is warmer and narrower when cooler, and so an accurate year by year record of the climate is available from the time the tree began to grow. From the historian's perspective, this can be very useful, so long as there are historical records of weather conditions to which the growth rings can be compared. An undated event referenced in a Renaissance manuscript referring to a particularly cold summer, for example, could be dated by counting back growth rings to an unusually narrow one which corresponded to the period in question. For events predating living trees, dendrochronology utilizes timber from ancient sites or wood preserved in bogland or permanently frozen ground. For events as far back as 1000 BC, however, dendrochronology runs into difficulty as historical records concerning local weather conditions are almost non-existent.

Nevertheless, it was by comparing radiocarbon dates with dates derived from dendrochronology that some archaeologists attempted to resolve the recalibration issue and so the controversy began. Firstly, they would obtain a radiocarbon date for a sample of ancient timber. Secondly, they would surmise from historical references that a cold summer or harsh winter may have occurred at a particular time. Thirdly, they would make an informed guess as to which narrow growth ring corresponded to the year in question. Having derived this date, they would radiocarbon date organic remains from the area to which the historical records were thought to refer and note by how many years the two dates diverged. Needless to say, many differing recalibration charts resulted and there is still no agreement as to precisely when the procedure should be used.

As a result, various archaeologists use various recalibration charts, some employing recalibration on radiocarbon dates obtained for as early as 1500 BC and others as late as 1000 BC, while others reject the recalibration theory altogether. To add to the confusion, when archaeologists quote radiocarbon dates when publishing findings some fail to mention that their dates are already recalibrated and colleagues unwittingly recalibrate the results for a second time. To make matters worse, the original radiocarbon date – given as X number of years ago – may even have been misinterpreted due to various renderings of the term 'before the present'. Some scholars use the term 'present' to refer to the time an item was dated, some use it to refer to the time of writing, and some use it to refer to 1950, the scientific 'standard year' used by technicians at radiocarbon laboratories. The result is that many archaeologists, historians and Egyptologists prefer to ignore radiocarbon dating altogether.

Chronology

BC – Approximate Chronology

3150–2686:	The Egyptian Archaic Period.
3100:	Narmer Palette – the oldest surviving historical record from Egypt.
3090:	Narmer's successor, Hor-Aha, establishes the First Dynasty and founds the capital city of Memphis.
2686–2181:	The Egyptian Old Kingdom.
2650:	The building of the first stepped pyramid for the pharaoh Zoser.
2570:	Construction begun on the pyramid of Cheops at Giza.
2470:	The Palermo Stone records a series of early kings.
2181–2040:	The Egyptian First Intermediate. Centralized government at Memphis is overthrown, and an age of continual fighting between local warlords and provincial rulers follows.
2040–1782:	The Egyptian Middle Kingdom. A fresh era emerges from a strong line of rulers from Thebes in Upper Egypt.
2000:	The birth of the Mari kingdom at Tell Hariri in Syria.
1890:	A wall painting in the tomb of the nobleman Khnumhotep shows a group of thirty-seven Semites with laden donkeys entering Egypt.
1782–1570:	The Egyptian Second Intermediate.
1750:	The Mari kingdom is invaded by the Babylonians.
1745:	A text from the reign of the pharaoh Sobekhotep III contains a list of seventy-nine household servants, of which forty-five seem to be Hyksos.

1745–1700:	Increasing numbers of Hyksos continue to settle in the Nile Delta, where the authority of the pharaohs is weak.
1720:	The whole of northern Egypt falls to the Hyksos.
1720–1570:	The Hyksos kings govern northern Egypt, making their own capital at Avaris at the eastern edge of the Nile Delta. Southern Egypt remains in the hands of the Theban princes.
	Hebrews first arrive in Egypt.
1660:	A circular alabaster jar, found at Knossos, is inscribed with the cartouche of the third Hyksos king, Khyan. Minoan wall paintings decorate the palace of the Hyksos kings in Avaris.
1570–1070:	The Egyptian New Kingdom.
1570:	The Theban prince Amosis reconquers northern Egypt. Expulsion of the Hyksos.
1567:	The god Re is assimilated with the god Amun. Temple cities of Karnak and nearby Luxor are expanded to an unprecedented size.
1500:	Royal List from the city of Karnak includes the names of the kings who preceded Tuthmosis III.
	The greatest expansion of the Egyptian empire under the pharaoh Tuthmosis III.
	Hebrews enslaved in Egypt.
	The oldest reference to the *Apiru*, on a scene from the tomb of Tuthmosis III's great herald Antef, which lists them among the prisoners of war captured during the pharaoh's campaigns.
1480:	The tomb of Queen Hatshepsut's chief minister, Senenmut, shows scenes of foreign envoys, each in their national costume. Some are called *Keftiu* and from the goods they bear it is clear that they are Minoans.
1475:	A scene on the tomb of the noble Puyemre at Thebes shows four men working a winepress and accompanying hieroglyphics read 'straining out wine by the *Apiru*'.
1450:	Minoan ships carry timber supplies from Lebanon to Egypt.
1430:	An inscribed stela at Memphis refers to 3,600 *Apiru*.
1390:	Central date for Thera eruption indicated by ice core samples.

1389–1364:	Reign of Amonhotep III.
1366:	Most likely date for eruption of Thera and the Israelite Exodus from Egypt.
	Amonhotep erects vast number of statues to the goddess Sekhmet.
1365:	Central date for the eruption of Thera indicated by the latest radiocarbon tests from Akrotiri.
1364–1347:	Reign of Akhenaten.
1364:	The Aten is installed as chief deity.
1360:	Central date for Thera eruption indicated by the first radiocarbon tests from Akrotiri.
1359:	Akhenaten changes his name from Amonhotep IV and founds the new city of Amarna.
1358:	Akhenaten moves his court to Amarna.
1357:	One of the Amarna letters, sent to Akhenaten by King Abimilki of Tyre, talks of the king's horror on visiting Ugarit to find the population gone and half the city washed away into the sea.
1355:	Akhenaten proscribes the Aten's association with Re-Herakhte.
1356:	Birth of Tutankhamun.
1352:	Death of Amonhotep III.
1350:	The likely deaths of Nefertiti, Queen Tiye and the princesses Meketaten and Neferneferure.
	Inscription on the Hermopolis Talatat refers to Tutankhamun as: 'The king's son of his loins'.
1349:	Smenkhkare appointed senior co-regent. Meritaten becomes Chief Queen.
	Persecution of Amun cult in Thebes. Desecration of the temple of Karnak.
1348:	Death of Kiya.
1347:	Death of Akhenaten.
	Smenkhkare reigns for less than a year.
	Tomb 55 desecrated.
1347–1338:	Reign of Tutankhamun and Queen Ankhesenpaaten.
1345:	Abandonment of Amarna.
	Amun and the old gods reinstated.
	Tutankhamun changes name from Tutankhaten.
1338:	Tutankhamun buried in the Valley of the Kings.

1338–1334:	Reign of the pharaoh Ay.
1334–1307:	Reign of Horemheb.
	Anti-Atenist reprisals.
	Israelites enter Canaan.
1315:	Central radiocarbon date for the burning of Jericho.
1307–1305:	Reign of Ramesses I.
1300:	First archaeological evidence for Israelites in Canaan.
1305–1292:	Reign of Seti I.
1300:	The *Apiru* are referenced in connection with a revolt at Beisham in Palestine.
	A Royal List from the city of Abydos names seventy-six kings who proceeded Seti I.
1292–1225:	Reign of Ramesses II.
1275:	Egyptian offensive against the Hittites.
1270:	*Apiru* used as hard labour to erect a pylon at Memphis and to make bricks at Miour in the province of Fayum.
1250:	The burning of Hazor.
1220:	Israel Stela mentions the Israelites having some kind of kingdom in Palestine.
	Royal Canon of Turin list of some 300 Egyptian kings.
1180:	*Apiru* listed as quarrymen and working on land sacred to the god Atum at Heliopolis.
	Philistines first recorded by Egyptians in eastern Mediterranean.
1070–332:	The Egyptian Late Period.
1000:	The Bible comes into historical context.
980:	King David and the unification of Israel.
960:	Solomon king of Israel and the building of Jerusalem Temple.
650:	Oldest known form of coinage used by the Lydians.
	Camels first used in Egypt.
	The books of the Pentateuch are written.
565:	Solon visits Egypt and hears Atlantis story.
332:	Alexander the Great annexes Egypt.
	The works of Manetho are written.
30:	Egypt's last pharaoh, Ptolemy XV, the son of Cleopatra, is murdered on the orders of Caesar Augustus and Egypt becomes the personal estate of the Roman Emperors.

AD – Egyptology and Archaeology

1799:	Discovery of the Rosetta Stone.
1816:	Giovanni Belzoni discovers the tomb of Ay.
1817:	Belzoni discovers tomb of Ramesses I.
1822:	The French scholar Jean François Champollion completes the decipherment of hieroglyphics.
1824:	The British explorer John Gardner Wilkinson makes first survey of rock tombs in Amarna.
1825:	The Scottish laird Robert Hay makes drawings of Amarna reliefs.
1840:	A German team led by Egyptologist Richard Lepsius make a number of detailed drawings of the tomb reliefs in Amarna.
1870:	The German archaeologist Heinrich Schliemann uncovers the remains of Troy at Hissarlik in Turkey.
1880:	Akhenaten's tomb discovered by an unknown Egyptian.
1882:	First pieces of jewellery from Akhenaten's tomb sold to the Reverend W. J. Loftie.
1887:	A peasant woman digging for fertilizer among the ancient ruins of Akhetaten unearths a cache of over 300 inscribed clay tablets, now called the Amarna Letters.
1890s:	The first archeological excavation of Amarna is conducted by Sir W. M. Flinders Petrie.
	Francis Llewelyn Griffith uncovers first evidence to suggest the co-regency between Akhenaten and Amonhotep IV – a stela from the chief servitor Pinhasy's mansion showing Amonhotep still alive in Amarna.
1891:	Alexandre Barsanti and a French expedition excavate Akhenaten's tomb.
1890s:	Over a period of six years, Norman de Garis Davies, the surveyor for the British-based Egypt Exploration Fund, painstakingly copies all the decorations that still survive in the cliff tombs in Amarna.
1898:	The mummy thought to be of Queen Tiye is found in the tomb of Amonhotep II.
	Tuthmosis III's tomb discovered by the French Egyptologist Victor Loret.

1901:	Boston archaeologist Harriet Boyd excavates Minoan remains at Gournia on the island of Crete.
1906:	Richard Seager excavates a Minoan port on the island of Mochlos.
1907:	Tomb 55 is discovered by the British archaeologists Edward Ayrton and Arthur Weigall, together with their American financier Theodore Davis.
1911:	The German archaeologist Ludwig Borchardt discovers Nefertiti bust in the studio of the royal sculptor Djhutmose at the Great Palace at Amarna.
1920:	The Greek archaeologist Stephanos Xanthoudidis uncovers the villa of Nirou Khani on the island of Crete.
1921:	Kiya's *Maru* temple discovered at Amarna by the British archaeologist Leonard Woolley.
1922:	Howard Carter discovers Tutankhamun's tomb.
1923:	The British archaeologist John Pendlebury discovers fragments of a carved tray bearing the name of Amonhotep III at Amarna.
1925:	While digging a drainage ditch at the Temple of Karnak workmen uncover the Akhenaten colossi.
1939:	Hermopolis Talatat discovered.
1956:	Geologists Dragoslav Ninkovich and Bruce Heezen of Columbia University conduct the *Vema* survey of the Mediterranean seabed.
1960:	Greek archaeologist Professor Nicholas Platon discovers the remains of Crete's easternmost Minoan palace at Kato Zakro.
1952:	The British archaeologist Dame Kathleen Kenyon excavates the Bronze Age fortification at Tell-es-Sultan near the Dead Sea, thought to be the site of ancient Jericho.
1955:	Israeli archaeologist Yigael Yadin excavates the site of ancient Hazor, modern Tell el-Qedah, some fourteen kilometres north of the Sea of Galilee.
1967:	Akrotiri excavations begun at Thera by Spyridon Marinatos.
1965:	Retired US foreign service officer Ray Wingfield Smith initiates the Akhenaten Temple Project.

1975:   Akhenaten Temple Project taken over by Professor Donald
             Redford of Toronto University.
1979:   Excavation of temple sanctuary on Mount Euptos, Crete.
1984:   Funerary vessel bearing the name of princess
             Neferneferure is discovered among rubble around the
             Amarna royal tomb by Egyptian archaeologist Dr Aly el
             Kouly.
1989:   French archaeologist Alain Zivie discovers the tomb of
             Aper-El at Saqqara.

References

CHAPTER ONE

Account of tomb opening taken from: Davis, T. M., *The Tomb of Queen Tiyi*, London, 1910. Ayrton, E. R., *The Tomb of Thy, Proceedings of the Society of Biblical Archaeology 29*, London, 1907. Weigall, A. E., *The Mummy of Akhenaten, Journal of Egyptian Archaeology 8*, London, 1922. Andrews, Emma, B., *Personal Diary*, Metropolitan Museum, New York.

Overall Perspective: Aldred, C., *Akhenaten: King of Egypt*, London, 1988. Weigall, A. E., *The Life and Times of Akhnaton*, London, 1922. Weigall, A. E., *The Treasury of Ancient Egypt*, London, 1911.

p. 3   Tomb of Tuthmosis IV: Davis, T. M., *The Tomb of Toutmosis IV*, London 1906. Romer, J., *Valley of the Kings*, London, 1981, ch. 18 & pp. 183–192

p. 10   Unwrapping of Mummy: Maspero, G., *New Light of Ancient Egypt*, London, 1908, ch. 19. Davis, T. M., *The Tomb of Queen Tiyi*, London, 1910.

p. 10   Unprofessional aftermath: Romer, J., *Valley of the Kings*, London, 1981, ch 20. Tyndale, W., *Below the Cataracts*, London, 1907.

p. 11   Ayrton finds seal: Andrews, *Personal Diary*. Weigall, *The Treasury of Ancient Egypt*. Aldred, *Akhenaten: King of Egypt*, pp. 196, 207.

p. 12   Arguments regarding identity of tomb occupant: Davis, *The Tomb of Queen Tiyi*. Weigall, A. E., *The Mummy of Akhenaten, Journal of Egyptian Archaeology 8*, London, 1922. Ayrton, E. R., *The Tomb of Thy, Proceedings of the Society of Biblical Archaeology 29*, London 1907. Andrews, *Personal Diary*. Aldred, *Akhenaten . . .*, p. 198–9.

p. 12   Tutankhamun's seal: Aldred, *Akhenaten ...*, p. 197.

p. 14   Magic Bricks: Romer, J., *Valley of the Kings*, London, 1981, p. 217. Aldred, *Akhenaten ...*, p. 199.

p. 14   Shrine panel: Drawn by Harold Jones in 1907 and reproduced in Romer, *Valley ...*, p. 215.

p. 15   Elliot Smith's examination of mummy: Smith, G. E., *The Royal Mummies*, Cairo, 1922.

p. 16   Vulture collar: Weigall, A. E., *The Life and Times of Akhenaten*, London, 1922, p. 248.

p. 16   Tomb 55 mummy: Harrison, R. G., *An Anatomical Examination of the Pharaonic Remains Purported to be Akhenaten, Journal of Egyptian Archaeology 52*, 1966.

p. 16   Tomb 55 mummy as Smenkhkare: Aldred, *Akhenaten ...*, ch. 18, pp. 204, 218. Clayton, P., *Chronicle of the Pharaohs*, London, 1994, pp. 126–7.

p. 17   Heads side by side: Cairo Museum J.E. 59294.

p. 17   Name in cartouche in Meryre's tomb: Davies, N. de G., *The Rock Tombs of El Amarna*, London, 1908.

p. 17   Length of Smenkhkare's reign: Aldred, *Akhenaten ...*, p. 293.

p. 18   Discs from Tutankhamun's tomb: Bosse-Griffiths, K., *Finds From the Tomb of Queen Tiye, Journal of Egyptian Archaeology 47*, 1961. Aldred, *Akhenaten ...*, pp. 209–300.

p. 19   Smenkhkare items in Tutankhamun's tomb: Reeves, N., *The Complete Tutankhamun*, London, 1990, pp. 109, 122. Aldred, *Akhenaten ...*, pl. 54. Desroches-Noblecourt, C., *Tutankhamun*, London, 1969, pp. 123, 124, 172.

p. 19   Jewellery around Tutankhamun's mummy: Reeves, N., *The Complete Tutankhamun*, London, 1990, p. 114. Aldred, *Akhenaten ...*, p. 300. Desroches-Noblecourt, *Tutankhamun*, pp. 123, 124, 172.

p. 19   Tutankhamun's second coffin as Smenkhkare likeness: Aldred, *Akhenaten ...*, p. 202.

p. 21   Shrine panels abandoned: *Ibid.*, pp. 196, 197, 208.

p. 21   Tools abandoned: Romer, *Valley ...*, p. 214.

p. 22   Female effects: *Ibid.*, p. 218. Aldred, *Akhenaten ...*, pp. 202, 203, 205.

p. 22   Mummy band: Desroches-Noblecourt, *Tutankhamun*, p. 172.

p. 23   One arm across chest: Samson, J., *Nefertiti and Cleopatra*, London, 1990, p. 94.

p. 23   Rolf Krauss: Aldred, *Akhenaten ...*, p. 205.

CHAPTER TWO

General history: Clayton, *Chronicle*... David, R., *Discovering Ancient Egypt*, London, 1933.

Akhenaten general: Aldred, *Akhenaten*... Redford, D. B., *Akhenaten: The Heretic King*, Princeton, 1987.

Dating: Clayton, *Chronicle*..., pp. 12–13.

p. 45   Akhenaten name removed, etc.: Aldred, *Akhenaten*..., pp. 198–9.
p. 48   Adapted for Akhenaten: *Ibid.*, p. 205.
p. 49   Atenist items in Tutankhamun's tomb: Desroches-Noblecourt, *Tutankhamun*, pp. 68, 69, 132, 195. Clayton, *Chronicle*..., p. 129. Reeves, *The Complete Tutankhamun*, pp. 113, 184, 185, 202, 203.
p. 49   Desecrations of inscriptions: Desroches-Noblecourt, *Tutankhamun*, pp. 208–12.
p. 49   Names omitted from king lists: Clayton, *Chronicle*..., p. 138.

CHAPTER THREE

General: Aldred, *Akhenaten*..., ch. 1. Redford, *Akhenaten*..., ch. 8. Samson, J., *Amarna: City of Akhenaten and Nefertiti*, London, 1972.

p. 51   Illustrations from tombs: Davies, *The Rock Tombs*... Petrie, W. M. F., *Tell el-Amarna*, London, 1894.
p. 55   Shrines: Aldred, *Akhenaten*..., p. 66
p. 55   Noble's tombs: Davies, *The Rock Tombs*...
p. 56   Window of Appearance: *Ibid.*, p.262. Redford, *Akhenaten*..., pp. 128–9.
p. 56   Boundary Stelae: *The Amarna Boundary Stelae Project, University of Chicago Oriental Institute Annual Report*, 1983. Aldred, *Akhenaten*..., ch. 4.
p. 60   Rock tombs: Davies, *The Rock Tombs*... Petrie, *Tell el-Amarna*. Weigall, *The Treasury*... Baikie, J., *The Amarna Age*, London, 1926. Gardiner, A. H., *A Later Allusion to Akhenaten, Journal of Egyptian Archaeology* 24, 1938.

p. 65   Amarna letters: Mercer, S. A. B., *The Tell el Amarna Tablets*, Toronto, 1939.

p. 66   Armed camp: Schulman, A. R., *Military Background of the Amarna Period, Journal of the American Research Centre in Egypt*, Vol. 3, 1964.

p. 66   Akhenaten physiology: Aldred, C., and Sandison, A. T., *The Pharaoh Akhenaten: A Problem in Egyptology and Pathology, Bulletin of the History of Medicine 36*, 1962. Aldred, *Akhenaten . . .*, ch. 20.

p. 70   Mummies analysis: Harrison. *An Anatomical Examination . . .*

p. 71   Hymn to the Aten: Aldred, *Akhenaten . . .*, pp. 241–3. Samson, *Nefertiti and Cleopatra*, pp. 29–32

p. 72   Goddess Mut: Ions, V., *Egyptian Mythology*, London, 1982, p. 100. Lurker, M., *The Gods and Symbols of Ancient Egypt*, London 1980, p. 82.

p. 74   Anti-Atenists: Redford, *Akhenaten . . .*, ch. 14.

CHAPTER FOUR

Amarna queens general: Lesko, *The Remarkable Women of Ancient Egypt*.

p. 77   Influence of Nefertiti: Samson, *Nefertiti and Cleopatra*.

p. 80   Boundary Stelae: *The Amarna Boundary Stelae Project . . .* Aldred, *Akhenaten . . .*, p. 48.

p. 80   Nefertiti images on sarcophagus: *Ibid.*, p. 42.

p. 80   Nefertiti hieroglyph: Samson, *Nefertiti and Cleopatra*, p. 62.

p. 80   Boundary stelae proclamation regarding Nefertiti: Aldred, *Akhenaten . . .*, p. 49.

p. 81   Ay as father of the god: Samson, *Nefertiti and Cleopatra*, p. 57. Aldred, *Akhenaten . . .*, p. 221.

p. 81   Ay as *Sem* priest: Reeves, *The Complete Tutankhamun*, pp. 72–3.

p. 81   Aper-El as father of the god: Zivie, A., *The Treasury of Aper-El, Egyptian Archaeology*, Summer, 1991, pp. 26–9.

p. 81   Tuya and Tiye titles: Aldred, *Akhenaten . . .*, p. 222.

p. 82   Mutemwiya: David, *Discovering Ancient Egypt*, p. 154. Clayton, *Chronicle . . .*, p. 115.

p. 82   Nefertiti bust: Samson, *Nefertiti and Cleopatra*, pp. 6–9.

p. 82   Knossos: Farnoux, A., *Knossos: Unearthing a Legend*, New York, 1996.

p. 82   Hyksos and Minoans: Clayton, *Chronicle*..., pp. 94–5. Biotic, M., *Avaris and Piramesses: Archaeological Exploration in the Eastern Delta, Proceedings of the British Academy, Vol. 65,* 1979.

p. 83   Keftiu and Senenmut's tomb: Clayton, *Chronicle*..., pp. 104–6. Wilson, I., *The Exodus Enigma,* London, 1985, p. 80.

p. 83   Malkata palace Minoan designs: Aldred, *Akhenaten*..., pl. 48 and 49. Heyes, W. C. *Inscriptions From the Palace of Amenhotep III, Journal of Near Eastern Studies 10,* 1953.

p. 83   Hittites: Dickinson, O., *The Aegean Bronze Age,* Cambridge, 1994.

p. 83   Minoan ships used to carry timber: Freeman-Grenville, *Chronology of World History,* p. 8.

p. 84   Nefertiti breaks taboos: Samson, *Nefertiti and Cleopatra,* p. 19.

p. 85   Mnevis Bull: Lurker, *The Gods and Symbols of Ancient Egypt,* p. 81. Ions, *Egyptian Mythology,* pp. 121–2.

p. 85   Bull references on boundary stelae: Aldred, *Akhenaten*..., pp. 47, 50.

p. 85   Bull's tail and Nefertiti head-dress: *Ibid.,* pp 46–7.

p. 86   Nefertiti's death: *Ibid.,* pp. 285, 288.

p. 86   Meketaten and Tiye's deaths: *Ibid.,* pp. 283, 284.

p. 87   Late Amarna art: *Ibid.,* pp. 234–5. Frankfort, H., *The Mural Painting of El-Amarna,* London, 1929.

p. 87   Smenkhkare Appointed Co-Regent: Thomas, A. P., *Akhenaten's Egypt,* London, 1996, p. 30. Aldred, C., *The Immediate Successors of Akhenaten, Cambridge Ancient History, Vol. II.* Aldred, *Akhenaten: King of Egypt,* pp. 289, 291.

p. 87   Princesses' tombs: *Ibid.,* ch. 3. Martin, G. T., *The Royal Tomb at Amarna,* London, 1974. El-Khouly, A. and Martin, G. T., *Excavations in the Royal Necropolis at El Amarna,* Cairo, 1985.

p. 89   Mayati letters: Mercer, *The Tell el Amarna Tablets.*

p. 90   Kiya: Aldred, *Akhenaten: King of Egypt,* pp. 285–288.

p. 92   Smenkhkare adopts Nefertiti's name: *Ibid.,* p. 192.

p. 92   Mutnodjme: *Ibid.,* pp. 222–3.

p. 93   Deaths of Akhenaten and Smenkhkare: *Ibid.,* p. 293.

p. 94   Kiya's monuments defaced: *Ibid.,* p. 204.

p. 94   Tomb 55 coffin: Perepelkin, G., *The Secret of the Gold Coffin,* Moscow, 1978.

p. 94   Footboard Text: Redford, *Akhenaten*..., pp. 189–90.

p. 95   Theory: Aldred, *Akhenaten*..., pp. 203–4.

p. 95   Krauss: *Ibid.,* p. 205.

p. 96   Band and coffin: *Ibid.*, p. 203.
p. 97   Smenkhkare drops epithet: *Ibid.*, p. 291.
p. 98   Anti-Amun: *Ibid.*, pp. 289–90
p. 99   Pairi tomb: *Ibid.*, p. 293. Clayton, *Chronicle...*, p. 126.

CHAPTER FIVE

General: Martin, *The Royal Tomb at Amarna*. Petrie, *Tell el-Amarna*. Aldred, *Akhenaten...*, ch. 3.

p. 108   Baby-carrying woman: *Ibid.*, p. 32.
p. 109   Niches: Aldred, *Akhenaten...*, p. 43.
p. 110   Magic bricks. Martin., *The Royal Tomb at Amarna*.
p. 110   Age of bricks. Romer, *Valley of the Kings*, p.217.
p. 113   Akhenaten's effects in Tutankhamun's tomb. Reeves., *The Complete Tutankhamun*, p. 169.
p. 114   Opening of Tutankhamun's tomb: Carter, H., *The Tomb of Tutankhamun*, London, 1933.
p. 115   Coffins and death mask: Reeves, *The Complete Tutankhamun*, pp. 106–14.
p. 117   Coffinettes: *Ibid.*, pp. 109, 122. pl. 54. Desroches-Noblecourt, *Tutankhamun*, pp. 123, 124, 161.
p. 118   Tutankhamun in obscurity: Howing, T., *Tutankhamun: The Untold Story*, pp. 266–7.
p. 119   Body jewellery made for Smenkhkare: Reeves, *The Complete Tutankhamun*, p. 114. Aldred, *Akhenaten...*, p. 300. Desroches-Noblecourt, *Tutankhamun*, pp. 123–4.
p. 119   Smenkhkare effects in Tutankhamun's tomb: Romer, J., *Valley of the Kings*, pp. 271,272, 275.
p. 120   Amun name removed: Aldred, *Akhenaten...*, pp. 289–90.

CHAPTER SIX

p. 127   Restoration Stela: Clayton, *Chronicle...*, p. 129.
p. 129   Throne: Reeves, *The Complete Tutankhamun*, p. 184.
p. 130   Skull cap: *Ibid.*, p. 113.
p. 130   Ay's tomb: Clayton, *Chronicle of the Pharaohs*, p. 137.

p. 130 Canopic Shrine: Carter, *The Tomb of Tutankhamun.*
p. 131 Memphis, Pentu, Minnakht and Neb: Aldred, *Akhenaten . . .*, p. 295.
p. 132 Kiya's daughter: *Ibid.*, p. 234.
p. 133 King's son: *Ibid.*, p. 287.
p. 133 Amonhotep III as Tutankhamun's father: *Ibid.*, p. 108.
p. 134 Griffith's stelae: *Ibid.*, pp. 66, 174.
p. 134 Tray: *Ibid.*, p. 101.
p. 135 Bek Aswan: *Ibid.*, pp.93–4.
p. 136 Living for ever: *Ibid.*, p. 174.
p. 136 Kheruef relief: *Ibid.*, p. 174
p. 136 Huya relief: *Ibid.*, p. 174.
p. 136 Amarna letters: *Ibid.*, ch. 17.
p. 137 Equal number of letters: *Ibid.*, p. 191.
p. 137 Wine: *Ibid.*, pp. 173–4.
p. 138 Amonhotep's death in Year 12: *Ibid.*, pp. 178–80.
p. 139 Isis and Sitamun: Clayton, *Chronicle . . .*, p. 115.
p. 139 Heirlooms in Tutankhamun's tomb: Reeves, *The Complete Tutankhamun*, pp. 168–9.
p. 140 Tiye's mummy. Aldred, *Akhenaten . . .*, p. 105.
p. 141 Huya, Meryre, etc.: Daves, *The Rock Tombs . . .*
p. 142 Bone in skull: Reeves, *The Complete Tutankhamun*, p. 118.
p. 142 Ankhesenamun letter: Desroches-Noblecourt, *Tutankhamun*, pp.202–3. Reeves, *The Complete Tutankhamun*, p. 23.
p. 143 Ay marries Ankhesenamun: Clayton. *Chronicle . . .*, pp. 136–137.
p. 144 Military activity: *Ibid.*, p. 130. Desroches-Noblecourt, *Tutankhamun*, pp. 144–147.
p. 144 Gesso box: Reeves, *The Complete Tutankhamun*, p. 189.
p. 144 Horemheb leads: Clayton *Chronicle . . .*, pp. 138–139.
p. 145 Horemheb marries Mutnodjme: *Ibid.*, p. 137.
p. 145 Ransacking: Redford, *Akhenaten: The Heretic King*, ch. 14.
p. 145 Kings' names expunged: Clayton, *Chronicle . . .*,. p. 138.
p. 146 Ay's tomb: *Ibid.*, pp. 136–137.
p. 146 Destruction of Tutankhamun's monuments: Desroches-Noblecourt, *Tutankhamun*, pp. 208–209.
p. 146 Dignitaries depicted at Tutankhamun's funeral: Reeves, *The Complete Tutankhamun*, p. 72.
p. 147 Robberies: *Ibid.*, pp. 95–96.
p. 148 Seals: *Ibid.*, pp. 92–94.
p. 148 Horemheb seals Tutankhamun's tomb: *Ibid.*, p. 97.

p. 148   Djohutymose: Clayton, *Chronicle* ..., p. 114.

p. 148   Maya – architect of Tutankhamun's tomb: Reeves, *The Complete Tutankhamun*, p. 71. Desroches-Noblecourt, *Tutankhamun*, p. 210.

p. 148   Curse: Reeves, *The Complete Tutankhamun*. pp. 62–63.

p. 150   Carter quotation: Carter, *The Tomb of Tutankhamun*.

p. 151   Stairwells of Tutankhamun's tomb: *Ibid.*

CHAPTER SEVEN

p. 155   Sudden emergence of Atenism: Aldred, *Akhenaten* ..., p. 244.

p. 155   Aten references: *Ibid.*, p. 239.

p. 156   Aten as sun disc: Lurker, *The Gods and Symbols* ..., p. 31.

p. 156   Aten not a god: Redford, *Akhenaten: The Heretic King*, p. 170.

p. 157   Talatat: Smith, R. W. and Redford, D. B., *The Akhenaten Temple Project*, Toronto, 1988.

p. 157   Ruler of Thebes: Aldred, *Akhenaten* ..., p. 21.

p. 158   Statues and temples: Thomas, A. P., *Akhenaten's Egypt*, London, 1996, ch.2.

p. 158   Aten name: Aldred, *Akhenaten* ..., p. 19.

p. 159   Name in cartouches: *Ibid.*, p 240.

p. 159   'May the good god ...': *Ibid.*, p. 47.

p. 160   'And may the Horus ...': *Ibid*, pp. 47–48.

p. 160   Akhenaten proscribes Re and Horus: *Ibid.*, pp. 240, 244. Redford, Akhenaten: The Heretic King, pp. 261, 262.

p. 160   History of Heliopolis: Hornung, E., *Conceptions of God in Ancient Egypt*.

p. 161   Heliopolis and the Aten: Aldred, *Akhenaten* ..., p. 259.

p. 161   Ben-Ben: *Ibid.*, p 265. Osman, A., *Moses: Pharaoh of Egypt*, London, 1990, p. 163.

p. 161   Greatest of seers: *Ibid.*, p. 163. Redford, *Akhenaten: The Heretic King*, p. 152.

p. 162   Parennefer's tomb: Aldred, *Akhenaten* ..., pp.91–92.

p. 162   Proscribes plural: *Ibid.*, p. 240.

p. 162   Akhenaten proscribes graven images: Aldred, *Akhenaten* ..., pp. 244, 245, 278.

p. 163   Aten as sunlight and graven images: *Ibid.*, pp. 261–262.

p. 163   'True king's son ...': Redford, *Akhenaten: The Heretic King*, p.59.

p. 166   Breasted: Breasted, J. H., *A History of the Ancient Egyptians*, London, 1920, pp. 232–235.

p. 166   Hymn to the Aten: Aldred, *Akhenaten . . .*, pp. 241–243. Samson, *Nefertiti and Cleopatra*, pp. 30–32.

p. 171   On and Joseph: Anderson, G. W., *The History and Religion of Israel*, Oxford, 1979, p. 25.

p. 171   Apion and Moses: Thackeray, H. (trans.), *Josephus's Against Apion*, London, 1926, p. 295.

p. 171   Freud: Freud, S., *Moses and Monotheism*, London, 1939.

p. 172   No evidence of Atenism before Akhenaten: Aldred, *Akhenaten . . .*, p. 244.

p. 173   Bronze bull: Amihay Mazor interviewed on *Time Travellers: The Mystery of the Israelites*, Arkios Productions 1992.

CHAPTER EIGHT

p. 177   No historical reference to Israelites in Egypt: Magnusson, M., *BC: The Archaeology of the Bible Land*, London, 1977, p. 43.

p. 180   Not same literary character: Anderson, *The History and Religion of Israel*, p. 3.

p. 181   Camels: Wilson, I., *The Exodus Enigma*, London, 1985, p. 15.

p. 181   Camels – oldest reference: Freeman-Grenville, *Chronology of World History*, p. 19.

p. 181   Camels – oldest reference in Egypt: *Ibid.*, p 24.

p. 181   Philistines first appear: Magnusson, *BC . . .*, p. 98.

p. 181   Philistines first in Canaan: *Ibid.*, p. 104.

p. 182   Lydians: Wilson, *The Exodus Enigma*, p. 61.

p. 182   Old Testament written: Redford, D. B. A., *A Study of the Biblical Story of Joseph*, Leiden, 1970.

p. 183   Israel Stelae: Breasted, J. H., *Ancient Records of Egypt*, Chicago, 1976.

p. 184   Kenyon excavations: Kenyon, K. M., *Digging up Jericho*, London, 1957.

p. 185   Dr Yadin's findings: Yadin, Y., *Hazor: Great Citadel of the Bible*, London 1963. Magnusson, *BC . . .*, pp. 84–88.

p. 189   Khnumhotep tomb illustration: Albright, W. F., *The Archaeology of Palestine*, Harmondsworth, 1956, p. 208.

p. 189   Long, sleeved robe: Magnusson, *BC . . .*, p.44.

p. 190   Mari: *Ibid.*, pp. 36–38.

p. 190 Hyksos – 'Desert Princes': Aldred, *Akhenaten* . . ., p. 117.

p. 193 Tell-el-Daba excavations: Magnusson, *BC* . . ., pp. 48–49.

p. 193 Bietak, M., *Tell-el-Daba II*, Vienna, 1975.

p. 194 Manetho: Waddell, W. G., *Manetho*, London, 1940.

p. 194 Yakob-aam: Clayton, *Chronicle* . . ., p. 95.

p. 196 Hyksos military: Yadin, Y., *The Art of Warfare in Biblical Lands in the Light of Archaeological Discovery*, London, 1963.

p. 197 Seqenenres's death: Wilson, *The Exodus Enigma*, p. 73.

p. 197 Inscription from the tomb of Ahmose: Pritchard, J. B., *Ancient Near Eastern Texts Relating to the Old Testament*, Princeton, 1969.

p. 197 Tuthmosis's campaigns: Clayton, *Chronicle* . . ., pp. 109–110.

p. 198 Rekhmire tomb: Davies, N de G., *The Tomb of Rekhmire at Thebes*, New York, 1944.

p. 199 Broken arms: Wilson. *The Exodus Enigma* p. 81.

p. 199 *Apiru*: Bucaille, M., *Moses and Pharaoh: The Hebrews in Egypt*, Tokyo, 1994, p. 55–56.

p. 200 *Habiru* in Mari texts: Magnusson, *BC* . . ., p 37.

p. 200 Origin of the name Hebrew: *Oxford Encyclopaedic English Dictionary*, Oxford, 1994, p.37.

CHAPTER NINE

p. 207 Amonhotep at the height of power: Clayton, *Chronicle* . . ., pp. 115–119. Aldred, *Akhenaten* . . ., ch. 15.

p. 209 Sekhmet statues: *Ibid.*, pp. 148–149, 283.

p. 209 British Museum statues: James, T. G. H., and Davies, W. K., *Egyptian Sculpture*, London, 1984.

p. 209 Legend of Sekhmet: Lurker, *The Gods and Symbols of Ancient Egypt*, p. 106. Ions, *Egyptian Mythology*, p. 104.

p. 209 Unrivalled numbers of Sekhmet statues: Masters, R., *The Goddess Sekhmet*, New York, 1988, p. 48.

p. 214 Ninkovich and Heezen: Ninkovich, D. and Heezen, B. C., *Submarine Geology and Geophysics, Colston Papers Vol. 17*, Bristol, 1965, pp. 413–452.

p. 214 Mount St Helens eruption: *Mount St Helens Holocaust*, Columbian Inc, Lubbock 1980. Lipman, P. W and Mullineaux, D. R., *The 1980 Eruptions of Mount St Helens, Washington*. US Geological Survey, Washington DC, 1981.

p. 215   Mount St Helens aftermath: Findley, R., *Mount St Helens, National Geographic 159*, 1981, pp.3–65. Findley, R., *Mount St Helens aftermath: the mountain that was and will be, National Geographic 160*, 1981, pp. 713–733.

p. 216   Krakatau eruption: Simkin, T. & Fiske, R. S., *Krakatau 1883: The Volcanic Eruption and its Effects*, Washington DC 1983. Fureaux, R., *Krakatau*, London, 1965.

p. 217   Thera eruption: Page, D. L., *The Santorini Volcano and the Desolation of Minoan Crete*, London 1970. Bullard, F. M., *Volcanoes in History, in Theory, in Eruption*, London, 1962.

p. 217   Harriot Boyd excavations: Hawes, H. B., *Gournia, Vasiliki and other Prehistorical Sites on the Isthmus of Hierapetra, Crete*, American Exploration Society, Philadelphia, 1908.

p. 218   Seager excavation: Seager, R. B., *Excavations on the Island of Mochlos, Crete, in 1908, American Journal of Archaeology 13*, 1909, pp. 273–303.

p. 218   Xanthoudidis excavation: Wilson, *The Exodus Enigma*, p. 89.

p. 220   Marinatos excavations: Marinatos, S., *Excavations at Thera, 7 Vols*, Athens, 1967–73.

p. 220   Platon excavations: Platon, N., *Zakros: The Discovery of a Lost Palace of Ancient Crete*, New York, 1971.

p. 222   No pumice beneath collapsed walls: Archaeologist Christos Dumas and vulcanologist Floyd Macoy interviewed on *Time Travellers: The Secrets of Minoan Crete*, Arkios Productions, 1992.

p. 222   Wilson, *The Exodus Enigma*, p. 113.

p. 223   Core samples: Ninkovich, D, and Heezen, B. C., *Submarine Geology and Geophysics, Colston Papers Vol 17*, Bristol, 1965, pp. 413–452.

p. 234   Thera *tsunami*: Galanopoulos, A. G., *Tsunamis Observed on the Coasts of Greece from Antiquity to the Present Time, Annali di Geofisica 13*, 1960, pp. 369–86.

p. 224   Lane, F. W., *The Violent Earth*, London, 1986, pp. 179–182.

p. 225   Plato: Jowett, B., *The Dialogues of Plato*, Oxford, 1892.

p. 225   Atlantis: Galanopoulos, A. G. & Bacon, E., *Atlantis: The Truth Behind the Legend*, London, 1969.

p. 228   Danish dating: Pichler, H. & Friedrich, W., *Radiocarbon dates of Santorini Volcanics, Nature 262*, 1976, pp. 373–374.

p. 229   Sarikay palace dendrochronology and controversy: Highfield, R., *History Uprooted by Trees, Daily Telegraph*, London, 3 July 1996.

p. 230 Jericho dating: Bruins, H. J. & van de Plicht, J., *The Exodus Enigma*, *Nature 382*, 1996, pp. 213–214.

p. 232 Amonhotep dating: Clayton, *Chronicle...*

p. 233 Volcanic atmospheric phenomena: Lane, F. W., *The Violent Earth*, London, 1986, p. 209.

p. 233 Sekhmet legend: Ions, *Egyptian Mythology*, pp. 80, 104.

p. 234 Tomb of Ramose: Aldred, *Akhenaten...*, p. 260.

CHAPTER TEN

Krakatau aftermath. Symons, G. J. (ed.), *The Eruption of Krakatau and Subsequent Phenomena*, London, 1988.

Mount St Helens fallout: Weintraub, B., *Fire and Ash: Darkness at Noon*, *National Geographic 162*, 1982, pp. 660–70, 676–84.

Thera eruption: Bullard, F. M., *Volcanoes in History, in Theory, in Eruption*. Sparks, R. S. J., *The Santorini Eruption and its Consequences*, *Endeavour 3*, 1979, pp. 27–31.

p. 245 Volcanic lightning: Anderson, R., *Electricity in Volcanic Clouds*, *Science 148*, 1965, pp. 1179–89.

p. 244 Wilson: Wilson, *The Exodus Enigma*, p. 121.

p. 245 Ecosystems and volcanoes: Sheets, D. P. & Grayson, D. K. (eds.), *Volcanic Activity and Human Ecology*, New York, 1979.

p. 245 Mount Pelee eruption: Kennan, G., *The Tragedy of Pelee*, New York, 1902. Perret, F. A., *The Eruption of Mount Pelee*, Washington DC 1932. Wilson, *The Exodus Enigma*, pp. 123–26.

p. 250 Volcanic *tsunami*: Galanopoulos, *Tsunamis Observed...*

p. 250 'A black cloud...': Symons, *The Eruption of Krakatau and Subsequent Phenomena*, p. 37.

p. 250 Thera plume: Wilson, *The Exodus Enigma*, p. 113.

p. 251 *Yam Suph*: Anderson, *The History and Religion of Israel*, pp. 23–24. Magnusson, *BC...*, pp. 64–65.

p. 254 Thera *tsunamis*: Bennett, J. G., *Geophysics and Human History*, *Systematics 1*, 1963, pp. 127–56.

p. 256 Sea withdrawal: Simkin and Fiske, *Krakatau 1883: The Volcanic Eruption and its Effects*. Wilson, *The Exodus Enigma*, pp. 132–135.

p. 257   King's son as governor of Memphis: Aldred, *Akhenaten: King of Egypt*, p. 259.

CHAPTER ELEVEN

p. 263   Early 19th dynasty history: Clayton, *Chronicle . . .*, pp. 140–158.

p. 270   Bietak excavations: Bietak, M., *Tell-el-Daba*, Vienna, 1975.

p. 270   Avaris as home town of Ramesses family: Clayton, *Chronicle . . .*, p. 140. Belzoni, G., *Narrative of the Operations and recent Discoveries within the Pyramids, Temples, Tombs and Excavations in Egypt and Nubia*, London, 1822.

p. 271   Manetho's account: Thackeray, H. (trans.), *Josephus: Against Apion*, London, 1926.

p. 272   Amonhotep, son of Hapu: Aldred, *Akhenaten . . .*, pp. 89, 148, 164–5.

p. 273   The greatest Egyptian army: Clayton, *Chronicle . . .* p. 150.

p. 273   Hazor dating: Magnusson, *BC . . .*, pp. 86–87.

p. 273   Jericho dating: Bruins, H. J., and van de Plicht, J., *The Exodus Enigma, Nature 382*, 1996. pp. 213–214. Radford, T., *Scientists Fix Date for Fall of Jericho, The Guardian*, London, 18 July 1996.

p. 274   Tuthmosis III campaign: Clayton, *Chronicle of the Pharaohs*, pp. 109–10.

p. 277   *Albatross* and *Vema* surveys: Ninkovich, D., and Heezen, B. C., *Submarine Geology and Geophysics, Colston Papers Vol. 17*, Bristol, 1965. pp. 413–452.

p. 277   1926 eruption: Wilson, *The Exodus Enigma*, p. 92.

p. 278   Ugarit excavations and Amarna letter: Curtis, A., *Ugarit: Ras Shamra*, Cambridge, 1985, pp. 43–44.

p. 279   Sacrificing duck: Aldred, *Akhenaten . . .*, pl. 62.

p. 279   Smiting scene: Redford, *Akhenaten . . .*, p. 62.

p. 279   'Good ruler . . .': Aldred, *Akhenaten . . .*, p. 305.

p. 280   Foreign legion: *Ibid.*, p. 265. Schulman, A. R., *Military Background of the Amarna Period, Journal of the American Research Centre in Egypt, Vol. 3*, 1964.

p. 280   Tomb of Aper-el: Zivie, A., *The Treasury of Aper-El, Egyptian Archaeology*, Summer 1991, pp. 26–29.

p. 282   A temple of Aten in Memphis: Aldred, *Akhenaten: King of Egypt*, p. 273.

p. 283   Moses' name: Osman, A., *Moses: Pharaoh of Egypt*, London, 1990, pp. 66–67.

p. 285   The Sargon myth: Magnusson, *BC* . . ., p. 58.

p. 285   Prince Tuthmosis: Aldred, *Akhenaten* . . ., p. 259.

p. 286   Whip: Clayton, *Chronicle* . . ., p. 120.

p. 286   'True king's son . . .': Redford, *Akhenaten* . . ., p. 59.

p. 286   Prince Tuthmosis tomb: Aldred, *Akhenaten* . . ., p. 298.

CHAPTER TWELVE

p. 296   Mafdet, Neith and Geb: Lurker, *The Gods and Symhols* . . .

p. 296   Saints: Chadwick, N. K., *The Age of Saints in the early Celtic Church*, London, 1981.

p. 300   Deaths of the royal women: Aldred, *Akhenaten* . . .,. p. 289.

p. 300   Deaths of chief ministers: *Ibid.*, p. 248.

p. 301   Plague in vassal states: *Ibid.*, p. 283.

p. 301   Plague in Hittite empire: *Ibid.*, p. 298.

p. 303   No pharaoh sires a male heir: Clayton, *Chronicle* . . ., pp. 120–142.

p. 303   Amarna women: Troy, L., *Patterns of Queenship in Ancient Egyptian Myth and History*, Uppsala, 1986, pp. 166–168.

Select Bibliography

Aharoni, Y., *The Land of the Bible: A Historical Geography*. London 1967.

Albright, W. F., *Archaeology and the Religion of Israel*. New York 1969.

Aldred, C., *Akhenaten and Nefertiti*. Brooklyn 1973.

    Akhenaten, Pharaoh of Egypt. London 1968.

    Tutankhamun's Egypt. London 1972.

    Akhenaten, King of Egypt. London 1986.

Anati, E., *Palestine Before the Hebrews*. London 1963.

Anderson, G. W., *The History of the Religion of Israel*. Oxford 1966.

Andrews, C., *Ancient Egyptian Jewellery*. London 1990.

Avi-Yonah, M. (ed.), *Encyclopaedia of Archaeological Excavations in the Holy Land*. Oxford 1976.

Bacon, E. (ed.), *The Great Archaeologists*. London 1976.

Bagnall, R. S., *Egypt in Later Antiquity*. Princeton 1993.

Baikie, J., *Egyptian Antiquities in the Nile Valley*. London 1932.

    The Amarna Age. London 1926.

Baines, J., and Malek, J., *Atlas of Ancient Egypt*. Oxford 1980.

Bean, G., *Aegean Turkey: An Archaeological Guide*. London 1966.

Beebe, H. K., *The Old Testament*. London 1970.

Bierbrier, M. L., *The Late New Kingdom in Egypt*. Warminster 1975.

Boardman, J., *The Greeks Overseas*. Harmondsworth 1964.

Brackman, A. C., *The Search for the Gold of Tutankhamun*. New York 1976.

Bramwell, J., *Lost Atlantis*. London 1937.

Brandon, S. G. F., *Creation Legends of the Ancient Near East*. London 1963.

Breasted, J. H., *Ancient Records of Egypt*. Chicago 1906.

Bright, J. A. *History of Israel*. London 1972.

Brotherstone, G., *World Archaeoastronomy*. Cambridge 1989.

Brown, F., *Hebrew and the English Lexicon of the Old Testament.* Oxford 1906.

Bryant, A. E., *Natural Disasters.* Cambridge 1991.

Bucaille, M., *Moses and Pharaoh: The Hebrews in Egypt.* Tokyo 1994.

Carter, H., *The Tomb of Tutankhamun.* London 1933.

Cassuto, U. *A Commentary on the Book of Exodus.* Jerusalem 1961.

Castledon, R., *Minoans: Life in Bronze Age Crete.* London 1990.

Cerny, J., *Hieratic Inscriptions from the Tomb of Tutankhamun.* Oxford 1965.

Chester, D., *Volcanoes and Society.* London 1993.

Clark, R.T., *Myth and Symbol in Ancient Egypt.* London 1978.

Clayton, P. A., *Chronicle of the Pharaohs.* London 1994.

Cone, P. (ed.), *The Discovery of Tutankhamun's Tomb.* New York 1976.

Cooney, J. D., *Amarna Reliefs from Hermopolis in American Collections.* Brooklyn 1965.

Cottrell, L., *Bull of Minos.* London 1955.

Cottrell, L., *The Secrets of Tutankhamun.* London 1978.

Curtis, A., *Ugarit: Ras Shamra.* Cambridge 1985.

D'Auria, Lacovara, S. P., and Roehrig, C. H., *Mummies and Magic: The Funerary Arts of Ancient Egypt.* Boston 1988.

Daiches, D., *Moses, Man in the Wilderness.* London 1975.

David, R., *Discovering Ancient Egypt.* London 1993.

David, R., and David, A. E., *A Biographical Dictionary of Ancient Egypt.* London 1992

Davidson, R., and Leaney, A. R. C., *The Penguin Guide to Modern Theology.* Harmondsworth 1970.

Davies, N., *The Tomb of the Two Sculptors at Thebes.* New York 1927.
  The Tomb of the Vizier Ramose. London 1941.

Davis, T. M., *The Tomb of Queen Tiyi.* London 1910

Dawson, W. R., and Uphill, E., *Who Was Who in Egyptology.* London 1972

Desroches-Noblecourt, C., *Tutankhamun: Life and Death of a Pharaoh.* London 1963.

Dickinson, O., *The Aegean Bronze Age.* Cambridge 1994.

Dodson, A., *The Canopic Equipment of the Kings of Egypt.* London 1994.

Dothan, T., *The Philistines and their Material Culture.* London 1982.

Doumas, C. G., *Thera, Pompeii of the Ancient Aegean.* London 1983.

Eaton-Krauss, M., and Graefe, E., *The Small Golden Shrine from the Tomb of Tutankhamun.* Oxford 1985.

Ebon, M., *Atlantis: The New Evidence.* New York 1977.

Edwards, I. E. S., *Tutankhamun.* London 1975.
  Treasures of Tutankhamun. New York 1976.

The Pyramids of Egypt. New York 1991.

Emery, W. B., *Archaic Egypt.* Harmondsworth 1961.

Evans, A. J., *The Palace of Minos.* London 1935.

Fagan, B. M., *The Rape of the Nile: Tomb Robbers, Tourists, and Archaeologists in Egypt.* London 1977.

Faulkner, R. O., *The Ancient Egyptian Coffin Texts.* Warminster 1977.

Fazzini, R., *Tutankhamun and the African Heritage: a View of Society in the Time of the Boy King.* New York 1978.

Frankfort, H., and Pendlebury, J., *The City of Akhenaten.* London 1933.

Frankfort, H., *Kingship and the Gods.* Chicago 1948.

    Ancient Egyptian Religion. New York 1961.

Freud, S., *Moses and Monotheism.* London 1939.

Friedlander, P., *Plato: An Introduction.* London 1958.

Gardiner, A., *Egyptian Grammar.* Oxford 1957.

    Egypt of the Pharaohs. Oxford 1961.

    The Royal Canon of Turin. Oxford 1959.

Giles, F J., *Ikhnaton: Legend and History.* London 1970.

Graves, R., *The Greek Myths.* Harmondsworth 1960.

Gray, J., *The Canaanites.* London 1964.

Greenberg, M., *The Hab/piru.* New Haven 1955.

Greener, L., *The Discovery of Egypt.* London 1968.

Habachi, L., *The Obelisks of Egypt; Skyscrapers of the Past.* London 1978.

Hanke, R., *Amarna-Reliefs aus Hermopolis.* Hildesheim 1978.

Harker, R., *Digging up the Bible Lands.* London 1972.

Harriss, J. E., and Wente, E. F. (eds), *An X-ray Atlas of the Royal Mummies.* Chicago 1980.

Hawkes, J., *Man and the Sun.* London 1962.

Hayes, W. C., *Royal Sarcophagi of the Eighteenth Dynasty. Princeton 1935.*

Herzog, C., and Gichon, M., *Battles of the Bible.* London 1978.

Hooker, J. T., *Mycenaean Greece.* London 1976.

Hornung, E., *Conceptions of God in Ancient Egypt.* London 1983.

    The Valley of the Kings: Horizon of Eternity. New York 1990.

Hoving. T., *Tutankhamun: The Untold Story.* Harmondsworth 1978.

Hutchison, R. W., *Prehistoric Crete.* Harmondsworth 1962.

Ions, V., *Egyptian Mythology.* London 1982.

James, E. O., *The Ancient Gods.* London 1960.

Josephus, Flavius, *Against Apion* (trans Thackeray, H.) London 1926.

Jowett, B., *The Dialogues of Plato.* Oxford 1892.

Keller, W., *The Bible as History.* London 1956.

Kemp, B. J., *Ancient Egypt: Anatomy of a Civilisation*. London 1989.

Kenyon, K. M., *Archaeology in the Holy Land*. London 1965.

   Digging Up Jericho. London 1957.

   Excavations at Jericho. London 1965.

   The Bible and Recent Archaeology. London 1978.

Khouly, A. el-, and Martin G. T., *Excavations in the Royal Necropolis at El-Amarna* Cairo 1987.

Leek, F. F., *The Human Remains from the Tomb of Tutankhamun*. Oxford 1972.

Lichtheim, M., *Ancient Egyptian Literature*. Berkeley 1980.

Lucas, A., and Harriss, J. R., *Ancient Egyptian Materials and Industries*. London 1989.

Magnusson, M., *BC: The Archaeology of the Bible Lands*. London 1977.

Marinatos, S., *Excavations at Thera*. Athens 1973.

Martin, G. T., *The Hidden Tombs of Memphis*. London 1990.

   The Royal Tomb at Amarna. London 1989.

May, H. G. (ed.), *Oxford Bible Atlas*. Oxford 1974.

Mayes, S., *The Great Belzoni*. London 1954.

Mercer, S. A. B., *The Religion of Ancient Egypt*. London 1949.

   The Tell el-Amarna Tablets. Toronto 1939

Moorey, P. R. S., *Biblical Lands*. London 1975.

Morrow, G. R., *Plato's Cretan City*. Princeton 1960.

Muck, O., *The Secret of Atlanis*. London 1979.

Murnane, W. J., *Ancient Egyptian Co-regencies*. Chicago 1977.

Murray, H., and Nuttall, M., *A Handlist to Howard Carter's Catalogue of Objects in Tutankhamun's Tomb*. Oxford 1963.

Negev, A. (ed.), *Archaeological Encyclopaedia of the Holy Land*. London 1973.

Nims, C. F., *Thebes of the Pharaohs*. London 1965.

Noth, M., *The History of Israel*. London 1960.

Osman, A., *Stranger in the Valley of the Kings*. London 1987.

   Moses: Pharaoh of Egypt. London 1990.

Page, D. L., *The Santorini Volcano and the Desolation of Minoan Crete*. London 1970.

Peet. T. E., *The City of Akhenaten*. London 1951.

Pellegrino, C., *Unearthing Atlantis*. New York 1991.

Pendlebury, J., *Tell el-Amarna*. London 1935.

Petrie, W. M. F., *Tell el-Amarna*. London 1894

   Researches in Sinai. London 1906.

Plankoff, A., *Egyptian Religious Texts and Representations*. Princeton 1968.

Playton, N., *Zakros: The Discovery of a Lost Palace of Ancient Crete*. New York 1971.

Porter, B., and Moss, R. L. B., *Topographical Bibliography of Ancient Egyptian Hieroglyphic Texts, Reliefs and Paintings. 1: The Theban Necropolis*. Oxford 1960.

Posener, G., *A Dictionary of Egyptian Civilisation*. London 1962.

Prichard, J. B., *Ancient near Eastern Texts Relating to the Old Testament*. Princeton 1969.

Pritchard, J. B. (ed.), *Ancient Near Eastern Texts*. Princeton 1969.

Ramage, E. S. (ed.), *Atlantis: Fact or Fiction*. Bloomington 1978.

Redford, D. B., *A Study of the Biblical Story of Joseph*. Leiden 1970.
   Egypt, Canaan, and Israel in Ancient Times. Princeton 1992.
   History and Chronology in the 18th Dynasty of Egypt. Toronto 1977.
   Pharaonic King-Lists, Annals and Day-Books. Ontario 1986.
   Akhenaten: The Heretic King. Princeton 1984.

Reeves, C. N. (ed.), *After Tutankhamun: Research and Excavation in the Royal Necropolis at Thebes*. London 1992.

Reeves, N., *The Complete Tutankhamun: The King, The Tomb, The Royal Treasure*. London 1990.

Renfrew, A. C., *Archaeology and Language*. London 1987.

Romer, J., *Valley of the Kings*. London 1981.

Rowley. H. H., *From Joseph to Joshua*. London 1950.

Samson, J, *Nefertiti and Cleopatra*. London 1990.
   Amarna: City of Akhenaten and Nefertiti. London 1978.

Schafer, H., *Principles of Egyptian Art*. Oxford 1947.

Schmidt, J. D., *Ramesses II*. London 1973.

Simkin, T., and Fiske, R. S., *Krakatau 1883: The Volcanic Eruption and its Effects*. Washington DC 1983.

Smith, E. G., *The Royal Mummies*. Cairo 1912.

Smith, R. W., and Redford, D. B., *The Akhenaten Temple Project*. Toronto 1988.

Spencer, A. J., *Early Egypt: The Rise of Civilisation in the Nile Valley*. London 1993.

Thomas, D. W. (ed.), *Documents from Old Testament Times*. London 1958.

Thomas, E., *The Royal Necropolis of Thebes*. Princeton 1966.

Van Seters, J., *The Hyksos*. London 1966.

Waddell, W. G. (trans), *Manetho*. London 1940.

Wainwright, G. A., *The Sky Religion in Egypt*. Cambridge 1938.

Weigall, A. *The Life and Times of Akhenaten*. London 1922.

Wilkinson, A., *Pharaonic Egypt: the Bible and Christianity.* Jerusalem 1985.
Winckler, H., *Tell el-Amarna Letters.* London 1896.
Winlock, H. E., *The Rise and Fall of the Middle Kingdom in Thebes.* New York 1947.
Wortham, J. D., *British Egyptology 1549–1906.* Newton Abbot 1972.
Wynne, B., *Behind the Mask of Tutankhamun.* London 1972.
Yadin, Y., *Hazor: Great Citadel of the Bible.* London 1975.
　The Art of War in Biblical Lands. London 1963.

Index